Property Valuation Principles

By the same authors

Property Development Appraisal and Finance (D. Isaac, J. O'Leary and M. Daley)
Property Investment (D. Isaac and J. O'Leary)
Property Finance (D. Isaac)
Property Valuation Techniques (D. Isaac and T. Steley)
The Valuation of Property Investments (N. Enever, D. Isaac and M. Daley)
Urban Economics: A Global Perspective (P. N. Balchin, D. Isaac and J. Chen)

Property Valuation Principles

2nd edition

David Isaac

Professor of Real Estate Management, School of Architecture, Design and Construction, University of Greenwich

John O'Leary

Senior Lecturer, School of Architecture, Design and Construction, University of Greenwich

First published 2012 by
PALGRAVE MACMILLAN

Palgrave Macmillan in the UK is an imprint of Macmillan Publishers Limited, registered in England, company number 785998, of Houndmills, Basingstoke, Hampshire RG21 6XS.

Palgrave Macmillan in the US is a division of St Martin's Press LLC, 175 Fifth Avenue, New York, NY 10010.

Palgrave Macmillan is the global academic imprint of the above companies and has companies and representatives throughout the world.

Palgrave® and Macmillan® are registered trademarks in the United States, the United Kingdom, Europe and other countries

ISBN-13: 978–0–230–35580–4 paperback

This book is printed on paper suitable for recycling and made from fully managed and sustained forest sources. Logging, pulping and manufacturing processes are expected to conform to the environmental regulations of the country of origin.

A catalogue record for this book is available from the British Library.

A catalog record for this book is available from the Library of Congress.

To Martin, brothers don't come any better.

Contents

Preface to the First Edition   xi

Preface to the Second Edition   xiii

Acknowledgements   xiv

List of abbreviations   xv

1 **Introduction**   1
   1.1 Introduction   2
   1.2 Current issues and dilemmas for property valuation   2
   1.3 The structure of the book   5
   1.4 Summary   7
        References   7

2 **The property market**   8
   2.1 Introduction   9
   2.2 Theory and the property market   10
   2.3 Owner-occupier and investment markets   11
   2.4 Property as an investment   13
   2.5 Property and investment portfolios   16
   2.6 Factors affecting property values   17
   2.7 The legal dimension   19
   2.8 Sources of finance   21
   2.9 Lending criteria   23
   2.10 The specialized nature of valuation work   25
   2.11 Summary   27
        References   27
        Self-assessment questions   28

3 **The role of the valuer**   29
   3.1 Introduction   30
   3.2 Types of valuation   31
   3.3 The Red Book and valuation bases   33
   3.4 Valuer qualifications and registration   37
   3.5 Market volatility   38
   3.6 Valuation accuracy and negligence   41
   3.7 Valuation tables and formulas   44
   3.8 Summary   51
        References   53
        Self-assessment questions   53

4 **The comparison method of valuation**   54
   4.1 Introduction   55
   4.2 Observations on the comparison method   55

4.3	Comparison and residential sales values	56
4.4	Comparison and commercial property rental values	58
4.5	Zoning of shops	61
4.6	Comparison and commercial property capital values	63
4.7	Comparison and development land	65
4.8	Summary	66
	References	67
	Self-assessment questions	67

5 The profits method of valuation **68**

5.1	Introduction	69
5.2	Principles, definitions and assumptions	69
5.3	Maintaining the wider perspective	72
5.4	Illustrating the process	73
5.5	The divisible balance, tenant's bid and turnover rents	76
5.6	Discounted cash flow and the profits method	77
5.7	Summary	78
	References	79
	Self-assessment questions	79

6 The contractor's method of valuation **81**

6.1	Introduction	82
6.2	The theory and stages in the DRC method	82
6.3	Applications of the DRC method	87
6.4	Fire insurance	90
6.5	Summary	91
	References	91
	Self-assessment questions	92

7 The residual method of valuation **93**

7.1	Introduction	94
7.2	The basic residual valuation model	95
7.3	Headings in the residual valuation	96
7.4	Adding detail to the residual valuation model	107
7.5	Factoring in affordable housing and infrastructure costs	109
7.6	Risk and change in variables	112
7.7	Sensitivity testing	115
7.8	Comparing refurbishment with redevelopment	116
7.9	Development potential and existing use value	117
7.10	A critique of the residual valuation method	118
7.11	Summary	122
	References	123
	Self-assessment questions	123

8 The investment method – traditional approach **125**

8.1	Introduction	126
8.2	Capitalizing using a yield	128
8.3	Freehold investment properties	130
8.4	Identifying the net rent	133

8.5	Term and reversion	136
8.6	The layer method	143
8.7	The equivalent yield	145
8.8	Over-rented property	149
8.9	Leaseholds and profit rents	152
8.10	Premiums	157
8.11	A critique of traditional investment methods	158
8.12	Summary	159
	References	160
	Self-assessment questions	160
9	**The investment method – discounted cash flow approaches**	**162**
9.1	Introduction	163
9.2	Traditional and DCF approaches to property investment valuation	164
9.3	Basic investment appraisal techniques	165
9.4	Discounting and DCF	167
9.5	DCF to identify net present value (NPV)	170
9.6	DCF to identify the internal rate of return (IRR)	174
9.7	Summary	179
	References	179
	Self-assessment questions	180
10	**Yields, gearing and growth**	**181**
10.1	Introduction	182
10.2	Inflation	182
10.3	Cost of capital	186
10.4	Risk premium	188
10.5	Gearing	189
10.6	The equated yield	192
10.7	The implied growth rate	195
10.8	Summary	197
	References	198
	Self-assessment questions	198
11	**Conclusions**	**200**
11.1	Introduction	200
11.2	Consolidation on some key themes	201
11.3	Issues and opportunities for valuers	203
11.4	Summary	206
	References	206
Solutions to self-assessment questions		**207**
Bibliography		223
Index		227

Preface to the First Edition

This book is intended to provide an introduction to property valuation. The general approach is that property appraisal is the overall aim and that this is divided into market valuation and investment analysis. It is in the area of market valuation that this text concentrates. The book covers five areas of study:

1 Valuation and markets.
2 Methods of valuation.
3 The investment method in detail.
4 Taxation and statutory valuations.
5 The development appraisal and finance.

The intention is to discuss the context of the market, show how valuation practice has developed within this context and explain the application of valuation methods in practice.

The book will be useful for both students and practitioners. For students it will provide a text at initial level (first- and second-year undergraduates) in estate management, property, surveying, planning, design and construction disciplines. Those in adjacent areas of study such as housing and economics will find this a useful introduction to the area of property valuation. Practitioners involved with property and real estate, and this includes a wide area of professionals, including surveyors, builders, construction managers, architects, engineers, estate managers and agents will find this a useful overview. Professional advisors such as bankers, financial advisors, accountants, investors, analysts and lawyers should also find this text useful as an aid to their dealings in the property sector.

I have aimed to reference the material as well as possible but apologies for any omissions. There are relatively few texts in the area of property compared to most other investment sectors and I have tried to reference existing ones as fully as possible to provide additional views and perspectives for the reader. Where possible, spreadsheet analysis has been used to explain and assist in the calculations. Each chapter has the overall aims set out at the beginning and also includes a summary at the end. Key terms are explained and exercise questions are included in relevant sections.

Finally, I would like to thank those who have assisted me in writing this book, Christopher Glennie, my publisher who has been patient with my progress and supportive in the book's development. I would also like to thank Terry Steley and Mark Daley of the University of Greenwich for their help and observations on the book. Finally, as ever, I am reliant on the continued support of the management and staff of the School of Land and Construction Management at the University of Greenwich in developing my studies and research and I am grateful for their help.

As a result of studying this book, students should attain the following objectives:

- understand property appraisal (valuation and analysis) in the context of property markets;
- understand and use the principle methods of valuation;
- understand the application of valuations in a variety of investment and development contexts; and
- begin to relate techniques of appraisal to a wider economic context related to property development, finance and the financial management of property projects.

David Isaac
University of Greenwich
School of Land and Construction Management
April 2001

Preface to the Second Edition

The first edition of this book was authored solely by David Isaac and published in 2002 as a user-friendly introduction to property valuation. The book subsequently established itself as one of a number used by tutors delivering undergraduate programmes in estate management, property, surveying, planning and construction. There was also a peripheral readership comprising students on adjacent programmes such as housing, business studies and economics. Some students on postgraduate conversion courses who were encountering the subject of property valuations for the first time also found the book useful.

The role played by the first edition of the book in helping to develop knowledge and a subject vocabulary is felt to remain as valid for this second edition, which is aimed at a readership similar to that for the first edition. David Isaac has been joined by John O'Leary for authoring this edition which has sought to update and emphasize the key elements from the first edition.

Student and tutor feedback on the first edition suggested that more space could be given to the five methods of valuation and worked examples. In this edition therefore the authors have tried to respond to those requests. The ambition has been to create a more logical progression through the material and to provoke some reflection by including self-assessment questions. It is hoped that tutors will find the book useful when structuring their courses and when directing students to particular chapters to support coursework development or exam revision.

Thanks to Mark Daley for providing helpful comments on a draft of Chapter 5 and to the referees who took the time to provide constructive comments which helped to shape the direction taken in this new edition. As ever, thanks go to our publisher Palgrave Macmillan and the team there: Helen Bugler, Neha Sharma and Alice Ferns who have provided helpful advice on steering the development of this edition. Thanks also to Martin Barr whose inputs enabled the manuscript to be put into production.

David Isaac and John O'Leary
School of Architecture, Design and Construction
University of Greenwich
2011

Acknowledgements

Every effort has been made to trace all the copyright holders, but if any have been inadvertently overlooked, the publishers will be pleased to make the necessary arrangements at the first opportunity.

Abbreviations

ASF	annual sinking fund
BCIS	Building Cost Information Service
BREEAM	Building Research Establishment Environmental Assessment Method
CGT	capital gains tax
CIL	Community Infrastructure Levy
CPI	Consumer Price Index
CSR	corporate social responsibility
DCF	discounted cash flow
DRC	depreciated replacement cost
EBITDA	earnings before interest, tax, depreciation and amortization
ERV	estimated rental value
EUV	existing use value
EUV-SH	existing use value for social housing
FRI	full repairing and insuring [lease]
GDV	gross development value
GIA	gross internal area
IPD	Investment Property Databank
IPF	Investment Property Forum
IRR	internal rate of return
IVSC	International Valuation Standards Council
LIBOR	London Interbank Offer Rate
LTV	loan to value ratio
NDV	net development value
NPV	net present value
PV	present value
REIT	Real Estate Investment Trust
RICS	Royal Institution of Chartered Surveyors
RPI	Retail Price Index
VOA	Valuation Office Agency
VRS	Valuer Registration Scheme
YP	Years' Purchase

1

Introduction

1.1 Introduction
1.2 Current issues and dilemmas for
    property valuation
1.3 The structure of the book
1.4 Summary
    References

Aims

As would be expected of an introduction, this short chapter airs some of the key concepts, expressions and dilemmas which will surface later in the book for more analysis and discussion. The chapter also summarizes the structure of the book by outlining the topics which will be discussed in each chapter.

Key terms

>> **Price** – the money paid by a purchaser to a vendor in a transaction where an asset such as a property is purchased. The price paid may become comparable market data for valuers to interpret when valuing other properties.

>> **Value** – in a property context this is the capital or rental value which a valuer places on a property in advance of an exchange to reflect what the valuer feels could be achieved if the asset were sold or leased.

>> **Worth** – is a subjective assessment of what an asset may be worth to a particular individual or organization reflecting their specific requirements. The worth attributed to an asset by an individual or organization reflects what they would be prepared to pay for it.

>> **Cost** – in a property context the cost encapsulates the expense required to develop or refurbish a property. For example, the cost to develop one house will be the sum of the construction costs, the fees, interest payments and contingencies plus the cost of the plot of land. The total cost to produce the house might be £100,000 but a valuer might subsequently value the house at £150,000 based on comparable market data and the characteristics of the house. The price subsequently achieved in a sale might then be £155,000 although one of the unsuccessful bidders thought the house was worth only £145,000.

1.1 Introduction

The ambition of this book is to explore the principles of property valuation from the perspective of those who may be new to the subject or are seeking to refresh or reinforce their understanding of the subject. The valuation principles discussed in the book have evolved over many years as a way of assessing the capital or rental value of properties. As for other fields of human endeavour, property valuation continues to develop and improve over time and readers will discover that there remain some grey areas in the methods and techniques which sometimes pose tricky dilemmas for valuers and valuation practice. The evolutionary process for valuation techniques is therefore ongoing.

1.2 Current issues and dilemmas for property valuation

It has only been in recent years that the concept of sustainability has moved from a fringe academic concern to a tangible issue for those involved in property. Most large organizations will now typically have corporate social responsibility policies which commit them to source or develop buildings which are sustainable and which will therefore perform well across the triple bottom line of social, economic and environmental criteria.

It is of course possible to accredit buildings to signify that they have achieved a degree of sustainability under BREEAM (Building Research Establishment Environmental Assessment Method) for commercial buildings and under the Code for Sustainable Homes for residential property. However, it is less straightforward for valuers to equate such an accreditation with a monetary value uplift, although there is some evidence to suggest that the market does value sustainable buildings over their unaccredited counterparts. This is one example of where there is a role for further research to shed light on how valuation practice could and should evolve further.

Readers will notice that in the discussion, reference is often made to the requirement for valuers to form judgements when using the valuation toolkit. Given the interplay of so many variables which affect property values and the uniqueness of each property, human judgement will always be required and it is doubtful that a software programme could ever be devised to render human judgement redundant in this field. Given that a lot rests on valuers to make the best possible judgements for their clients, the valuer's professional body, the RICS, has not been complacent and in 2010 it introduced a registration scheme to exert more control over the conduct of RICS members who offer their services as valuers. The RICS also regularly updates its advice to valuers in the Red Book whose formal title is the *RICS Valuation Standards* (2011).

Capturing the value of a property can be more elusive than might first appear. A price may crystallize in a market transaction but this may not always equate with the valuation previously put on a property. The difference between price and valuation can arise because the market place for property is said to be imperfect, a characteristic which is shared with many other markets. For instance it is a straightforward task to ascertain the current share price for a publicly listed company from the internet or a daily newspaper. However valuing an office building, for example, is a far more difficult challenge. Even where there has recently been a sale of a similar office block, there will remain be a whole plethora of differences between the market comparable and the subject property. The valuer will seldom be in possession of all the facts but will still be expected to do the best job possible in interpreting and adjusting for these differences. The latter will typically necessitate comparisons between the subject property and available market comparables in term of their relative size, age, specification, condition, tenure, letting status and quality of the subject property.

Sometimes a valuer will be faced with a difficult dilemma in that there will have been no comparable transactions to provide any sort of benchmark to work from and this is one of a number of imperfections found in the property market. Even when there have been recent and broadly comparable transactions the motives and power relationships between the parties in any particular deal will never be fully understood by a third party. The economic context for property transactions is constantly changing so that the shelf life of a valuation can be quite limited in rapidly changing markets.

Markets are an effective way of bringing buyers and sellers together and in that way they can be very efficient at allocating resources. However markets and particularly property markets can move in different directions making them appear fickle and capricious. This is particularly true for those who purchase at the top of a market only to find several years later that the property is no longer worth what it once was. The consolation for such purchasers is that, over the longer term, property values have shown the ability to outperform the inflation rate, so property recessions are not permanent and can be ridden out.

Perhaps a little controversially it might be suggested that, given the risks posed by upward and downward market movements, a little too much faith is sometimes placed in property valuations. What is clear is that there is some misunderstanding on the part of some clients regarding what a property valuation really signifies. Some clients of valuers believe that just because the value of a property falls they can successfully sue a valuer for providing misleading information. Such an action is unlikely to succeed unless there is clear evidence of negligence in the process which a valuer followed and which led to an erroneous valuation. At this early point in the book it might be helpful to think about a valuation as an estimate of the price which a property could be expected to achieve when sold in the market. A valuation is not however an insurance policy which guarantees that the value of a property will never fall below the datum provided by the valuation.

Although a valuation report will usually refer to a specific sum of money which represents the value of a property, there is in fact a reasonable tolerance attached to such figures to reflect their status as estimates rather than actual figures. The concept of a tolerance is used in fields such as engineering, where it is recognized that it is either technically very difficult, or not practical or necessary to achieve absolute precision. Thus an allowance between acceptable parameters of plus or minus a particular value around a core figure is accepted to be the practical tolerance for the particular situation. In valuations the tolerance is referred to as 'the bracket' and for very straightforward valuations the acceptable bracket has been found by the courts and tribunals to be 5 per cent either side of the valuer's figure. For more complicated and challenging valuations the courts will accept a wider bracket of say 10 per cent either side of the valuation, or wider than that where there are particularly challenging circumstances. A lot will depend on the particular circumstances and market conditions and there is no absolute scale which can be conveniently read off in this respect.

It will be mentioned in the text that valuation is more of an art than a science and it might therefore be thought of as predicting a realistic figure rather than an absolutely precise figure. Indeed for some types of valuation such as those for developments, the RICS (2008: 17) agree that it permissible for a valuer, with the agreement of a client, to report an array of figures and to attach a degree of probability to the most likely central ground within the array.

Although valuers do strive to be as accurate as possible, valuation is not just about predicting the precise price that a property will exchange for; it is as much about providing a realistic estimation which can act as an aid to decision-making. The latter is illustrated by the practice of most banks who, when considering high value property loans, will normally obtain two independent valuations. Decision-makers within the bank will then mull over where they feel the value of the asset is felt to lie within that bracket suggested by the two valuations. The valuations will have helped the bank to frame the decision ultimately reached and in that respect the valuations will have served their purpose by helping to improve the decision taken.

As Figure 1.1 below illustrates, a valuation is an estimate made before a transaction takes place hence the expression *ex ante* which means 'predicted before the event' and in this context the event is the sale of a property. In that context a valuer will usually be working from comparable data which has emerged from the market to make this prediction. Thus when a valuer is called upon to establish the value, say, of a terraced house, recent transactions on similar houses will obviously provide a very good guide to the value of the subject property.

In contrast, the expression *ex post* in Figure 1.1 below means 'after the event' and in this context it can mean the investment returns expected to flow from an investment property, such as a shop or office block. If the property were a house being purchased as somebody's primary residence, then it is unlikely that the purchaser will be thinking about *ex post* benefits in monetary terms. It is more likely that the householder will be interested in the property because of what economists call its *utility*, which is the combination of benefits derived from living in the house and the area.

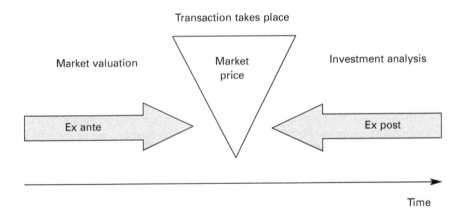

Figure 1.1 Market valuation and investment analysis

It will be explained in Chapter 9 that for investment properties, i.e. those which the owner is not intending to use directly, that a valuation can be based upon an anticipation of what might credibly happen in the *ex post* period. This can be done by bringing together expected future income and capital growth from a property to arrive at a valuation of worth. This type of exercise requires reasoned assumptions to be made about future growth potential of the asset, juxtaposed with an individual investor's profit expectations. The outcome is the identification of the present value of the asset from the point of view of a particular investor and given the specific set of assumptions made.

The process of investment analysis which factors in a specific investor's requirements comes very close to forecasting and it certainly moves the exercise away from a market valuation based upon previous comparable deals in the market place. There are thus some distinctions to be drawn between constructing future oriented financial modelling exercises which is part of investment analysis and reflecting what participants in the market have been prepared to pay for similar assets in the past in a market valuation. These distinctions will resurface later in the book when examples of the different types of approach will be given clearer definition and illustrated in examples.

1.3 The structure of the book

In Chapter 2, the property market is considered as it is the domain in which property valuers work. There are in fact several different property markets, separated by both tenure and property type. Thus there is a market where the freeholds of commercial properties such as shops and offices are purchased for capital values. There is also a rental market where businesses rent commercial properties under commercial leases. There is a residential market where housing is bought and sold for occupation and where properties may also be purchased by investors who wish to become residential landlords by letting the properties in the private rented market. Imperfections can be found in all of these branches of the property market and these serve to make the job of the valuer more challenging.

Chapter 2 will also explain that property valuations are sought for a wide variety of reasons in a wide variety of contexts. For example, valuations are often needed to support the purchase or sale of commercial or residential properties; they may be needed for mortgage purposes, or to establish the collateral value of a development to support borrowing, or to determine the compensation payable when property it to be compulsorily purchased. Credible valuations in whatever situation are based upon a valuer's knowledge, technical competence and experience of dealing with the particular property type. Valuers therefore have to have a good understanding of the context and basis for the valuation stemming from a client's instruction. The chapter will explain that valuation is therefore a specialized activity and it is not, for example, reasonable to expect a valuer who is conversant with valuing large urban commercial properties to value a farm.

Chapter 3 looks at the role of the valuer in trying to value in turbulent markets and where market imperfections of one sort or another require that valuers form judgements and make credible assumptions in the circumstances encountered. The chapter will also explain the role played by the Red Book and by the recently introduced valuer registration system. The thorny issue of valuation accuracy and potential negligence is also outlined in the chapter. The chapter will also explain that while valuers do not have to be mathematically gifted, they will have to develop confidence in using valuations tables, formulas and their abbreviations.

Chapter 4 begins the review of what are often referred to as the five methods of valuation, by considering the *comparison method* of valuation. It will be explained that valuers have to exercise judgement on which particular method to use in the circumstances which they encounter. In this respect it will be explained that the comparison method will usually be one of the first considerations. The method is relatively straightforward and relies on market evidence in the form of capital values and rents of properties that have recently been sold or let.

Chapter 5 examines the *profits method* which is based on the assumption that the value of a property can be deduced from identifying the profit produced by the business using the premises. This method is often used to value leisure industry properties such as hotels, pubs, golf clubs, casinos and nightclubs where the comparison method could not be relied upon because of a lack of comparable market transactions.

Chapter 6 looks at the *contractor's method* of valuation which is more formally known as the depreciated replacement cost method and which is based on the cost of construction in circumstances where there is no market for the particular type of property. The contractor's method comes into play when a value is required for properties such as schools, public libraries or fire stations.

Chapter 7 explores the *residual method* of valuation which is used in development situations. The method works backwards from an assessment of the value of a completed development from which development costs and profit are deducted to arrive at a residual balance, which is a sum of money which can be used to purchase the land. The residual valuation can be restructured if necessary to identify the developer's profit if the land value is already known.

Chapter 8 discusses the traditional *investment method* of valuation, which is used to identify the capital value of investment properties. This method uses a multiplier called the years' purchase to capitalize rental income to arrive at a capital value.

Chapter 9 continues the exploration of the *investment method* but brings to it the use of discounted cash flows (DCF) which many feel are a more transparent way to structure investment valuations. It will be explained that the traditional and DCF approaches to investment valuation are both in widespread use and that this does not contradict RICS guidance and nor does it suggest that one approach is superior to the other. Readers will be able to make up their own minds on which approach to investment valuation they find most convincing.

Chapter 10 considers specialized topics which affect valuations and which include yield calibration, gearing and inflation rates. Chapter 11 concludes by bringing together some of the key themes arising from the book. Chapters 2–10 each have five self-assessment questions at the end, the model answers for which can be found at the back of the book.

1.4 Summary

This chapter has introduced some themes which will be explored later in the book and which illustrate that there remain dilemmas within the body of valuation knowledge and techniques. It was suggested that the art of valuation continues to evolve and that there are research agendas such as how to attribute monetary value to sustainability. The chapter also outlined the content of the chapters which are to follow and for example Chapter 2 which follows will be setting the scene by discussing the property market in which valuers earn a living.

References

RICS (2008) *Valuation of Development Land: Valuation Information Paper 12* (London: RICS).

RICS (2011) *RICS Valuation Standards – Global and UK* (7th edn, Coventry: RICS).

2

The property market

2.1 Introduction
2.2 Theory and the property market
2.3 Owner-occupier and investment markets
2.4 Property as an investment
2.5 Property and investment portfolios
2.6 Factors affecting property values

2.7 The legal dimension
2.8 Sources of finance
2.9 Lending criteria
2.10 The specialized nature of valuation work
2.11 Summary
Self-assessment questions

Aims

This chapter will explore the property market which is the context in which valuers work. It will be discovered that the market is not a single cohesive entity but that it is in fact segregated between residential and commercial property. The latter is further subdivided into different types of commercial property such as offices, retail, industrial and leisure property. The chapter will explain that tenure differences also give rise to separate markets for owner occupation and rental properties. The latter is referred to as the property investment market in which landlords acquire property not for use but for financial performance.

The chapter will also consider how property values reflect the interplay of a number of different influences. One of the themes in the chapter is vocabulary building, as some of the terms and expressions will surface again in later chapters which focus upon different valuation techniques.

Key terms

>> **Investment properties** – are those purchased by an investor such as a pension fund or wealthy individual and then leased to a business or a household for rental income. Investors are attracted to property because it can provide rental income and potentially capital growth. Investment properties come in all shapes and sizes and could for example be a whole shopping centre or an office block or a buy-to-let apartment.

>> **Portfolio diversification** – a portfolio is a collection of different investments such as shares, gilts, cash and property held by either wealthy individuals or corporate investors. Portfolio diversification is based on the

principle that different types of asset exhibit different income and capital growth patterns and that a prudent investor would seek exposure to these different patterns rather than be overexposed to the performance of just one type of asset.

>> **Collateral** – most property developments and transactions will require loans from banks or other lenders. Loans will be provided under certain conditions which normally include the requirement for the borrower to provide collateral which the bank will then have first charge over. If anything goes wrong, the bank can take possession of the collateral so that it can be sold to redeem any remaining debt. Collateral can be used creatively by large organizations to support prudent borrowing needed to expand the business. Thus uncharged properties owned by an organization could be seen as valuable and exploitable collateral assets.

>> **Corporate social responsibility (CSR)** – in a property context CSR implies that developers, purchasers and users of property will have regard to how sustainable a property is when measured against the triple bottom line, i.e. is the property sustainable in economic, environmental and social terms. The ability to calibrate the monetary value of a property against these three dimensions is still in its infancy, although there is some tentative evidence to suggest that buildings which have a sustainability accreditation will tend to perform better financially.

2.1 Introduction

Property valuers operate at the interface between clients, the providers of finance and property assets and they therefore fulfil a pivotal and responsible role. Valuers undertake this role in the various branches of the property market for different types of employer or client. For example valuers may be directly employed by a property company or investment fund where valuation work is used internally or they may work in a professional practice where they may be responding to the instructions of a wide variety of public, private and voluntary sector clients. In the public sector valuers may be employed by local authorities, central government departments or an agency of government.

To be effective in the settings in which they work, valuers will normally have developed a good understanding of the characteristics of types of properties that they are customarily asked to value and the objectives of their clients or employers when they seek valuation advice.

The property market, which is the domain in which valuers work is in fact a number of different property markets, segregated by property type and tenure. Within these market sectors properties have different qualities and characteristics which affect value. When viewed as an investment asset, property is quite different from a number of other investment opportunities with which it competes. However, these differences can appeal to some corporate investors and particularly those looking to diversify, i.e. reduce the risk to large investment portfolios.

The chapter considers the financial dimension where valuations are often sought to support property related loan applications to banks by borrowers. The chapter rounds up by discussing some of the many types of valuations which clients procure in relation to commercial and residential property.

2.2 Theory and the property market

Compared to an idealized perfect market, the property market is said to exhibit various imperfections which make it less efficient than it might otherwise be. There is said to be imperfect knowledge in the property market, although the availability of Land Registry data on the internet and contributions made by various property websites has in recent years improved the information flow and transparency in the market.

The property market is said to be fragmented and unlike commodities markets or central stock exchanges there is no central dealing room or focus for the property market. Property is diverse and each property has unique characteristics including location and so the market is by its nature decentralized and diffused.

There is restriction of movement into and out of the property market because of the constraints of time, legal and financial considerations. While there can occasionally be very fast transactions when both the purchaser and vendor are motivated and make a special effort, on average a commercial or residential property transaction will take around three months to complete. For much of that time there is no guarantee that the transaction will complete on the terms initially agreed and the situation only really becomes certain with the exchange of contracts towards the end of the process.

Properties with a high unit cost are prone to illiquidity. It can be very difficult to dispose of large commercial properties such as shopping centres, hotels and office blocks because of the limited number of potential purchasers in the market at any one time who are capable of making the scale of investment required. The so called 'lotting size' issue does reduce flexibility in that ordinarily the whole property needs to be purchased, although joint ventures can to some extent overcome the indivisibility issue.

In the short run the supply of property is inelastic as reflected in Figure 2.1 which depicts the theoretical relationship between supply and demand for land.

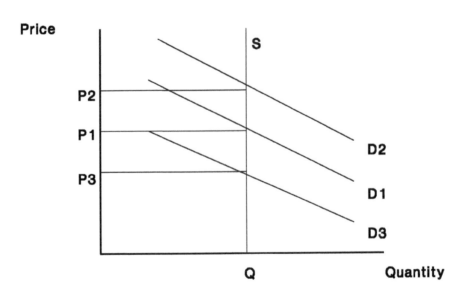

Figure 2.1 The supply of land

The vertical alignment of the supply schedule: S reflects the fact that land is a scarce resource. The use of land can of course be changed in order to increase the supply of a particular type of property. The supply of development land is not totally inelastic as the supply schedule below suggests, as local planning authorities can gradually release land in response to population pressures which necessitate the gradual expansion of towns and cities. The price mechanism plays a part in this process as the planning system has been reformed in recent years so that it is now more responsive to, but not dominated by price signals.

While there is some elasticity in the supply of land, ultimately the supply of land is finite. It is against this backdrop of overall scarcity that land is only released for development when absolutely necessary and when that decision can be shown to be the most sustainable option. Given constraints on the land supply, increases in demand such as represented below by the shift from D1 to D2 will cause significant increases in price in the short term as illustrated by the shift from P1 to P2.

Inelasticity in the supply of land also has consequences where demand falls away and thus in Figure 2.1 above the price would drop quite dramatically to P3 if demand fell to D3. This is effectively what happens during a recession when property values will tend to fall quite sharply, often after a number of years of steady growth in property values fuelled by consistent demand. It is not necessary here to delve into the causes of property cycles and readers could for example consult Balchin *et al.* (2000: 360–5) for a summary of that subject.

Property markets bring buyers and sellers together to enable exchanges and in that respect they fulfil a valuable clearing house role. However markets are also fickle and there will always be an element of risk regarding the financial performance of properties. The expression 'buyer beware' was coined because markets and the transactions which take place within them are inherently risk prone. Despite the risks and recurrent peaks and troughs in the property market, the longer term financial performance of property suggests that it can outperform the inflation rate to exhibit real growth. This presupposes sensible stock selection, adequate property maintenance and the need to take a longer term perspective.

Of course when looked at in detail, all markets for investments, commodities or services will have imperfections of one kind or another. It is unrealistic to expect that real markets for goods or services will conform to the conceptual ideals of the perfect market where imperfections do not exist. Given that imperfections are inevitable in the workings of any market, then imperfections will be encountered in the property market where they will present challenges for valuers when undertaking their work. In later chapters when valuation techniques are discussed it will become evident that one way of overcoming some of the imperfections encountered, is to create a number of reasoned assumptions or hypothetical constructs in order to arrive at a defensible value for a property.

2.3 Owner-occupier and investment markets

Property has an important use value for businesses and households and it can also play the role of an investment asset that produces both income and capital growth, the latter is realized when the asset is disposed of. The property investment market comes about through the collective action of individual and corporate investors who purchase existing properties or develop new ones so that they can be leased to other parties in return for rental income. In the UK the Investment Property Forum (2005) has estimated that approximately 43 per cent of all commercial property is leased and thus the balance of approximately 57 per cent is owner occupied by the relevant business.

In the commercial property sector there is a correlation between the size of the property and the propensity for it to be an investment rather than an owner occupied property. Larger commercial properties are more likely to be investments owned by large corporate landlords. Thus the office towers which can be seen on the horizon of most large cities will tend to be owned by corporate property investors, such as pension funds or real estate investment trusts. The floorspace within such towers could be leased to one corporate occupier such as a financial services or insurance company. However in the majority of cases, office towers are multi-let to numerous business tenants, who may take a floor, or a number of floors or parts of floors on occupational leases.

Similarly large shopping centres will also tend to be owned by institutional investors who let the individual shops to retailers. The same is true of large edge of town and city business and retail parks where there may be an institutional landlord who owns the whole site and who has granted occupational leases of varying lengths to the business occupiers. Given the size of some of these developments there are sometimes joint venture arrangements where two or more corporate landlords take proportionate shares in the freehold relative to the stake invested. Alternatively the freeholds of specific plots may be sold off to different investors who then have responsibility for leasing the buildings on their particular plot or plots.

Regarding residential property, statistics published by the Department for Communities (2011) reveal that in 2009 the private rented sector accounted for 4.2 million of the total of 27.1 million dwellings in the UK. Thus the invested stock of residential properties accounts for approximately 15.5 per cent of all dwellings. Most of the private rented residential stock is held by small investors many of whom have become buy-to-let investors over the last 10 years, attracted by the potential gains from this type of investment activity.

Whether in a residential or commercial property context, the property investment market relies upon rights and responsibilities defined in landlord and tenant law which has evolved over a long period. Perhaps understandably the law has evolved differently for residential and commercial property but in essence it reflects the fact that for some companies and households it is sometimes more practical to rent rather than buy property. The tendency to rent is stronger in the commercial property sector where for example, financial services, professional practices, manufacturing, distribution and retailing firms may find it more financially viable to rent rather than own the properties they occupy.

The UK therefore has an established commercial property investment market populated mainly by corporate landlords who include financial institutions, property companies and Real Estate Investment Trusts (REITS). These organizations trade investment grade properties on the basis of their income producing ability and capital growth potential. In recent years this market has seen some large companies dispose of the freehold of their properties and then to lease them back for operational purposes, so that the capital freed up in a sale and leaseback can be used to develop the particular business. The tendency for a company to rent its premises or to acquire premises as an owner occupier will depend on a number of factors including the stage of development that a company has reached and what its corporate strategy and expansion plans may be.

The circumstances are different in the housing sector, where home ownership is a reasonable ambition held by most people, reflected in the fact that nearly 70 per cent of the housing stock is already owner occupied. Technically, a large proportion of those households will not yet own their homes outright but will be at some intermediate stage of paying off a mortgage, but most will successfully make that journey to ultimately become home owners in a real sense. For statistical purposes however they are already deemed to be home owners.

2.4 Property as an investment

Property as an investment asset is in competition with alternative investment opportunities which all have different combinations of risk and reward and management responsibilities. Property investment presents some risks and it is relatively more costly and difficult to purchase and divest of than most other investments. Property also presents ongoing management obligations and while these may be contracted out to asset management companies, there will be some costs to be borne in transferring the responsibilities. There is no escaping the fact that property investment is different from other types of investment because the ownership of physical assets such as real property is more complex than the ownership of a share certificate.

Given that there are more stock selection, verification and ownership responsibilities arising for property than arise for many other forms of investment, a rational investor would need the incentive of an attractive rate of return for investing in property. That rate of return is traditionally benchmarked against what is sometimes referred to as the risk free rate. The latter is the return that could be earned from investing in an asset which had virtually no risk and no ongoing management obligations, such as depositing funds in a building society account or buying gilt edged stock.

Investors also have different attitudes to risk; some will be willing to expose a proportion of their investable funds to higher risks and thereby expect to earn higher returns for the additional risk exposure. Smaller investors, who perhaps have more to lose, will tend to be more risk averse and could not therefore expect to earn high returns for making more cautious investment choices. It is a truism that all investors are risk averse to some extent in that they will act rationally in trying to reduce risks while maintaining the best rate of return possible. Thus if an investor has £50,000 invested in asset A which is earning a 5 per cent per annum return and £50,000 in asset B which is also earning 5 per cent per annum but some risks appear which threaten the returns on asset B, most rational investors would divest of asset B and reinvest the money in safer asset A, at least until the risk profiles equalized.

The extent to which an investor could be characterized as risk seeking or entirely risk averse is linked to expectations about investments and how willing an investor is to accept divergence from the perfect hypothetical investment which would have the following characteristics.

- There would be total security of capital.
- There would be perfect liquidity enabling the asset to be disposed of very easily.
- There would be a regular and secure income stream from the capital invested.
- There would be negligible cost involved in acquiring and then divesting of the asset.
- The investment would be divisible, enabling part of it to be sold if necessary.
- There would be security in real terms, so that increases in the investment's value kept pace with or exceeded the rate of inflation.

In reality it would be very difficult if not impossible to find an investment which met all of these characteristics and even if it could be found, the rate of return given the high degree of security would probably be negligible. In reality investors have to settle for some of the idealized characteristics while forgoing others. Thus a very risk-averse investor might choose an asset which had total capital security and a regular income but where the rate of return was modest and might not always be as good as the rate of inflation. A risk-seeking investor might forgo security of capital when seeking higher but potentially variable income returns than the risk-averse investor could expect for taking a more cautious approach.

Table 2.1 opposite considers some of the key investment characteristics of a typical residential buy-to-let investment property in comparison to competing investment assets. For example a key variable is whether an investment achieves real security in that the capital value will not fall in real terms after inflation has been accounted for. Real values can be thought of in terms of purchasing power, if this declines in terms of capital value or income then the real value return is falling and the investment is inflation-prone (as opposed to inflation-proof).

The comparison above says something about the relationship between risk and return for each investment opportunity. Thus investments which pose greater risk should offer a higher return and conversely the low risk options could not be expected to earn high returns. For example the capital invested in premium bonds is not at risk but there is only an outside probability that the bonds will earn anything. Shares are considered more risky than property and so the expectation is that a portfolio of shares in the leading companies should earn higher returns than less risky property.

Some investments will inevitably out-perform others in the simple comparison in Table 2.1 opposite, although the type of investment chosen is also influenced by an investor's characteristics. For example investors have different tax status, so that one or other of the investments will become more or less appealing to them. There may also be ethical considerations which affect investment choices. Investors will differ in their expectations regarding the timing of returns, some will require early cash flow while others might be able to take a longer term view to realize capital growth. Finally, risk and return is related to the liquidity and asset management responsibilities which some investors may be able to tolerate while others will not.

Table 2.1 The characteristics of different investment opportunities

Characteristics of investment	Type of investment				
	A buy-to-let house	Shares	Gilt edged stock	Building society accounts	Premium bonds
Security of capital	Reasonably secure although market downturns will reduce capital values.	Some risk, shares can lose value.	Very secure.	Very secure.	Very secure.
Security of income	Not guaranteed, letting will require marketing, vetting and management.	Not guaranteed, depends on company performance.	Very secure.	Very secure.	No, requires winning numbers to be drawn.
Regularity of income	If let, yes.	Yes, if dividends are issued.	Yes.	Yes.	No.
Ease of purchase and disposal	No, takes time and expense to buy and sell.	Yes.	Yes.	Yes.	Yes.
Divisibility	No.	Yes.	Yes.	Yes.	Yes.
Real growth (hedge against inflation)	Normally but depends on the property and the holding period.	Depends on company performance.	Normally but not always.	Depends on the account.	No.

2.5 Property and investment portfolios

Property and in particular commercial property, is one of a number of competing investment media for large corporate investors such as pension funds and insurance companies. These investors will typically assemble portfolios of investment assets to generate returns although they will also be aware of the need to reduce risk through diversifying the collection of assets in their portfolios.

Although property can play a risk reduction role in investment portfolios, the role of property should not be overstated, as most major investment portfolios are dominated by more conventional investment media such as equities, gilts and cash. Large corporate investors will however tend to hold some investment properties which will make up a small proportion of the overall value of a portfolio of investments. Prudent investors will seek to manage their exposure to the performance of any particular asset through diversification so that in simple terms they do not have 'all of their eggs in one basket'. Diversifying a portfolio of investments is an effective way of reducing risk and thus corporate investors will keep their investment portfolios constantly under review by considering both the spectrum of investments and the effect that the acquisition or disposal of an asset will have on the other investments held.

For example if an investor already has assets A, B and C in a portfolio and is then offered asset D, it is the effect on the overall portfolio by adding D that is critical, rather than its particular performance. Asset D could be a very risky property but if changes in its value over time follow a different pattern to those for assets A, B and C then the inclusion of D might make the portfolio less risky. The principle of diversification has led authors such as Baum (2009) to consider the correlation of returns from property with other asset classes. While there is no need here to investigate this concept in depth, there is some evidence to suggest that investment properties have a low correlation with the financial performance of gilts and equities. This suggests that for corporate investors, property is a good diversifier and therefore risk reducer.

Pension funds and insurance companies are not the only large corporate investors who buy and sell investment properties, as there are also established property companies with significant budgets to support the acquisition and sometimes development of major commercial properties. In recent years a number of the UK's leading property companies such as British Land, Land Securities, SEGRO, Hammerson, Great Portland Estates and Derwent London have converted into Real Estate Investment Trusts (REITs) in order to benefit from reduced taxation. To stay within the more favourable tax regime created by the government, REITs must concentrate on their property trading and rental activities so that development becomes a minor part of the business. REITs have to pass on to shareholders the majority of their earnings from owning and managing thousands of commercial properties which include shopping centres, office blocks, industrial and warehouse units both in the UK and overseas.

The property portfolios held by leading REITs show the practical application of the principle of diversification. These property portfolios, which run into billions of pounds by value, exhibit in different ways both a geographical and sector spread which prevents over-exposure to the performance of one particular sector of the property market. The sheer volume of properties held by these organizations also helps with diversification as financial performance is then less reliant on high value flagship properties in a portfolio.

2.6 Factors affecting property values

It is intriguing sometimes to pause and ponder on the question: where does value emanate from? The price that an asset achieves in a sale provides concrete evidence that somebody valued an asset up to a certain price and that they were willing to pay that sum of money to enjoy the 'value' bestowed by the asset. The price obtained by the vendor crystallizes the value of the asset and it is often a valuer's role to try to predict what that value is in advance of a transaction.

The value of a property is subliminally underpinned by a number of factors some of which enhance value and some of which detract from value. Take for example the value of a major hotel in the tourist district of a famous city. Its value will reflect subjective interpretation and almost unconscious synthesis of a number of factors.

For example, a large part of the hotel's business will probably rely on international tourists who will make decisions on whether to travel based upon economic stability in their own countries and advantageous exchange rates. A major hotel's business and therefore its value will tend to decline when there is a global recession, general economic uncertainty and exchange rate turbulence. There is also a supply and demand relationship between the number of bed-spaces provided by hotels of a particular quality and the demand for those bed-spaces. Where new hotels are developed the supply and demand relationship could be disturbed to the detriment of existing providers if there is already sufficient supply in the market.

In the residential sector housing values are less affected by the arrival of new stock because new developments only represent a tiny proportion of the millions of dwellings which already exist and which tend therefore to set the tone for housing values. Housing values are more likely to be influenced by mortgage credit availability, interest rates, changes in stamp duty thresholds and the confidence of borrowers to be able to take on and meet loan repayments. The latter is a factor of job security and employment rates generally.

As well as macro economic factors which set the general tone for housing values, the specific property characteristics also play their part in determining what somebody will pay for a property. Thus obvious factors come into play such as the age, style, design, architectural detailing, quality and size of external spaces and the presence or absence of on-site parking. The state of repair will affect value as will the availability of services such as central heating. Housing values are also sensitive to the proximity to good schools and other services and improvements in transport infrastructure can boost residential property values significantly. Gradual gentrification of an area where homeowners are improving the housing stock can create very fashionable enclaves where housing values increase sharply.

Tenure will also affect property values and in the residential sector there will generally be a preference for freehold rather than leasehold property. The latter can be difficult to sell in some situations when the lease has less than 80 years remaining and where there may also be high annual service charges combined with ground rent payments. Where a property is being evaluated as a buy-to-let prospect, the above characteristics are also relevant but in addition factors such as the government's tax policies on capital gains and income derived from rents also come into play.

In commercial property the value of freeholds will tend to be significantly higher than leasehold interests and this area of valuation is discussed and illustrated in later chapters. The potential for extension, renovation, reuse and redevelopment will affect the value. The ease of purchase and sale will also affect the property price and there is a tendency for the price to fall when the marketing process is lengthy and unsuccessful.

In recent years the concept of Corporate Social Responsibility has surfaced on the agenda of most large companies and this will increasingly mean that the properties which are developed, purchased or leased must achieve some wider social and environmental benefits as well as satisfying economic criteria. In order to hold their value or outperform their peer group, properties will increasingly need to demonstrate through some form of recognized accreditation that they are sustainable.

The RICS (2009: 66) advice to its valuers on the topic of sustainability is that they should take full account of the economic, social and environmental dimensions of sustainability when assessing the value of properties. For example, new and retro-fitted commercial buildings in the UK may attract a sustainability rating under BREEAM (Building Research Establishment Environmental Assessment Method) which awards standards such as 'good', 'very good' and 'excellent'. In the residential sector the counterpart for BREEAM is the government's Code for Sustainable Homes which awards a star rating up to six stars and which is a zero carbon home. At present there is no straightforward method or formula which a valuer can use to automatically convert the sustainability accreditations which a building may have into a monetary value.

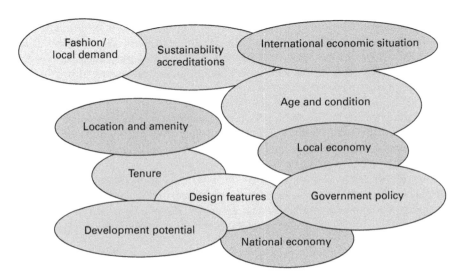

Figure 2.2 What affects property values?

However researchers such as Lorenz (2009) suggest that the value added through enhanced sustainability will become more mainstream in valuation work, as investors and occupiers begin to expect sustainability accreditations in the buildings they pay for.

Leading property companies in the UK including those that have converted into REITs, have already taken ownership of the concept of sustainability and this implies that they are beginning to see a connection between financial performance and the sustainability of the assets which they acquire, develop or refurbish. For example Derwent London plc (2010: 15) is one such company and it has a corporate policy commitment that its developments of over 5,000 m² must achieve a minimum BREEAM rating of 'very good'. Figure 2.2 above provides a summary of the factors such as sustainability which affect property values.

2.7 The legal dimension

When valuing properties valuers have to be aware of whether they are dealing with freehold or leasehold, which are the two principal interests in land. Other interests include restrictive covenants and easements which are restrictions on the use of land by a freeholder or leaseholder. A covenant is a contractual obligation in a deed while an easement is a right under common law that burdens one piece of land for the benefit of another. Easements include rights of way, rights of support and rights of light and ventilation. Interests in land have to be distinguished from permission to enter upon land such as licences. There is no need to delve too deeply into legal nuances beyond the broad point that property acquisition requires legal advice so that there is no discrepancy between the rights in land sought by an investor and those that are actually being purchased.

Freeholds are properties in which the owners hold ownership absolutely and in perpetuity. The owner is either in possession of the property as an owner occupier or derives rents arising from leases or tenancies granted as a property investor. Leasehold properties are subject to legal agreements allowing the lessees rights over the property for a term of years. Freehold and leasehold interests are defined as legal estates by the Law of Property Act 1925 and these are enforceable against anyone. Other interests are termed equitable interests and can be enforced against some people only. Leasehold and equitable interests are carved out of the freehold interest. At the end of a lease there is a reversion to the landlord (that is the property ownership reverts back to him). However, the Landlord and Tenant Acts provide powers in certain circumstances for commercial tenants to extend or renew their leases.

There are two principal types of lease:

- The *building* or *ground lease*, where the lessee (the person who takes the lease) erects buildings such as a block of flats or a shopping centre on a freeholder's site. These leases tend to be long because of the commitment made in building and depending on the development the lease length may be 99 or 125 years but could be as much as 999 years.
- The *occupational lease*, where the lease is of both land and buildings for occupation. These leases are very common in commercial property where for

example a retail firm will take a lease on a retail warehouse the freehold of which is owned by a corporate property investor. In recent years the average length of these leases has been gradually reducing and is now fewer than 10 years although it is still possible to encounter new business leases with a 25-year term. In virtually all cases there will be provision in a commercial lease for rent reviews which will normally take place every five years although given shorter leases the frequency may be three years.

Subleases are granted by lessees and carved from their leasehold interest. The nature of leases and subleases is shown in Figure 2.3 below.

Beside the legal interests in land, government statutes may act to constrain land in one way or another. For example the government can intervene in respect of lessees and tenants of certain properties, both to give security of tenure and to control levels of rent. The government also intervenes through its fiscal policy to tax income and capital gains arising from land. Local authorities have statutory control over the development and use of land through the Town and Country Planning Acts and over the construction of buildings through the Building Regulations. There is a myriad of legislation relating to the use and condition of premises including the Offices, Shops and Railway Premises Act, the Factories Act, the Fire Precautions Act, the Housing Acts and Health and Safety legislation.

Valuers are not lawyers and they cannot be expected to know all of the details of legislation that can affect land and buildings. However they have a duty of care towards their clients and must conduct reasonable investigations and

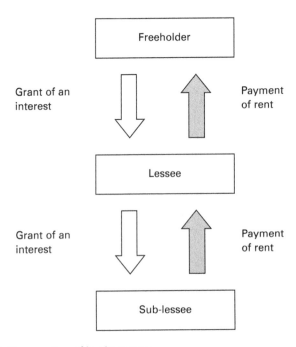

Figure 2.3 The granting of legal interests

Figure 2.4 The Courthouse pub in Dartford

consult legal advisors (who are probably already acting for a client) to ensure that if there are legal constraints then they must be reflected in the value ascribed to a property. For example in a high street setting properties have a particular use class under the Town and Country Planning Use Classes Order. A valuer would therefore verify whether a subject property was for example Use Class A1, which is the shops use class, or A2 which is the use class for financial services or A3, the restaurants use class, or A4 for drinking establishments or A5 for hot food takeaways.

The pub above in Figure 2.4 is now in Use Class A4 but would have needed a change of use consent from the local authority as well as a licence to enable the conversion from the building's original use as a courthouse. The latter would have been considered *sui generis* which signifies a unique use which does not easily fit within the existing use classes. Changes between use classes generate numerous permutations which are beyond the scope of this book, however the point is that a valuer would be expected to make reasonable inquiries to confirm the specific use class for the property being valued.

2.8 Sources of finance

Property transactions will normally consume large sums of money, a large proportion of which is likely to be borrowed. Where loans are required, property valuers will normally be involved acting for either the borrower or the lender. In the world of property, finance is generally raised by corporate entities, such as property companies and REITs using existing assets as collateral for new borrowing. Collateral can be properties which are already owned but as yet uncharged in that they will not have previously been put forward as collateral to support borrowing. However collateral does not necessarily have to be real estate and other combinations of assets could be offered to a lender by a borrower to support a loan application.

Conventionally most property transactions of any scale will rely upon some debt finance i.e. borrowing. Given the benefits of gearing (discussed in Chapter 10) borrowers might be relying on lending to fund the major part of the costs to acquire a property or to undertake development, sourcing the funds from the corporate lending divisions of the major banks. Financial institutions such as insurance companies and pension funds might also provide loans to developers where there is already a partnership established around a specific development. This enables the institution to attach conditions to the funding provided so that a degree of control is exerted over a developer to ensure that the development meets the particular specification of the fund. The funder may have agreed a pre-sale with the developer under which the fund takes over the completed development on pre-agreed terms in order to manage the investment over the longer term.

Historically banks have tended to dominate the market for short term lending on developments while financial institutions have come to specialize in the selective acquisition of property investments which they then manage over the medium to long term for rental income and capital growth.

Banks can make considerable profits from lending on property developments and transactions of various sorts and over the last 50 years they have shown considerable enthusiasm for becoming involved in particularly commercial property, despite periodic property recessions. The process has become global and developers are able to source the best loan deals by shopping in the international finance markets. For example the development of the Shard of Glass office tower at London Bridge is a very risky mega project which commenced in 2009 just when the global economy was shaking off the worst effects of the credit crunch. The loans sourced by the developer to support that development were obtained from a consortium of Middle Eastern banks.

While property offers the potential for large rewards for banks, there are of course significant risks which lenders naturally seek to manage. Lenders try to avoid becoming over-exposed to the activities of one developer or the capriciousness of the property market generally and they will therefore try to establish an exit route in the event that ventures do not go as well as forecast at the outset. Thus before agreeing to fund major development projects or property acquisitions, lenders such as banks will normally commission at least two independent valuations against which they will benchmark their loan to value offer to the borrower. Thus if the lower of two valuations of a commercial development suggests that it will be worth £30 million when complete a bank might be prepared to lend up to 65 per cent of that figure in return for a first charge on the scheme. This provides some comfort for the bank in that if the developer fails and the scheme is taken into possession to be sold to recover debt, it would take a fairly dramatic collapse in property values for the scheme not to realize 65 per cent of £30 million which is £19.5 million. Following the credit crunch and the over-exposure of some banks to property because of causal lending practices, it is likely that more scrutiny will be brought to bear upon developer loan applications in future.

2.9 Lending criteria

The cost and availability of lending is a function of the value of a particular project and the amount of cost to be financed. The nature of the development in terms of its location, design, combination of uses and likely demand are all factors which a lender will need to be reassured on. A lender will also want to know whether a development has been fully or partly pre-let or is entirely speculative. For example the Walbrook office building shown in Figure 2.5 below is available to let after having emerged on to the City of London office market. Thus it was a speculative scheme, although the risks are significantly reduced because of its address and convenient transport connections. There is therefore risk to the lender because the scheme is speculative but this risk is mitigated because of the location where there is a strong likelihood that the building will find business tenants.

Where some or all of the lettings have been secured, a lender will be interested in the quality of the tenants who will be providing the cash flow to support the re-financing of a development. Other important criteria are the track record of the developer, the duration of the loan and the frequency and

Figure 2.5 The Walbrook office development in the City of London

size of repayments prior to redemption. The scrutiny process that a lender brings to bear on a loan application to acquire or develop property can be summarized under the four 'Cs' as follows:

- character;
- cashstake;
- capability; and
- collateral.

Character

This relates to the trading history or development experience of a borrower. In respect of a property developer or an investment company the lender will want to know whether the borrower has the experience to complete the development or manage the investment. Established developers and property investors will have no difficulty in showing that they have the necessary experience to carry out the particular venture, as they will probably have a successful track record to draw upon. It will be more difficult for unknown or new companies to convince a bank that they have the experience and staying power to carry the responsibilities which go with large projects and large loans. Banks will usually examine the corporate credit ratings of loan applicants and returns to Companies House where they exist.

Cashstake

This relates to how much equity the borrower is going to contribute to the development or acquisition. A bank will normally conduct sufficient investigations to satisfy itself that the equity is not money borrowed from another source and that it is not tied up in another venture. Due diligence would be undertaken to ensure that the money was clean and not a notional accounting surplus which could not actually contribute the project in hand.

Capability

The lender will seek assurances that the borrower has the capability to service the loan by meeting repayments when required. A bank would therefore look at the borrowers accounts or business plan so that a clear relationship could be established between the estimated cash flow from the project and the loan repayment obligations. A loan cover margin would normally be built in so that if the known repayments per quarter were £X then the cash flow arising from the project to meet those repayment obligations would have to be demonstrated to be at least $1.25 \times £X$.

Collateral

The lender will want to know what security will be offered for the loan, its value and its saleability. The lender will want to know who valued the security and on what basis. The lender will then assess the extent of the loan that would be exposed against the value of the security. The importance of collateral has already been mentioned earlier in this chapter and it will surface again below when examples to illustrate the specialized nature of valuation work are considered.

2.10 The specialized nature of valuation work

Valuers will tend to become specialists in a particular field and in a particular geographic area and when they step outside of that domain they have a professional obligation to ask themselves whether they are really equipped to carry out a client's instruction effectively. Sometimes the answer is that the commission can be undertaken but will need a specific contribution from another valuer or specialist to bridge a gap in knowledge or local market awareness. Sometimes the answer to the question will be 'no' and thus the commission should be passed on to another valuer who is experienced and capable of carrying out the job.

In simple terms a valuer who becomes expert at valuing agricultural land and equipment in Yorkshire could not be expected to competently value a multi million pound hotel in the west end of London. Similarly a valuer who was equipped to tackle the hotel valuation could not be expected to value open cast mineral workings in Devon. The valuer who is equipped to tackle the latter valuation would not be the best specialist to approach to value an affordable housing development in Manchester.

It is not possible in this text to explore all of the possible permutations in which a valuation may be sought and those readers who wish to develop their understanding of this matter further, could go on to examine more specialized and advanced valuations texts such as Askham (2003) Hayward (2008) or Baum *et al.* (2007). This section of the chapter has more modest ambitions to set out some examples of the contexts in which valuations are sought by clients to support their property transactions. A glimpse is therefore provided of some of the interesting and specialized career paths that valuers can take. In subsequent chapters when different methods of valuation are explored the scope will be widened on the variety of circumstances where valuers are called upon for their expertise.

In commercial property markets, valuers could find themselves working for landlords or tenants in trying to determine the value of any of the different types of investment which produce different patterns of income. There are market rented freeholds, reversionary properties, secure ground rents, short leasehold profit rents, turnover rents and a valuer could be called upon to value any one of these types of property. For example a valuer may be asked by a major corporate landlord to value the freehold interests in a portfolio of properties for annual accounts purposes.

Valuers might also be instructed to value freehold properties which are to be disposed of. A valuer could also be instructed by a business tenant who wishes to verify the rental value of a property in the context of lease negotiations or rent reviews. Sometimes a valuer will be asked to place a value on a leasehold interest in a commercial property which has a finite life until the lease expires and therefore cannot be expected to be worth the same as the freehold equivalent. Examples of these types of valuations will be illustrated in later chapters when different valuation methods are explored.

In the residential sector, valuers will be active valuing properties for sale and in providing mortgage valuations for lenders such as building societies. As Baldwin *et al.* (2003) and RICS (2011: 149–51) explain there is also specialized work for valuers in the affordable housing sector for housing associations, who are also referred to as registered providers. These clients will sometimes require a valuation of part of their stock which is being put forward as collateral to support borrowing. Loans secured from banks or building societies play an important role in enabling housing associations to part fund the development or acquisition of new properties. By using un-charged dwelling stock in this way, a housing association is able to expand and meet its business objectives.

Housing association properties being evaluated as collateral are likely to remain in social housing use in which guise their income generating ability is limited. This is simply because the raison d'être for these properties is to provide affordable housing and charging high rents would be contrary to that objective. It is coincidental that those parts of an association's stock which remain uncharged may be used as collateral to support prudent borrowing but it is not a reason for housing associations to ramp up their rents beyond government guidelines.

Valuers who undertake work for housing association clients will therefore structure their valuations to reflect the assumption that the dwellings will remain in use as social housing for the foreseeable future. The valuation of this type of stock is therefore on the basis their *existing use value for social housing* (EUV–SH) and it involves a discounted cash flow of the net rental income arising from continued payment of affordable rents. The value arising for dwellings under EUV–SH will tend to be significantly lower than for similar properties with vacant possession and which could be sold for full market value.

Where a developer or housing association is producing a mixed tenure development containing a combination of open market housing, shared ownership and social rented properties, the valuation becomes more complicated. In this context a valuer will essentially combine the value streams from each constituent part of the scheme. Sales receipts from open market housing and the portion of shared ownership properties which have been sold are combined with the discounted cash flows of net rental income from the social rented properties and the unsold (but rented) part of the shared ownership properties. The RICS (2010) provides guidance to its valuers on this particular type of valuation.

Valuers may also become in involved at a later stage in such schemes when an occupier of a shared ownership unit wishes to buy a further tranche of the equity. A formal independent valuation is required at that point, so that the housing association achieves a fair return for selling an additional slice of a property's equity. The process is referred to as staircasing out to full ownership although it can take a long time, as not all shared ownership occupiers are equally motivated or financially able to staircase out to full ownership. These examples of types of valuation have been included to illustrate the specialized nature of valuation work, which rests upon technical knowledge of valuation techniques and contextual knowledge of the particular property sector and the client's overall objectives.

2.11 Summary

This chapter has examined the property market which is the imperfect domain in which valuers work. It was explained that in fact, there is no such thing as one homogeneous property market because it is divided between residential and commercial property and then between owner-occupied and rental properties. Rented property is more common in the commercial property sector where approaching half of the total stock of buildings are owned by property investors and leased out to business tenants. This is something of a marriage of convenience because some businesses need the flexibility associated with renting and do not wish to have large sums of capital tied up in properties when that money could better be spent on running and possibly expanding a business.

As well as playing the role of commercial landlords, commercial property investors will often be behind the development of very large properties such as shopping centres and office blocks. The latter pose considerable risks and the scale of investment required will normally exceed the capacities of individual companies who may wish to rent some space in these developments.

Circumstances are different in the residential sector where the lot size issue does not present itself to the same degree and where there is a reasonable expectation on the part of most households that they will ultimately become home owners. Despite the expansion of buy-to-let in recent years, the invested residential stock remains at around 15.5 per cent of all dwellings and it is unlikely to climb very much higher than that level. Valuers in the residential sector are therefore more likely to be providing valuations for sale or mortgage purposes to facilitate a purchase of a dwelling by an aspirant home owner.

Risk was found to be an ever present factor in the various branches of the property market because property values are not fixed nor subject to automatic growth. This is because property values reflect the inter-play of various economic forces and a constantly shifting relationship between supply and demand. Some wrongly believe that because a valuation has been placed on a property at a particular point in time that its value will never fall below that datum. Periodic property recessions prove that this is not the case and while valuations should be correct at the date when they are produced, subsequent valuations of the same property will be influenced by different market conditions. This might mean that valuations can sometimes be tracking the market downwards as well as upwards.

The chapter rounded up by considering some of the specialized areas where valuers work such as at the interface between banks and those wishing to borrow money against property. Some specialized areas of valuations were also discussed to illustrate how valuers develop knowledge about specific property contexts, client objectives and property characteristics. It is not possible to map all of the possible permutations, however the discussion in subsequent chapters contains scenarios and examples which will reveal a number of other contexts where valuers have carved out rewarding careers.

References

Askham, P. (2003) *Valuation: Special Properties and Purposes* (London: Estates Gazette).

Balchin, P., Isaac, D. and Chen, J. (2000) *Urban Economics: A Global Perspective* (Basingstoke: Palgrave).

Baldwin, C., Davies, F. and Petty, R. (2003) *A Valuation for All Seasons: A Practical Guide to Valuation for Housing Associations* (London: National Housing Federation).

Baum, A., Sams, G., Ellis, J., Hampson, C. and Stevens, D. (2007) *Statutory Valuations* (4th edn, London: EG Books).

Baum, A. (2009) *Commercial Real Estate Investment: A Strategic Approach* (2nd edn, London: EG Books).

Department for Communities (2011) *Table 101 Dwelling Stock: By Tenure, United Kingdom* (historical series) (London: Department for Communities and Local Government). Available in e-format at: www.communities.gov.uk

Derwent London plc (2010) *Report and Accounts 2010* (London: Derwent London plc).

Hayward, R. (ed.) (2008) *Valuation: Principles into Practice* (6th edn, London: EG Books).

Investment Property Forum (2005) *The Size and Structure of the UK Property Market* (London: Investment Property Forum).

Lorenz, D. (2009) *The Application of Sustainable Development Principles to the Theory and Practice of Property Valuation* (Karlsruhe: University of Karlsruhe).

RICS (2009) *Sustainability and the RICS Property Lifecycle* (London: RICS).

RICS (2010) *Valuation of Land for Affordable Housing* (London: RICS).

RICS (2011) *RICS Valuation Standards – Global and UK* (7th edn, London: RICS).

Self-assessment questions for Chapter 2

1 List some of the key factors which combine to affect property values and which a property valuer would normally be aware of.

2 The expression 'invested stock' is sometimes used in property context. What is the stock and who are the investors?

3 Explain some of the common circumstances in which a property lender such as a bank might become the client of a valuer?

4 What are the four Cs and why are they important in a property lending context?

5 What connections could be made between the work of a property valuer and CSR and BREEAM?

Outline answers are included at the back of the book.

3

The role of the valuer

3.1 Introduction
3.2 Types of valuation
3.3 The Red Book and valuation bases
3.4 Valuer qualifications and registration
3.5 Market volatility

3.6 Valuation accuracy and negligence
3.7 Valuation tables and formulas
3.8 Summary
References
Self-assessment questions

Aims

This chapter examines the different contexts, purposes and bases upon which clients request valuations of property. The chapter also looks at the attributes that valuers need in order to take on the responsibility of determining the value of a property. The chapter will explain that registered valuers are expected to work within the framework of the RICS *Valuation Standards* which is also known as the Red Book. Given that judgments will always need to be made in valuation work, the chapter will consider the acceptable degree of accuracy in valuation.

Finally the chapter rounds up by looking at an important tool which valuers use and which is the valuation tables and their underpinning formulas. That section of the chapter acts as a prelude to subsequent chapters where the mathematics is applied within different valuations methods.

Key terms

>> **Red Book** – the familiar name for the *RICS Valuation Standards* (2011) which sets out the terms, definitions and framework within which registered valuers should operate when carrying out valuations for clients.

>> **The bracket** – a term used by the courts when considering valuation accuracy and which is the acceptable tolerance either side of what a notionally competent valuer would have achieved. The width of the bracket will vary depending on the type of property being valued. For standard uncomplicated properties the courts have suggested that 10 per cent either side of the true value of a property is an acceptable degree of valuation accuracy.

>> **Basis of value** – the Red Book recognizes four bases of value which can be reported in valuations and these are *market value, market rent, worth or investment value* and *fair value*. The definitions of these bases are provided

below in this chapter. It is important that clients and valuers discuss and confirm instructions at the outset, so that there is no misunderstanding on the basis upon which a valuation is to be conducted.

3.1 Introduction

This chapter begins by looking at the variety of contexts and purposes for which clients seek valuations on properties. The discussion will explain that a property's value could be determined on any one of four valuation bases, although the majority of valuations are carried out to determine *market value* (for a sale) or *market rent* (for a letting). Some clients however require a valuation on the basis of *worth* given their specific investment expectations and resources. Finally *fair value* might be needed where there is a special transaction between two specific parties who already have a connection with a property and where in effect the rest of the market has been locked out.

Having summarized the purposes for which valuations are produced, the chapter considers the role, qualifications and responsibilities of valuers. In this discussion the term valuer refers to chartered surveyors who work as valuers and who since 2010 are required to register with their professional body: the RICS in order to practise as *registered valuers*. These individuals work in a wide variety of fields and much of the work which they undertake needs to comply with the standards set out in the RICS *Valuation Standards* (2011) which is more familiarly known as the Red Book. Even where the specific valuation being undertaken falls outside of the remit of the Red Book, such as valuation for certain types of agency work, the valuer will still be guided by the core principles in the Red Book and the rules of the Valuer Registration Scheme. These core principles include maintaining independence and integrity and avoiding conflicts of interest.

The guidelines in the Red Book and the availability of valuation techniques (which will be discussed in later chapters) provide the framework and toolkit for valuers; however, valuation is ultimately a matter of opinion. Despite internet accessible databases containing comparable market information and spreadsheets and software packages which make valuation calculations easier, valuation remains an art requiring an individual's subjective assessment of relevant factors.

The role of the valuer comes with significant responsibility for the obvious reason that if a property valuation is too low there is the possibility of a significant loss for a client, whereas a valuation which is too high will probably result in a property languishing on the market and a sale may not materialize. Faith is also placed in valuations by banks and building societies when they lend significant sums of money against residential and commercial property and so errors in valuation work can potentially lead to significant losses for those clients.

Valuers have an obvious duty of care which any professional owes to a client, and they must try to achieve high standards of accuracy because if those standards are not met they face the double risk of deregistration by the RICS and litigation from clients on the grounds of negligence. It will be explained however that if a valuer does a competent job he or she cannot be held liable for subsequent market fluctuations which will result in property values moving up or down over time.

At the end of the chapter there is a summary of the valuation tables and the formulas which generate the constants in those tables. The tables and the formulas are an important part of the valuer's toolkit because they form important elements in the various valuation methods. Although valuers do not have to be mathematically gifted, they do have to develop their numeracy skills to a certain standard in order to practice competently. Concluding the chapter on the valuation tables provides a logical platform for subsequent chapters where the valuation methods which rely upon the tables and formulas are discussed.

3.2 Types of valuation

Valuations are commissioned by clients from valuers in a variety of different contexts, although it is possible to identify two broad categories and which are *statutory* and *non-statutory* valuations. A summary of some of the main types of valuation under each heading is shown in Table 3.1 below however this list is not exhaustive and there are numerous other specialized areas where valuations are required. For example shared ownership is becoming a popular housing format provided by housing associations and a valuation is needed when a part-owner wishes to purchase a further share in a property.

Table 3.1 Statutory and non-statutory purposes for valuation

Types of valuation	
Statutory	*Non-statutory*
• rating and council tax • compulsory purchase and compensation • taxation generally where there is a property dimension • fair rents for dwellings • residential lease extensions and enfranchisements • aspects of commercial leases arising from landlord and tenant legislation	• purchase or disposal of a property • to establish rental value • reinstatement cost for fire insurance • residential and commercial mortgage valuations • valuation for company accounts • development appraisals and to secure development loans

There follows a brief summary of the different types of valuation identified in Table 3.1 above and which begins with the statutory valuations shown in the left-hand side of the table.

Statutory valuations

These types of valuations are conducted because either an Act specifically requires a valuation for a specific purpose or that the implementation of an Act or other statutory instrument has a financial consequence which triggers the need for a valuation. Because legislation is involved there will also be statutory rules and case law to interpret and this makes each branch of statutory valuation very specialized. For example Bond and Brown (2006) have produced a specialized text which just focuses on rating valuation. It is not possible or necessary in this text to explain all of the branches and intricacies of statutory valuations and so a brief summary of the main areas is provided below. However readers who want to explore the topic further could consult Baum *et al.* (2007). The main branches of statutory valuation are:

- *Valuations for rating* undertaken by officers who work for the Valuation Office Agency (VOA). The VOA is an executive agency of HM Revenue & Customs and it is responsible for among other things, assessing the rateable value of non-domestic properties based upon their annual market rental value. The VOA has an obligation to update the rating list every five years which triggers cycles of revaluation. The rateable value identified by the VOA is multiplied by a rate in the £1 set by central government but collected by local councils. The residential equivalent to business rates is the council tax which is based upon capital value bandings. To ensure fairness and transparency, there is an appeals process whereby businesses or residents who believe their rateable value or council tax assessment is incorrect can challenge the value identified by the VOA.
- Valuations for compulsory purchase and compensation are undertaken when land is to be acquired for regeneration purposes or to accommodate new transport infrastructure or to enable the construction of a nationally important project such as the Olympics venue in East London. The valuations undertaken play an important part in determining the compensation to be paid to those who have had part or all of their land acquired. Valuations are also needed to assess the compensation payable to those whose land has been adversely affected by severance or injurious affection.
- *Valuations for tax purposes* include assessment of the liability for capital gains tax on property assets and stamp duty land tax where interests in property are to exchange above certain value thresholds.
- *Assessments of fair rents* for rented dwellings.
- *Valuations in the context of residential leasehold enfranchisement* or where the tenants of long leasehold flats wish to exercise their right to extend a lease.
- *Valuations under Part II of the Landlord and Tenant Act 1954* where there are transactions involving commercial leases.

Statutory valuations are based on market valuations but there are often special assumptions made to reflect the special circumstances involved. For example, valuations for compulsory purchase compensation are required to ignore the potential effects of the scheme of development for which the compulsory purchase is being made. In those circumstances the expression 'valuing in the no-scheme world' is used.

Examples of non-statutory valuations are:

- *Valuations to establish market value in the context of a sale* and where the valuation is an estimate of what a property would change hands for on the valuation date between a willing buyer and seller.

- *Valuations to identify market rent* where a property is to be let or where a business is contemplating taking a commercial lease.
- *Valuations for fire insurance* based on the construction costs of reinstating a property which has been destroyed by fire.
- *Mortgage valuations* in the context of a mortgage loan application by a purchaser where the lender wishes to know if the property represents sufficient security for the size of the loan sought. These types of valuations may also be carried out where a residential property is being used as security for another transaction.
- *Valuation for company accounts* given that most businesses of any scale will have some value tied up in real property in one form or another.
- *Development appraisals* which are a specialized type of valuation to establish whether an envisaged development would be viable from a developer's perspective. These types of appraisal can be structured to identify the value of the land or the profit margin if the land value is already known. Development appraisals can also be used to support development loan applications, enabling a bank to assess the scale of loan which could be advanced against a developer's scheme. For major schemes where large loans are sought, it is likely that a bank will obtain two valuations and may lend a proportion of the value identified by the lower of the two valuations to reduce the bank's risk exposure to a scheme. Large housing associations who are active developers will sometimes wish to secure loans against the net rental income stream from properties subject to particular tenancy conditions and that will require a specialized type of valuation.

3.3 The Red Book and valuation bases

Much or what a valuer does is governed by the framework provided by the RICS's 'Red Book' whose full title is the *RICS Valuation Standards – Global and UK* and which by 2011 had reached its 7th edition. There is also a twin volume written specifically for India. The Red Book does not tell valuers how to value in each and every case and valuers are left to judge which techniques should best be employed in the particular circumstances encountered. However the Red Book does set professional and ethical standards which need to be met and it provides core definitions to provide consistency and to avoid misunderstanding around what valuers do for clients. Specific *Valuation Standards* within the Red Book specify such things as the minimum requirements which need to be met when reporting a valuation. There are also specialized *Guidance Notes* in the Red Book which deal with particular aspects of valuation.

Many of the principles and definitions regarding property valuation in the Red Book have global applicability. It is for this reason that in recent years, property valuers from different countries have been working together to try to harmonize these principles under the auspices of the International Valuation Standards Council (IVSC). This could be seen as an aspect of globalization involving the convergence and standardization of rules and procedures so that ultimately a client or bank anywhere in the world can place the same reliance on the professional standards of the valuation carried out.

A key area in the Red Book relates to the definition of four bases of valuation, because it is recognized that it is possible to report the value of a property in four different ways depending on the circumstances. Thus a valuation might be needed to confirm:

1 The capital value of a property, where that property is to be sold or where the value needs to be recorded for accounts purposes or to provide confirmation of the value of collateral for lending purposes.
2 The rental value of a property, where it is to be leased or because the rental value provides the basis for calculating the business rates payable on the property.
3 The investment value of a property, where a specific client wishes to know if a particular property will meet specific investment expectations.
4 The value of an interest in property in which two parties already have a commitment which effectively excludes the open maker but where a further transaction is envisaged which would release marriage or synergistic value which is to be shared between the parties.

In each of these four cases the Red Book provides a definition and these can now be considered in turn.

Market value

Market value is the first and most commonly referred to basis of value defined in the Red Book and it is one of the definitions agreed between the IVSC and the RICS and is as follows:

> The estimated amount for which a property should exchange on the date of valuation between a willing buyer and a willing seller in an arm's-length transaction after proper marketing wherein the parties had each acted knowledgeably, prudently and without compulsion. (2011: 27)

This relatively straightforward definition provides the basis for a lot of the work which valuers undertake and that is why Valuation Standard 3.2 in the Red Book (RICS, 2011: 27) expects valuers to adopt and work to this concept.

Given the importance attached to the concept of market value the RICS (2011: 28–9) has expanded upon some of the phrases used in the definition. For example the definition begins with the beguiling simply expression '*The estimated amount* ...' which the RICS explain is the best price reasonably obtainable by the seller and the most advantageous price reasonably obtainable by the buyer in the prevailing market conditions. No account is to be given to any special concessions or the ulterior motives of either of the parties, as what is assumed is an uncomplicated arm's-length transaction where the independence of the buyer and seller is not distorted by any special factors. It would therefore be entirely wrong under the definition to take account of special relationships between the buyer and seller, such as where a subsidiary company was purchasing a property from a parent company under special conditions.

The market value definition also assumes that neither party is in an undue hurry where they might make rash decisions just to achieve a quick transaction, which would almost certainly distort the price. The definition assumes that both parties are fully aware of the characteristics of the property that is to be exchanged, so that they are not acting in ignorance when making or accepting an offer on a property. It is also assumed in the definition that the property has been given adequate market exposure before the buyer and seller finally come together to agree the exchange price.

When trying to identify the market value of a property, a valuer is therefore working to an idealized set of circumstances which although they may be approximated in reality they are seldom found to the degree of perfection implied by the definition. However, despite the imperfections often found in the real marketplace, the definition of market value does help valuers screen out distractions, suppositions and speculation about what might happen in different scenarios. The definition therefore enables the valuer to be clear-minded so that a focus can be brought to bear on the subject property in order to identify its market value.

Market rent

The definition of *market value* above is fundamentally concerned with capital value and it can apply where a property is to be sold. The counterpart to market value where the rental value of a property needs to be identified is *market rent* which the RICS (2011: 31) Red Book defines as:

> The estimated amount for which a property, or space within a property, should lease (let) on the date of the valuation between a willing lessor and a willing lessee on appropriate lease terms in an arm's-length transaction after proper marketing wherein the parties had acted knowledgeably, prudently and without compulsion.
>
> Whenever market rent is provided the 'appropriate lease terms' which it reflects should also be stated.

This is also a definition adopted by the IVSC because it has global applicability and Valuation Standard 3.3 in the Red Book therefore expects valuers to adopt this definition when carrying out rental valuations. As might be expected because this definition is dealing with rental value, the phraseology changes from 'buyer and seller' to 'lessor and lessee'. There is also a supplementary sentence referring to 'appropriate lease terms' so that the valuer focuses on key issues such as the remaining duration of the lease, whether there are break clauses and rent review clauses and who under the lease is responsible for building insurance and repairs. The lease terms will combine to affect the market rent for the property, an issue which will be explored in a little more depth in Chapter 8 where investment properties are considered.

Worth and investment value

This is the third basis of valuation in the Red Book and when discussing it there is a deliberate change in terminology because while most valuations will use market reference points to identify capital and rental value, this basis of value stems from an individual purchaser's perspective. The Red Book defines the basis of a valuation for worth or investment value as follows:

The value of property to a particular owner, investor, or class of investors for identified investment or operational objectives. (2011: 32)

For example the market value of a London hotel might be £100 million. However an international hotel operator who wants to establish a presence in the London hotel market might be willing to pay more than that to acquire the property, subject to the transaction achieving the hotel operator's minimum rate of return. Given the required rate of return and the instruction to carry out the valuation on that basis, a valuer could determine what the hotel might be worth to the specific hotel operator. If the hotel operator is willing to accept a lower rate of return than the peer group of international hotel operators, then it is likely that a value of worth to the investor will be higher than the market is willing to pay and the investor may well be able to acquire the hotel.

A valuation of worth to a specific investor could also be very similar to market value. Alternatively and to extend the discussion above, there might be other hotel operators who already have significant exposure in the London market and would only contemplate the acquisition of a further hotel at a price where the annual returns would represent an above normal rate of return on capital invested. A valuation of worth for those types of client would probably generate a bid below the market value of £100 million, representing those investors' ambivalence about acquiring another London hotel.

To illustrate the difference which can arise between market value and worth, assume that a developer has just completed and let an office unit on a business park which is producing a net market rental income from a business tenant of £70,000 per annum. A market valuation of this asset for Investor A would interpret market information to arrive at a yield of say 7 per cent in order to produce a capital value for the asset of £1,000,300 as shown in Table 3.2 below.

However the cost of capital for Investor B is 5 per cent and for this class of asset the investor requires an additional risk premium of 3 per cent and so expects the return or yield to be 8 per cent. Investor B already has a number of similar properties in the portfolio and so there is no particular appetite or special reason to vary the corporate policy expectation of an 8 per cent yield. Investor B's valuation of worth for this investment asset is therefore £875,000 which is below the market value. Investor B's bid is therefore unlikely to be successful, although if the property remained unsold and the price gradually fell to around £875,000 Investor B might well reactivate the offer.

Investor C has a lower cost of capital at 4 per cent and for properties like this which are not currently held in the portfolio, the risk premium can be as low as

Table 3.2 The difference between market value and worth

Valuation basis	Client	Yield (capitalization rate)	YP in perp. (1/yield)	Net annual rental income	Capital value
Market Value	Investor A	7%	14.29	£70,000	£1,000,300
Worth	Investor B	8%	12.50	£70,000	£875,000
Worth	Investor C	6%	16.67	£70,000	£1,166,900

2 per cent producing a yield of 6 per cent and a capital value of £1,166,900. Investor C could therefore outbid the market as a higher worth is being placed on the asset by this particular investor who is willing to accept a lower yield than competitor bidders.

A valuation for market value is therefore taking its key reference points from what the market in general expects and which can be deduced from comparable data. In contrast, a valuation for worth develops from a specific investor's capacities and investment expectations.

The example used here has deliberately simplified the relationship between the yield and the overall rate of return to illustrate the differences between market value and worth. Although Investor C might be content with a 6 per cent return, in all probability the combination of future rental and capital growth would mean that 6 per cent was really only the starting point (sometimes referred to as the initial yield) and that in the longer term a higher rate of return would actually be achieved. This issue will be explored in more depth in Chapter 8.

Fair value

The fourth basis upon which a valuer might report the value of an asset and which is recognized in RICS's Red Book is *fair value,* which is defined as:

> The amount for which an asset could be exchanged, between knowledgeable, willing parties, in an arm's-length transaction. (2011: 32)

This valuation basis applies in special contexts where the two independent parties have prior knowledge and some pre-existing commitment to a property and where there is no intention that the property be offered to the wider market. It could apply in situations where an existing business tenant wishes to surrender and renew a lease. In certain circumstances there can be a win–win scenario releasing what is known as synergistic or marriage value and all that needs to be agreed is a fair value for the parties to proceed.

3.4 Valuer qualifications and registration

The RICS Red Book (2011: 14) Valuation Standard 1.5 explains that if valuations are to be carried out to the standards required by the Red Book, then the valuer must be appropriately qualified and accept responsibility for the valuation. The Red Book explains that to be appropriately qualified a person must possess the following attributes:

- academic/professional qualifications, demonstrating technical competence;
- membership of a professional body, demonstrating a commitment to ethical standards;
- practical experience as a valuer;
- compliance with any state legal regulations governing the right to practice valuation; and
- where the valuer is a member of the RICS, registration in accordance with the Valuer Registration Scheme (VRS).

Valuation Standard 1.6 also requires valuers to have sufficient knowledge of the particular market and the requisite skills to undertake the valuation in a competent fashion. This has a geographic dimension in that the valuer must be familiar with the way the market operates in the relevant locality and the valuer must have experience with the type and purpose of the valuation. Thus where a client's instruction requires a valuer to extend beyond their particular specialism or operating context, the valuer must consider whether the commission should be referred to a relevant specialist or whether a relevant specialist could be brought into to assist with the relevant aspect of the work.

The requirement in Valuation Standard 1.5 for valuers to register under the RICS *Valuer Registration Scheme* (VRS) was introduced from 2010 and is seen as a step in strengthening the reputation of valuers (RICS, 2011a). The VRS is also a means by which the RICS can monitor the professionalism and standards of service provided by valuers to their clients. The VRS rules (RICS, 2010) place obligations on valuers which in many ways reassert those found in the RICS valuation standards and so for example a registered valuer shall:

> At all times act with integrity and avoid conflicts of interest and avoid any actions or situations that are inconsistent with their professional obligations. (RICS, 2010: 3)

Under the VRS rules valuers are also reminded of their duty of care to their clients and for example are expected to:

> Carry out their professional work with due skill, care and diligence and with proper regard for the technical standards expected of them. (RICS, 2010: 3)

Valuers are reminded about maintaining adequate professional indemnity insurance and to have in place a complaints handling procedure for clients. The key to the VRS however is that it makes explicit the RICS's ability to call in the records of valuers for scrutiny. The RICS may de-register a valuer or firm of valuers if it is found that adequate standards are not being maintained.

3.5 Market volatility

Commercial and residential property markets have shown themselves prone to periods of two or three years of 'market correction' when prices fall, often following much longer periods when prices have risen at or above the general rate of inflation. The longer periods of growth in property markets seem to create a false sense of security that property values will continue to grow indefinitely at a rate above the general rates of growth in the economy. This is not sustainable, as property would ultimately become so expensive that it would become an unaffordable luxury good. Thus periods of market correction may be financially painful for some participants in property markets but they are necessary to restore the real value relationship with the rest of the economy.

During periods of market correction when prices fall there are a number of different effects depending on a number of variables such as whether a property is residential or commercial, when the property was purchased and whether there are short-term plans to dispose of the property. For example, purchasers of a £100,000 house ten years before a property recession which caused residential values to fall 15 per cent, would probably only experience the effects in a notional way. This is because even if the value of the house had only grown at a relatively modest average of 6 per cent per annum over the 10 years leading up to the recession, it would have become worth close to £179,000 (the product of $1.06^{10} \times £100,000$).

If the home owners wanted to move during the downturn they might achieve a sale which reflected a reduction of 15 per cent on £179,000 to say £152,000 which is still of course considerably higher than the £100,000 originally paid for the house. However it is unlikely that the house which they were moving to would have been immune from the market fall of 15 per cent. The notional loss of £27,000 should not be an insurmountable problem given that they were probably purchasing a property that had also fallen in value by a similar margin.

As well as prevailing market movements having a similar effect on all properties, price adjustments are also known to have ripple effects up and down housing chains. Properties which remain overvalued when the rest of the market has fallen will tend to remain unsold until such time as they 'get in line' with market movements. Of course this would have a material effect if the home owners were planning to sell up and emigrate, as they would be extracting less value than they might have done if they had sold before the onset of the recession.

If in the scenario above there were no pressing need to move house, it would be possible to ride out the recession, as it would only need the return of a very modest annual growth rate of say 4 per cent over four years for the notional value of £152,000 to climb back to close to where it was before: $1.04^{4} \times £152,000 = £178,000$ (rounded up).

However, a fall in value of £27,000 could be very significant for first-time buyers who had purchased a £179,000 property at the height of the market with a 90 per cent loan (£161,100) only to see the value of the property fall below the mortgage debt. Although the same principle of riding out the market applies, this particular group of purchasers are most vulnerable in the first two years of a purchase when there might be an imperative to move or to achieve a sale to offset mounting financial problems. Negative equity also has a corrosive effect which destabilizes the relationship between borrowers and lenders and repossessions because of defaults on mortgage repayments may ensue.

The principle of riding out a recession discussed above in a residential context has some relevance to commercial property markets, where if there is no imperative to dispose of property during a recession then it is obviously better to wait until values recover. Some of the better performing real estate investment trusts and property companies have been those that rely on their rental income during recessionary periods and then switch to capital sales during stronger markets. However, similar problems to negative equity can arise in commercial property markets where significant bank loans were taken out at the height of the market to fund investment acquisitions and property development only for subsequent values to fall below what had been borrowed. Because of the large lot sizes involved and the very large capital values, many millions can disappear from just one venture.

The discussion above confirms that property markets are volatile and risky places and that valuing in those markets can therefore present difficulties. Not surprisingly, the criticisms of valuers and valuation practice tend to peak when the property market goes into recession, such as in the credit crunch broadly between 2008 and 2009 when property values fell significantly. It is also not surprising that when the property market experiences periods of growth the complaints against valuers tend to diminish, suggesting that there might be something of a counter-cyclical relationship at work.

Like the credit crunch, the early 1990s was a period when property values fell and when some clients of valuers tried to recover their losses by pinning the blame on valuers in high-profile negligence cases. In response to these cases and rumblings of discontent in the property industry, the RICS commissioned the Mallinson Report (RICS, 1994) which investigated the process and practice of commercial property valuation. The report found that misunderstandings could arise on the part of clients regarding the status of valuations, as some believed (and still do) that just because a Red Book valuation has been obtained that it will, in some mysterious manner, prevent the value of a property from ever falling.

The Mallinson Report confirmed that valuation is in fact a written opinion as to the value of a property on a particular basis at the valuation date and it is therefore a snapshot picture of the price that would be achieved in the market at one point in time. Mallinson felt that misunderstandings like this could be resolved by better communication between the valuer and the client.

The Mallinson Report proposed that there were four key areas where valuers could improve the service which they provided when undertaking commercial property valuations and these were:

1 Valuers needed to demonstrate to clients that, although it was possible for valuers to make different judgements, all work took place against a common body of knowledge, application and expression. Differences should therefore be as narrow as possible, and where they did occur they should be reasonable and explicable, not perverse or chaotic.
2 Valuers needed to demonstrate to clients that the profession was regulated, not in a purely bureaucratic sense, but that valuers perform their task in an organized manner, not in a maverick or inspirational way, that they take care to educate themselves, and that they are subject to discipline.
3 Valuers needed to express more clearly what they do and what they do not do. It is not possible to 'make clients understand', nor is it tenable to urge that 'clients should be educated'. Care and precision in explanation will do much to achieve both ends.
4 Valuers needed to improve the technical element of their skill, updating and extending their mathematical models, their access to and use of data, and their expression of the relativities of their judgement. They should not assume their task to be limited to the production, as if from a hat, of a final figure.

The main proposals which arose from the Mallinson Report were therefore that there should be a greater dialogue between valuers and their clients leading to clearer instructions, a summary of which would accompany the valuation figure.

The report also recommended that valuations needed to contain more comment on valuation risk factors, price trends and economic factors. The use of discounted cash flow techniques and research on concepts of 'worth' needed to be developed further. Most of the Mallinson Report recommendations duly made their way into the Red Book edition at that time and which has since evolved further to reach the 7th edition by 2011 (RICS, 2011).

The Red Book has therefore evolved in response to practice issues surfacing and as a result of debate and opinion within the profession and from academia. For example there has been a debate on whether a valuation should provide both the value of an asset at the valuation date *and* an estimate of the value at some future date, say in six months or one year's time. A contribution on this issue by Law and Gershinson (1995) suggested that a valuation report should be an appraisal with emphasis on the risks attached to the performance of the property during the period of a loan granted as a result of a valuation. However, even this relatively modest proposal would presuppose a static market unless the valuer was aware of factors which would affect the value of an asset in the future, and if so, then those factors should have been taken into account in the initial valuation. Having considered various cases on the subject, Murdoch (2008: 583) confirms that it is the valuer's task to determine the market value of an asset at the valuation date and not to try to predict future market movements.

If a valuer became drawn into forecasting valuation figures at a future date, those forecasts would inevitably have to be based upon some special insight into future market conditions, which is a very risky basis upon which to predicate figures. It is also questionable whether a valuer should become involved in forecasting as this is not a specialism for which they are recognized. There is therefore general agreement that valuers should not be trying to value into the future as this would probably raise unrealistic client expectations and open up valuers to a whole raft of litigation risks in the event that forecasted values did not subsequently materialize.

3.6 Valuation accuracy and negligence

As noted above, particularly when property markets have dipped into recession, there has been a tendency on the part of some clients to try to pin the blame on valuers for the losses which have been incurred because the market has fallen. As Figure 3.1 shows, there are a number of scenarios and potential pinch points where difficulties can arise. One such pinch point is obviously when a sale or letting has been achieved very soon after a valuation, and when there is a reasonable expectation that the valuation and sale figures will be reasonably close. There is some discussion below on what the acceptable margin of error or '*bracket*' can be in this type of situation.

Another pinch point shown in Figure 3.1 arises out of a common scenario in property recessions when corporate lenders such as banks, building societies and insurance companies have become directly exposed to the falling value of properties, because borrowers have gone into liquidation or defaulted on large loans. The lender in possession then has to sell the asset in a fallen market and in turn tries to sue the valuer for the gap between what was originally lent and what was realized on a sale in a recessionary market. For large commercial properties this gap can amount to many millions and while all claims against valuers

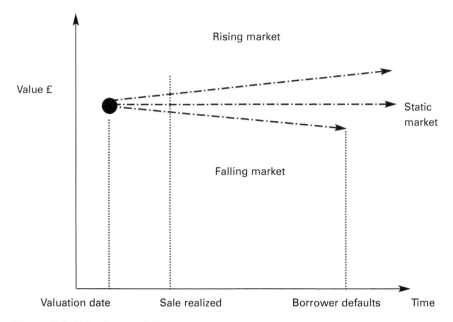

Figure 3.1 Valuations and time

in these circumstances will not succeed, it is obviously important for valuers (and a requirement of the RICS) that they maintain professional indemnity insurance cover which is commensurate with the risks posed by the type of work undertaken.

Some clients may have wrongly been interpreting a Red Book valuation as an insurance policy, so that if the value of a property subsequently falls, then the valuer may be sued for the gap between the valuation and what was actually realized in a sale or letting. Murdoch (2008: 577–96) has usefully reviewed some of the leading cases in this area from which a number of principles have emerged. Readers who wish to delve into these cases could consult Murdoch directly and follow up the cases. However, for the purposes of this discussion, it is only necessary to summarize some of the key points which have arisen.

In the first instance the courts have shown enthusiasm for the concept of the bracket, which is the acceptable tolerance between the value placed on a property by a valuer and the price subsequently realized in a sale or letting. The courts and tribunals recognize that because there will inevitably be a time lapse between a valuation and a sale and because valuer judgements are involved, it is unlikely that a valuation will be exactly the same as the sale price. This is explicitly recognized by the RICS in its Guidance Note 1 which forms part of the Red Book:

> All valuations are professional opinions on a stated basis, coupled with any appropriate assumptions or special assumptions. A valuation is not a fact, it is an estimate. The degree of subjectivity involved will inevitably vary

from case to case, as will the degree of certainty – that is, the probability that the valuer's opinion of Market Value would exactly coincide with the price achieved were there an actual sale at the *date of valuation*. (2011: 80)

Decisions in the courts have suggested that for relatively straightforward valuations of standard property types, the bracket within which a valuation should fall is within 10 per cent of what is achieved in a sale. However, the acceptable bracket can extend beyond 10 per cent where the circumstances become more challenging for the valuer, given the specific characteristics of the property and the market context.

As Murdoch points out (2008: 584) where the courts are able to identify an acceptable bracket for a subject property, a valuation which falls outside of that raises a presumption of negligence which the valuer then has to disprove. In this context expert witnesses are often relied upon to provide a view on the acceptable breadth of the bracket (or margin of error) and thus what a hypothetical valuer who was reasonably competent should have achieved. Thus the opinion of what the 'real value' should have been comes down to another valuer's judgement given the same set of circumstances. Given that valuation is as much an art as it is a science, it is not surprising that there can arise some variance between one valuer's opinion and another's regarding the value of a property. It is therefore difficult to be categorical on what the actual datum of 'true value' is and what the margin of error should be in each and every case.

The above does not mean that allegations of valuation negligence can always be argued away because it is difficult to pin down in absolute terms the value of a property. Like any other professional, valuers owe a duty of care to their clients, and thus they are expected to act in a diligent and competent manner when undertaking valuation work. If a valuer overlooked key facts which a hypothetically competent valuer would not have missed and which lead to a significantly higher or lower value which causes loss to a client, it is likely that the client will have a case against the valuer. For example, overlooking relevant market comparables in arriving at a valuation which encouraged a bank to lend considerable sums on a commercial property, which when valued later, revealed errors which had led to an inflated valuation (and a higher than necessary loan exposure) the valuer will be is some difficulty.

As a general rule in cases where negligence is proven, Murdoch (2008: 587) confirms that the valuer will have to meet the loss as measured in the difference between what would have been loaned on a property and what was loaned. There may be a fallback position where liability might to some extent be limited, such as by showing some contributory negligence by the client. As a general principle, however, no valuer would want to put him or herself in that position in the first instance.

On the other hand, there can be defaulting borrowers and the necessity for lenders to dispose of properties in a fallen market creating large losses but where the original valuation is found to be flawless. In those cases the valuer cannot be held liable for subsequent market movements which have caused a loss to the client. As in all markets, there are risks of fluctuations over time. For example it would not be credible to try to sue a stock broker because some shares which were purchased at what seemed to be a good price at one point in time, subsequently saw falls in value because of market movements. In that sense Red Book valuations are good for the valuation date but they cannot be used as a guarantee that a property's value will never fall below that datum.

3.7 Valuation tables and formulas

At this point in the chapter the attention turns to one of the core resources which valuers rely upon when conducting their work and this is the valuation tables. The tables and the formulas used to compile them enable the compounding or discounting of capital sums or income streams over whatever time period and interest rate is applicable to the project. It is expected that professionals and particularly valuers who work at the interface between finance and property will have acquired a good grasp of these principles. For example, property investment is essentially the purchase of an asset which will produce an income stream over a period of time and the valuation tables or their formulaic counterparts can be used to assist the conversion of the value of the anticipated income stream into a present capital sum.

The different types of appraisals which valuers use will be explained in later chapters, however common to all of those techniques is reliance, to a greater or lesser extent on the valuation tables or their formula equivalents.

Long before the advent of the pocket calculator and Excel spreadsheets valuation calculations could be time-consuming and prone to error and so it was not surprising that published valuation tables emerged as a way of providing reliability and reducing the need for repetitive calculations. Now a valuer could probably carry out a complex discounted cash flow valuation virtually anywhere using an ipad but that convenience was not always available. Some property professionals still prefer to use published valuation tables, the most well known of which is *Parry's Valuation and Investment Tables* (Davidson, 2002). Even those who prefer to use formulas in spreadsheets for valuation work might still refer to a copy of the valuation tables to check accuracy.

The subsections which follow try to summarize with examples the most frequently used valuation tables and formulas. The tables deal with the process of compounding and discounting and for example the first subsection will examine the Amount of £1 table which adds compound interest to an initial sum to give a future capital sum. The main options of conversion are:

- capital to income and vice versa;
- present sums to future sums and vice versa; and
- the compounding of sums into the future, and discounting back to the present.

Amount of £1

This table provides the sum which £1 will accumulate into over n years at an annual interest rate of i. It thus compounds up from a present capital sum to a future capital sum. This is commonly known as compound interest and the formula is A (Amount of £1) = $(1 + i)^n$. In many ways this formula is the fundamental building block of the valuation tables and it is used quite widely in a financial and property context.

For example a saver plans to invest £10,000 in a tax-free savings account earning interest at 5 per cent and to leave the money in the account for the next six years. The formula could therefore be used to compound the sum by inserting 5 per cent in decimalized form (which is 0.05) into the formula in place of i and 6 to replace n for the time period as follows.

$$(1 + 0.05)^6 \times £10,000 = £13,401 \text{ rounded up}$$

The saver could check the outcome in Parry's Tables (Davidson, 2002) by looking up the multiplier in the Amount of £1 tables where 5 per cent over six years reveals the constant 1.3401 which when multiplied by £10,000 produces £13,401. The saver could also go to the trouble of checking the result longhand as follows.

Year	Starting balance	Annual interest @ 5%	End balance	Comments
1	£10,000	£500	£10,500	First year's interest added to original sum
2	£10,500	£525	£11,025	Second year's interest added to starting balance
3	£11,025	£551	£11,576	Third year's interest added to starting balance
4	£11,576	£579	£12,155	Fourth year's interest added to starting balance
5	£12,155	£608	£12,763	Fifth year's interest added to starting balance
6	£12,763	£638	£13,401	Sixth year's interest added to starting balance
End balance therefore			*£13,401*	

In the example above compound interest has been applied to savings, i.e. credit but it can also apply to borrowing or debt to identify the interest charges which accumulate on a compound basis over time. This is very common in property contexts where because of the large sums required to purchase or develop property, there will tend to be at least some reliance on borrowing. Borrowed money therefore accumulates interest charges on a compound basis usually at a higher rate of interest than for credit and prudent property developers and investors would normally establish at the outset how this will affect their schemes.

For example a developer plans to purchase a site for £500,000 on borrowed money at 9 per cent and then to carry out a development before selling the completed scheme two years later when the capital spent on the land with rolled-up interest will need to be repaid to the bank. There will of course be other costs arising from the development but here the focus is on the land element. The developer could use the compound interest formula to work out how much the bank will be expecting when the scheme is completed in two years' time as follows.

$$(1 + 0.09)^2 \times £500,000 = £594,050$$

The value of n in the formula and those that follow can of course represent months or quarters if interest rates are presented in those terms. Thus in the example above where £500,000 had been borrowed over two years but the bank levied interest rates on a quarterly basis the first step would be to establish the relationship between the quarterly rate and the annual rate. Because compounding is involved this step is not as straightforward as just diving the annual rate by four to identify the quarterly rate as this would give an incorrect result. The quarterly equivalent rate of 9 per cent per annum is: $1 - ((1 + 0.09)^{(1/4)}) = 2.178$ per cent rounded up. That quarterly rate could then be inserted into the compound interest formula remembering to adjust n to represent eight quarters as two years as follows.

$$(1 + 0.02178)^8 \times £500,000 = £594,058$$
(a slight difference occurs because of rounding)

Incidentally if a borrower were presented with a quarterly rate and wanted to check the annual equivalent rate they could reverse the conversion formula as follows: $1 - ((1 + 0.02178)^4) = 9$ per cent.

Similarly if a bank levied interest rates on a monthly basis for this type of loan the monthly equivalent rate of 9 per cent per annum is: $1 - ((1 + 0.09)^{(1/12)}) = 0.721$ per cent rounded up. That figure could then be transposed into the compound interest formula where n becomes 24 months (two years) as follows.

$$(1 + 0.00721)^{24} \times £500,000 = £594,088$$

Present Value of £1

The present value of £1 gives the sum which needs to be invested at the interest rate i to accumulate to £1 in n years. The process discounts a future capital sum to a present capital sum and it is the reverse of compounding considered above under the Amount of £1. The formula for the Present Value of £1 is: $1/A$ and it is often used in a property context to evaluate the present value of future capital values.

For example a developer who is expecting to realize £13 million from the sale of a completed scheme in two years' time might need to establish for accounts purposes the present value of that sum in the context of interest rates at 8 per cent. The variables would be inserted into the formula as follows.

$$(1/(1 + 0.08)^2) \times £13,000,000 = £11,145,404$$

The developer could check the accuracy if required by consulting Parry's Tables (Davidson, 2002) wherein the constant for the Present Value of £1 in two years at 8 per cent is 0.8573388 which when multiplied by £13,000,000 produces £11,145,404. If the developer required a further check, the principle can operate in reverse by compounding £11,145,404 at 8 per cent over two years to prove that it would compound into £13 million as follows.

$$(1 + 0.08)^2 \times £11,145,404 = £13,000,000 \text{ rounded up}$$

Amount of £1 per annum

This is the amount that £1 invested annually will accumulate into over n years. It is thus compounding a present income stream to a future capital sum and the formula is $(A - 1)/i$. Because property leases commit tenants to paying annual rents which are fixed for a number of years this formula has application to property as the following example illustrates. A property investor has let a modest property to a business tenant for five years at a rent of £10,000 receivable annually in arrears. Rather than consume the annual income the investor plans to invest it in a tax-free savings account which earns 6 per cent interest per annum and is curious to know what the income will have compounded into after five years. The particular variables could be inserted into the formula as follows:

$$(((((1 + 0.06)^5) - 1)/0.06) \times £10,000 = £56,371 \text{ rounded up}$$

If the investor wanted to check that a mistake had not been made in the application of the formula Parry's Tables (Davidson, 2002) could be consulted wherein the Amount of £1 per annum at 6 per cent for five years reveals the constant of 5.6371. The latter multiplied by the actual sum of £10,000 produces £56,371. Alternatively the investor could produce a year-by-year compound interest calculation which would look as follows but which would obviously become very tedious if the timescales extended much beyond five years.

End of year	Annual income received	Compound at 6% per annum	Resulting sum	Comments
1	£10,000	1.2625	£12,625	Compounds for 4 years
2	£10,000	1.1910	£11,910	Compounds for 3 years
3	£10,000	1.1236	£11,236	Compounds for 2 years
4	£10,000	1.0600	£10,600	Compounds for 1 years
5	£10,000	1	£10,000	Received year end and does not compound
		Total	£56,371	

The table above confirms that the assumption underpinning the valuation tables is that incomes from properties are receivable annually in arrears. This is something of a fiction in that under most commercial leases the rent is paid quarterly in advance. While Parry's Tables do contain quarterly in advance equivalents it is fair to say that partly for continuity and partly because if inertia a lot of straightforward valuation work continues to be done on an annual in arrears basis. The issue of quarterly in advance is stretching beyond the scope of this introductory text but those readers who want to go further on this topic could examine Banfield (2009) for example.

Annual sinking fund (ASF) to produce £1

This is the amount which needs to be invested annually to accumulate to £1 in n years at interest rate i. It thus discounts back the future capital sum to a present income stream. The formula is: $i/(A − 1)$ and it is thought to be of value to property investors who invest in short leases. Because the latter are wasting assets a prudent investor would put aside a sum each year so that when the lease expired the original capital sum had been replaced. This issue is revisited in Chapter 8 where the effects of tax on an annual sinking fund are considered but here a simple example is provided which assumes a tax-free sinking fund account.

An investor has purchased a lease on a shop which only has six years remaining for £50,000 but which is producing an income of £20,000 per annum. Using the sinking fund formula the investor could calculate how much of the £20,000 income would need to be put into a sinking fund earning 5 per cent per annum so that the original investment of £50,000 was recovered when the lease expires in five' years time. The variables could be inserted into the formula as follows:

$$(0.05/(((1 + 0.05)^6) − 1)) \times £50,000 = £7,351 \text{ rounded up}$$

The investor could check the accuracy by using Parry's Tables (Davidson, 2002) where the constant of 0.1470175 is shown Annual Sinking Fund tables for six years at 5 per cent and which when multiplied by £50,000 produces £7,351 rounded up.

Annuity £1 will purchase

This is the income stream that will be generated over n years by an original investment of £1. The income produced will be consumed as part capital and part interest on capital. Assuming the rates of consumption are the same, a single rate approach gives an equation $i/(1 − PV)$. If the rates differ, then the formula $(i + s)$ needs to be used, where s is the annual sinking fund formula above at a different interest rate from i. Note that this is the way a mortgage is calculated as the building society provides the initial capital sum and expects repayments of equal amounts throughout the loan period (assuming fixed-rate money), but the repayments consist of interest and capital (that is, the sinking fund).

For example, assume a borrower has taken a £150,000 mortgage loan to purchase a flat at a fixed rate of 5 per cent on capital and interest repayment terms over 25 years. By inserting the variables into the formula as follows, the annual (and therefore monthly) repayments which the borrower will have to meet can be calculated and which is known as the amortization of the loan.

$$(0.05/(1 − (1/(1 + 0.05)^{25})) \times £150,000 = \text{annual repayments} = £10,643 \text{ rounded up}$$

In Parry's Tables the Annuity £1 will purchase (single rate) tables for 5 per cent over 25 years reveals the constant 0.0709525 which when multiplied by the loan of £150,000 confirms that annual repayments will have to be of the order of £10,643 rounded up. This equates to approximate monthly repayments of £887 so that the borrower has a rough idea of whether those obligations can be met when set against monthly income.

There are mortgage instalment tables in Parry's which could also be used should a third check be required and which can identify the monthly repayments based on a notional loan of £100. Those tables reveal a constant of 0.5913 i.e. 59 pence which would be the sum which a borrower would need to repay each month for 25 years at a 5 per cent fixed-rate loan if they had initially borrowed only £100. Of course the actual loan is £150,000 or 1,500 times £100 and so the constant is multiplied by 1,500 to identify the monthly repayments of £886.95. That monthly repayment multiplied by 12 produces the annual equivalent obligation previously identified by formula and which is £10,643.

Present value of £1 per annum

The present value of £1 per annum is more commonly known as the years' purchase for n years or simply: YP. The YP formula is: $(1 - PV)/i$ and it calculates the present value of the right to receive £1 each year for n years. The formula discounts a future income stream back to present value, which is the opposite of the annuity calculation previously considered. There is also what is referred to as a 'dual rate' version of the PV formula which applies when an investor is using a sinking fund to recover money spent on acquiring a lease which is gradually running down and will ultimately expire. That specific issue was touched upon above and is discussed more fully in Chapter 8 but here the focus is on the so-called single-rate version described above.

The PV formula is often used in a property context when investors are trying to ascertain what to pay for a lease which is producing a rent. For example an investor might want to establish the maximum that could be paid to acquire a lease which had five years remaining and under which a business tenant was paying £50,000 per annum. The investor might have a minimum rate of return as an expectation for this type of asset and which might be 7 per cent. The formula could then be used to establish the present value of the five-year income stream, i.e. the maximum that could be bid by the investor while preserving a 7 per cent return. Transposing the variables from this scenario into the formula would produce the following.

$$(1- (1/((1 + 0.07)^5))/0.07 \times £50,000 = £205,010 \text{ rounded up}$$

In other words if the investor paid £205,010 for this wasting asset the income from it over the next five years of £50,000 per annum would repay the investor's outlay plus providing the equivalent of a 7 per cent per annum return on that investment. The investor could also check that a mistake had not been made in the application of the formula by consulting Parry's Tables where the Present Value of £1 per annum or Years' Purchase Single Rate tables where 7 per cent over five years provides a constant of 4.1002 which when multiplied by £50,000 will produce £205,010.

As will be seen in Chapter 9 the PV formula replicates what a discounted cash flow (DCF) does. A DCF is however more versatile because it can deal with varying incomes juxtaposed with varying costs over time, whereas the PV formula can only work on the basis that a constant income is receivable for a specific time period.

Years' purchase in perpetuity

It is not surprising that those coming new to the subject can find valuation terminology and abbreviations confusing. For example in the section above the Present Value of £1 per annum was discussed where it was discovered that in practice this title is not used because another title: Years' Purchase for *n* years is preferred and which is then used in the abbreviated form: YP. To confuse matters further this section is discussing another YP but this time a 'YP in perpetuity' which is abbreviated to 'YP in perp.'. This version of the YP does not deal with specific time frames because the word 'perpetuity' has been added to reflect an assumption that the present income will continue uninterrupted for the foreseeable future. The formula for YP in perp. is much simpler than those considered so far and is $1/i$.

The YP in perp. formula is regularly used in property valuations and for example it can apply where an investor is interested in purchasing the freehold of a commercial property which has recently been let at a market rent to a business tenant. The expectation is that this type of property will have an income-producing future at least as good as at present and thus the investor is considering the purchase of an asset whose income will continue for the foreseeable future and which could be sold at some point in the future to realize a capital gain. Clearly this type of asset could be very valuable and the YP in perp. formula: $1/i$ is used to determine that value. The interest rate *i* in the formula is also referred to as the *all risks yield* and which will be discussed more fully in Chapter 8. However, at this stage the interest rate is more likely to be market derived, reflecting what investors expect in terms of a return on the particular class of property assets.

For example, the freehold of a commercial property recently let for a market rent of £50,000 per annum is to be sold. The market perceives this type of investment to warrant a 7 per cent all risks yield and so property investors could use the YP in perp. formula to ascertain that the capital value of this asset is likely to be in the region of:

$$(1/0.07) \times £50,000 = £714,285$$

If the investor wanted to ensure that there had been no mistake in the calculation, a check in Parry's Tables under Years' Purchase in Perpetuity would reveal the multiplier at 7 per cent to be 14.2857. When the current annual income on the property of £50,000 is multiplied by 14.2857 the capital value of £714,285 is identified. Note that there is a difference of £509,275 between the capital value of this freehold asset which is earning £50,000 per annum and what investors were willing to pay for an annual income also of £50,000 in the previous example but where there was only five years remaining on a lease. The differences between freehold and leasehold investment properties from a valuation perspective are explored further in Chapter 8.

Table 3.3 A summary of the valuation tables

Option	Cash flow		Formula
	Now	*Future*	
Amount of £1 (A)	Capital sum $\xrightarrow{\text{compounding}}$ Capital sum		$A = (1 + i)^n$
Present value of £1 (PV)	Capital sum $\xleftarrow{\text{discounting}}$ Capital sum		$PV = 1/A$
Amount of £1 pa	Income $\xrightarrow{\text{compounding}}$ Capital sum		$(A - 1)/i$
ASF to produce £1 (ASF)	Income $\xleftarrow{\text{discounting}}$ Capital sum		$ASF = i/(A - 1)$
Annuity £1 will purchase	Capital sum $\xrightarrow{\text{compounding}}$ Income		$i/(1 - PV)$
PV of £1 per annum (YP)	Capital sum $\xleftarrow{\text{discounting}}$ Income		$YP = (1 - PV)/i$ (single rate)
Years' Purchase in Perpetuity (YP in perp.)	Capital sum $\xleftarrow{\text{discounting}}$ Income		YP in perp. $= 1/i$

Having discussed and illustrated the main valuation tables and formulas Table 3.3 above provides a summary of the options considered.

3.8 Summary

This chapter began by looking at the various contexts in which valuations are sought by clients and a broad distinction was made between statutory valuations and non-statutory valuations. Statutory valuations are those undertaken to fulfil the purposes of legislation and include valuations to determine the rateable value of a property or those to assess the compensation payable where land is to be compulsorily purchased. Non-statutory valuations include those to support a loan application for a residential mortgage or to fund a commercial development.

Not only are there different contexts in which valuations are sought but that the valuation can be conducted and reported on one of four bases of value. Perhaps the most common and easily understood basis is *market value* which reflects what the market would be willing to pay to acquire a property on the valuation date. The second basis of value is *market rent* which as the name implies is the rental value of a property, given its particular lease terms. Third, there is *worth or investment value* which instead of taking a 'what the market would pay' perspective looks at what a particular investor would pay given the worth which they attribute to the property. The fourth basis of value is *fair value* which applies where two parties already hold a stake in a property and wish to conduct a further transaction such as renewing the lease. In effect the market is locked out in these situations but a fair value still needs to be determined to satisfy both parties to the transaction.

The precise definitions of these bases of value are set out in the RICS's Red Book whose formal title is the *RICS Valuation Standards – Global and UK* and which by 2011 had reached its seventh edition. The Red Book contains advice and a framework within which valuers are expected to work. Since 2010 valuers have been required to register with the RICS so that it can monitor whether the standards set out in the Red Book are being complied with. In return valuers are able to distinguish themselves to clients as 'Registered Valuers' so that the overall effect is expected to be both the maintenance of satisfactory valuation standards and enhanced status for valuers.

It was explained that because property markets can be volatile and that valuation is an art requiring judgement rather than an absolute science there will inevitably be some discrepancy between the value placed on a property and the price subsequently realized in a sale or letting. When disputes have arisen, the courts have applied a bracket to reflect a reasonable tolerance within which a valuation produced by a hypothetically competent valuer would fall. Where valuations have fallen outside of the bracket there arises a presumption of negligence which a valuer has to defend against.

However where a valuation has been carried out correctly, clients cannot expect to be successful in trying to sue a valuer just because the property market subsequently fell and a loss on a property was made. As in the purchase of any asset there is the risk that values can rise or fall and a Red Book valuation should not be seen by clients as an insurance policy which can be cashed in by suing the valuer in the event that values fall at some future date. No matter how accurate a Red Book valuation may be, it cannot prevent the operation of the market.

Towards the end of the chapter the valuation tables and their formulas were explored because they are an important part of the valuer's toolkit as will become clear in subsequent chapters where the various valuation methods are discussed.

Finally for those who are new to this topic, some of the phrases and definitions which surfaced in this chapter will appear as a slightly baffling exercise in semantics. There is no escaping the fact that there is a specialized vocabulary to engage with and that parts of this vocabulary have accumulated over a long period of time with the result that there are some arcane terms. Some of these terms appear very similar and for some concepts there is confusingly two ways of expressing the same thing. It might therefore take several readings of texts like this before fluency and confidence emerges around the terms and expressions which valuers use.

References

Banfield, A. (2009) *Valuation on Quarterly in Advance Basis and True Equivalent Yield* (Reading: College of Estate Management).

Baum, A., Sams, G., Ellis, J., Hampson, C. and Stevens, D. (2007) *Statutory Valuations* (4th edn, London: EG Books).

Bond, P. and Brown, P. (2006) *Rating Valuation: Principles and Practice* (2nd edn, London: EG Books).

Davidson, A. W. (2002) *Parry's Valuation and Investment Tables* (12th edn, London: EG Books).

Law, D. and Gershinson, J. (1995) 'Whatever Happened to ERP?', *Estates Gazette*, 16 September, pp. 164–5.

Murdoch, J. (2008) 'Negligence and Valuations', in R. Hayward (ed.), *Valuation: Principles into Practice* (6th edn, London: EG Books).

RICS (1994) *President's Working Party on Commercial Property Valuations: the Mallinson Report* (London: RICS).

RICS (2010) *Rules for the Regulation of Schemes, 01 September 2010, Version 2* (London: RICS).

RICS (2011) *RICS Valuation Standards – Global and UK* (7th edn, Coventry: RICS).

RICS (2011a) *Why Use a Registered Valuer?* (London: RICS). Available in e-format at: www.rics.org/vrs

Self-assessment questions for Chapter 3

1 A client has threatened to sue a valuer for £1 million because two years previously the valuer had provided a Red Book valuation of £5.5 million on an investment property which having been purchased is now worth £4.5 million. The client claims that a competent valuer would have valued the property at £5 million thus significantly reducing the scale of the loss. Should the valuer be concerned?

2 In general terms explain what a *statutory valuation* is and provide three examples where this type of valuation would be undertaken.

3 In your own words try to fill in the gaps in the following statement.

The _____ which is more familiarly known as the Red Book recognizes four _____ which are:

A valuation to determine _____ .
A valuation to determine _____ .
A valuation to determine _____ .
A valuation to determine _____ .

4 What it the VRS, who does it apply to and why?

5 Identify the correct formula and calculate the following:

   (a) If £5,000 is invested in an account earning annual interest at 9 per cent, how much will have accumulated after 12 years?

   (b) What is today's value of £17,000 receivable in 6 years time when the discount rate is 8 per cent per annum?

   (c) If £10,000 is invested each year at 7 per cent per annum how much will have been accumulated after 12 years?

Outline answers are included at the back of the book.

4

The comparison method of valuation

4.1 Introduction
4.2 Observations on the comparison method
4.3 Comparison and residential sales values
4.4 Comparison and commercial property rental values

4.5 Zoning of shops
4.6 Comparison and commercial property capital values
4.7 Comparison and development land
4.8 Summary
References
Self-assessment questions

Aims

Using examples, the aim of this chapter is to explore the use of the comparison method of property valuation which is thought to be the most straightforward method in the valuation toolkit. The chapter will discuss the most appropriate property contexts in which the comparison method can legitimately be used.

The chapter will also explain that there are boundaries beyond which direct comparison ceases to be credible but where comparison may still play a secondary role by helping to calibrate key variables which play a part in a more complex valuation.

Key terms

>> **Comparables** – transactions which have taken place in the property market, the data from which can be analysed by a valuer to assist in the valuation process.

>> **Units of comparison** – the rendering of comparable data into transferable units which can be used in a valuation and which depending on the subject property, might be the price per hectare of development land or the rental value per square metre of commercial floorspace or the yield to be used to find the capital value of commercial investment properties.

>> **Zoning** – a particular type of comparable valuation which is used to identify the rental value of high street shops. The unit of comparison which arises in this type of valuation is referred to as the rental value per square

metre in terms of Zone A which is thought to be the most valuable part of a shop.

4.1 Introduction

The comparison method is perhaps the most straightforward method available to a valuer and as its name suggests, it relies upon the analysis of previous transactions so that a value can be placed on the subject property. As a general principle the comparison method is one of the first considerations for a valuer, as the courts and valuation tribunals have shown a preference for its use before more complex methods are considered.

The comparison method is relatively simple and transparent and it can be used to identify rental or capital values. The use of the method however has it limits and there comes a point where properties do not have direct comparables either because of their use, location or other unique characteristics or that there have been no recent transaction and there are no comparisons to analyse. However even where the comparison method is passed over because a more specialized technique is required, comparison will still play a supporting role by helping to calibrate the variables in other more complex methods.

4.2 Observations on the comparison method

The comparison method requires analysis of rental and/or capital value transactions which have taken place in the property market. The method is most applicable in sectors of the property market where there are regular transactions to provide the data and where the properties are similar in nature, so that a like for like comparison can be made. As those ideal conditions deteriorate so does the reliability of the comparison method and other more specialized valuation methods may then be needed.

As Shapiro *et al.* (2009: 51) confirm, there are limits to the extent to which the direct comparison principle can be used in property valuation and they suggest that it is most applicable to residential valuation, the valuation of some types of development land and agricultural land. This is not to say that the comparison does not come into play when valuing commercial property as it does have a role in identifying units of comparison such as rental value per square metre and the investment yield which then become key components in the valuation calculation for the subject property.

In the residential property market, data arising from residential sales for owner-occupation will obviously be relevant for valuing housing. However, valuing residential property for investment purposes will also require some knowledge of the rental values which could be achieved in the residential lettings market. In the commercial property markets there is also a lettings market for occupiers from which rental values may be derived and an investment market where capital values can be identified. There are thus two types of comparables which are consulted, and these are rental deals and investment deals.

Whichever the market, the art of the comparison method is to identify relevant data and to analyse it appropriately. Given that comparison is based upon deals which have already taken place, the analysis is always dealing with past events and so the process is backward looking even when comparables are relatively recent. To overcome this problem valuers are expected to make adjustments which reflect current market circumstances and not to simply mimic historic patterns. Adjustments will also need to be made to reflect the differences between the subject property and the properties from which comparable data were gleaned, as in the end, all properties are unique. The challenge lies in making credible adjustments to the comparable data to support the valuation of the subject property.

4.3 Comparison and residential sales values

Most readers will at one time or other in their lives become involved in buying or selling a house or flat and normally that will be handled through an estate agent. The latter will, in consultation with the vendor, market the property for a particular asking price. That value will have been arrived at by comparison with the sales of similar properties with adjustments made for the particular characteristics of the subject property. There are thus a number of influences feeding into the process; comparable sales suggest what purchasers in the market have been willing to pay for similar properties, the vendor may have a subjective view of what they want for the property and the agent will have a sense of the peer group of properties and what their asking prices are.

There is no formula which condenses these variables to produce the 'definitive valuation' and hence a residential property's first appearance on the market will, within reason, tend to give the benefit of the doubt to the vendor and expressions such as 'Offers in excess of £200,000' might appear or 'Offers in the region of £200,000'. Unless the vendor wants to make a quick sale, a property will be marketed at the top end of expectations until such time as the market has shown its disinterest at that price and thus what started out as 'Offers in excess of £200,000' may two months later become 'Offers in the region of £180,000' to see if that will stimulate a sale.

As Mackmin (2008: 45) confirms, since the Land Registry records of sales transactions have become publicly available online, comparable data can easily be assessed by buyers, sellers or estate agents. Indeed websites such as Zoopla have made the material very user-friendly so that browsers can easily ascertain a pattern of sales and current valuations (asking prices) in any particular street over recent time. The material is also linked to indices so that changes in the general pattern of residential values can be seen over time as the property market fluctuates.

When using these websites to examine the sales patterns for a particular street, it soon becomes evident that there are wide variations in value even for properties which appear to be identical because they were built in the same period and have the same floor area and number of bedrooms.

Shapiro *et al.* (2009: 49) confirm that one of the key factors causing this type of variation are locational differences which can have dramatic value consequences over very short distances. Thus a house which is next to a pub or a busy junction or access road to the local supermarket will probably have a value which is significantly lower than for housing of almost identical quality but in a position in the street where they are not directly affected. Planners use the term 'amenity' to encapsulate the overall environmental quality of an area and amenity, however defined, plays a large part in framing residential values.

Even within blocks of flats such as those with a riverside setting shown below in Figure 4.1, the flats may have similar floor plans, internal space, maintenance charges, ground rents and lease terms, but the specific position within the block can have a significant effect on value. Ground floor flats will tend to have the lowest values as they are harder to sell in comparison with those on the top floor, benefiting from better views. Some flats will only have single aspect while others will benefit from double or even triple aspect and the presence or absence of a balcony will also affect value. The presence or absence of an on-site parking space will also have a large effect on value.

The condition of a property will obviously affect its value and poorly main-tained property will be much harder to sell unless reductions are made in the asking price relative to the value of well-maintained properties in the same street. Subjectively buyers will discount properties by a notional sum which would put a property back into a position similar to more marketable property.

Other obvious factors will be whether there is off street parking, the size of the garden, the standard of décor, the capacity and condition of the central heating system, the presence or absence of double glazing and the condition of internal fixtures and fittings.

Where extensions have been added to properties they can have a positive or negative effect on value depending on whether the work was undertaken by competent builders. Some extensions and internal 'improvements' of older properties, such as chimney breast removal and repositioning of staircases, can destabilize the structural integrity of properties leading to cracking and an unsaleable house. Extensions with flat roofs or those with faulty or non-existent damp-proof membranes only serve to create problems which are detected by a building survey and which require expensive remediation works, devaluing the property by a similar amount. Period houses often require expensive timber treatments to be undertaken under guarantee.

Figure 4.1 Riverside apartments on the Isle of Dogs, London

Legislation now requires that an Energy Performance Certificate is displayed in a property's marketing material so that potential buyers have some idea of how energy efficient or inefficient a property is. This provides a notional benchmark on how costly it is likely to be to heat a property and it also sends a signal as to whether the energy efficiency of a property needs to be upgraded. At present it is not clear that this information is having a significant effect on residential sales values but as the sustainability agenda gathers momentum and fuel cost inflation begins to take effect, it is likely that at the margin, energy-efficient properties will begin to have a value advantage.

As Mackmin (2008: 48) suggests, it is possible to capture the key data arising from residential property transactions in a systematic manner on a sales schedule. The latter would bring together similar properties and record the date and asking price when each property was first marketed followed by the subsequent sales value achieved and how long it took for each sale to materialize. The core characteristics of each property could be recorded including the number of bedrooms, aspect, general condition and whether money had recently been spend on a new kitchen or bathroom, etc. The schedule would show each properties' gross internal area (GIA) and from that the value per square metre could be shown.

The sales schedule approach would be best practice and represent methodical record keeping which would bring more confidence to the instinctive values discussed between an estate agent and vendor. However, those who value properties for estate agents (and who are not always chartered surveyors) will tend to work on a more instinctive basis having absorbed this type of comparative data through their engagement with the local market.

It will have become apparent by now that there are numerous variables which interact to influence residential sales values so that it is not possible to be overly definitive on the process followed. In the end it comes down to what somebody is willing to pay for a property and whether that price is acceptable to the vendor. The presence of recent comparable data is very helpful in providing a general value framework which sets the context for marketing property. However, even though the data may be recent, it will still need some interpretation in the light of the specific characteristics of the subject property. Local estate agents become experienced in this process and can quickly reach an opinion on what a property will ultimately sell for in current market conditions.

4.4 Comparison and commercial property rental values

The rents achieved on recent lettings and rent reviews for commercial properties such as shops offices, warehouses and factories are an obvious and important source of comparison for the valuer. In general terms the RICS (2006: 1) confirm that evidence arising from new leases should be given more weight than the rental values arising from rent reviews, although taken together it is possible for an experienced commercial property valuer to build a picture of the general tone of market rents. This information can then be used to inform negotiations around new lettings and rent reviews or it may be factored into more complex investment valuations for accounts purposes or for development appraisals where the value of an as yet undeveloped scheme is required.

In recent years the availability of this type of data has improved considerably, given that companies such as CoStar with their Focusnet online subscription service are able to provide updated market information on investment and rental deals for all types of commercial property. For example recent rental values arising from lettings and rent reviews or the yields arising from recent capital sales in the Canary Wharf office cluster shown in Figure 4.2 below can be sourced online and used in the next valuation. Of course data capture companies cannot make up for slow markets or where there simply have been no comparable transactions for a number of years. In those circumstances valuers have to dig deep into their experience and instincts by taking a view on how to build and justify values.

Assuming sufficient market data is available rental valuations can proceed on a comparative basis. For example if comparable data suggests that prime office property in a particular city centre has recently been letting at an average rental value of £300 per m^2 this is obviously very helpful in determining the value of the next office block to be valued. However, deals also have to be examined to ensure that there are comparable lease terms. This issue will be revisited in Chapter 8 in which the investment method of valuation is examined, but at this juncture a simple example will serve to illustrate the general principle of rendering commercial rents on a like for like basis.

Offices have been let on full repairing and insuring (FRI) terms as follows:

Annual rent:	£50,000
Internal and external repairs estimated at @ 15% of rent:	£7,500
Insurance estimated @ 2.5% of rent:	£1,250
Core annual property expenditure by the tenant therefore:	£58,750

Although the tenant's direct annual property outgoings are £58,750 there will also be property taxes (rates) and water rates, which in multiple letting

Figure 4.2 The Canary Wharf office cluster on the Isle of Dogs, London

situations the landlord may pay and then apportion and recover the costs from the tenants. Multi-letting situations will also give rise to commercial service charges which include the maintenance of common areas and lifts within office blocks.

However the focus here is on the effects of the lease terms upon the rental payments which can be illustrated by contrasting the above situation with a lease on internal repairing terms. In that situation the landlord becomes responsible for external repairs and insurance and the tenant is responsible for internal repairs. For this type of lease the gross rent which the landlord receives should put the landlord in the same financial position as if an FRI (full repairing and insurance) lease existed as shown below.

Expected rent on internal repairing terms:

Net annual income:	£50,000
External repairs allowance @ 10% of rent:	£5,000
Insurance @ 2.5% of rent:	£1,250
Management fee @ 5% of rent plus repairs and insurance:	£2,813
Expected rent therefore	£59,063

The relative responsibility between the parties under a lease for property repairs and insurance premiums will therefore determine the rent which will pass on the property. In modern FRI leases, the rent will already be net of these outgoings and it is the net income which is used in comparison and in investment valuations which are the subject of Chapter 8. Given that the cost of repairs will play a part in determining the net rent it is worth briefly considering how these costs are arrived at in a comparison valuation. Repair costs should be costed in detail, however general parameters have emerged from the property market and which are benchmarked against the rent as shown in Table 4.1 below.

The cost of insurance premiums to provide fire insurance cover is based on the reinstatement cost of the building calculated by multiplying the gross internal area of the building by the cost of construction per square metre. The premium is a percentage of the reinstatement cost but a rough approximation is 2.5 per cent of the rent.

As shown in the example above a management charge has been made where the lease terms are on internal repairing-only basis. This is because in that scenario the landlord is accepting management responsibility beyond the ordinary process of monitoring rent collection and checking that the tenant is in occupation under the terms of the lease. If a net income is being received by

Table 4.1 Examples of annual property repair costs

Property type	External repairs as a proportion of rent	Internal repairs as a proportion of rent
Offices and commercial	10%	5%
Shops	5%	5%
Residential	30%	10%

the landlord (i.e. on an FRI lease), sometimes a deduction for management is not made. Where a charge is made it is benchmarked at 10 per cent of the rent reducing to 5 per cent on property that is easy to manage.

4.5 Zoning of shops

Zoning is a valuation procedure used to identify the rental value of shops. The value arrived at using this method reflects the different areas of activity in the shop, placing a higher value on those parts of a shop which are thought to contribute more to sales. The latter is thought to be at the front of the shop which attracts customers in contrast to the rear of the shop where few customers may venture and where space may be used for storage.

As illustrated in Figure 4.3 below shops with more frontage relative to depth are able to announce more of a corporate presence through window displays and signage and this helps to generate more trade. Assuming the premises are in a busy high street or successful mall, the broader frontage will normally mean that the premises are more sought after by retailers than narrow frontage premises in the same setting.

The application of the zoning method will place a higher value on a shop which has more frontage relative to depth, so although Shops A and B in Figure 4.4 below may have exactly the same floor area, Shop A will have a higher value. This is because Shop A can advertise its presence in the high street with window displays to a greater extent than is possible for Shop B.

Shop A in Figure 4.4 also has a greater proportion of its floorspace in Zone A which extends back 6 metres and which was originally based upon 20 feet. The latter is actually closer to 6.1 metres which as Bond and Brown (2006: 223) explain is still used in valuation for rating purposes. However most valuers have dispensed with the 0.1m and use 6 metre zone depths as shown in Figure 4.4 for this type of valuation. In fact whether 6 metres or 6.1 metres is used will make very little difference to the final value, so long as a consistent approach is

Figure 4.3 Shops in the Broadway at Bexleyheath

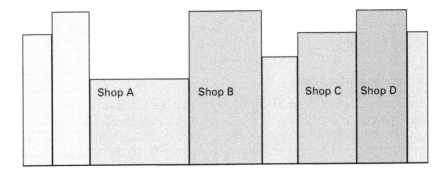

High Street

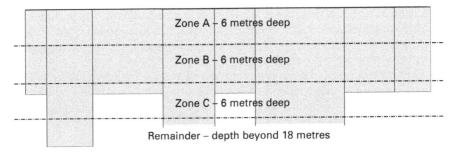

Figure 4.4 Zoning to identify the rental value of high street shops

taken to analysing the comparable property and then building up the value of the subject property.

The zoning process is explored in the following example where the convention is to halve the value attributed to each subsequent zone. The expression 'remainder' is used to describe any parts of a shop which extends beyond the boundary of Zone C, i.e. beyond 18 metres deep.

Shop D in the high street shown in Figure 4.4 above has a frontage of 7 metres and a depth of 20 metres and it was recently let for an annual rent of £35,000. Shop D is thought to provide a good comparable for its neighbour Shop C which has a frontage of 8 metres and a depth of 18 metres. The approach to valuing Shop C would begin by analyzing the transaction which has taken place on Shop D to identify the rental value in terms of zone A (ITZA). As shown in Figure 4.4, 6 metre zone depths have been used in the analysis as follows.

Analysis of Shop D

Let value per m^2 ITZA = X

Zone A:	$7m \times 6m = 42m^2$ @ £X/m^2	= 42X
Zone B:	$7m \times 6m = 42m^2$ @ £0.5X/m^2	= 21X
Zone C:	$7m \times 6m = 42m^2$ @ £0.25X/m^2	= 10.5X
Remainder:	$7m \times 2m = 14m^2$ @ £0.125X/m^2	= 1.75
Total depth = 20m		75.25X

In this rental $75.25X$ equates to £35,000, therefore $X = £35,000/75.25 =$ £465 per m^2 ITZA rounded to the nearest pound.

Valuation of Shop C

Rent per m^2 ITZA from the comparable = £465

Zone A:	8m × 6m = 48m^2 @ Xm^2	= 48X
Zone B:	8m × 6m = 48m^2 @ 0.5X/m^2	= 24X
Zone C:	8m × 6m = 48m^2 @ 0.25X/m^2	= 12X
Total depth = 18m		84X

The rental value of Shop C is therefore 84 × £465 per m^2 = £39,060

Corner shops in high-value settings which have a return frontage may be valued at a higher than Zone A rent depending on the evidence. Retail warehouses and large retail units with good circulation are not normally valued using a zoning approach and a comparison with rental value per square metre will therefore be made with other large stores or retail warehouses.

4.6 Comparison and commercial property capital values

As well as determining the rental value of commercial properties comparison can also be used to identify the capital value of commercial investment properties. This issue is looked at in a little more depth in Chapter 8 where the investment method of valuation is discussed, however at this point the purpose is to identify how comparables can help build up a picture of yield patterns. The yield is sometimes referred to as the capitalization rate because it is used to produce a multiplier called the Year's Purchase in perpetuity (YP in perp.) as follows:

$$1/Yield = YP \text{ in perp.}$$

For example if the yield were 5 per cent the YP in perp. would be 20 as $1/0.05$ = 20. When the YP in perp. is known it can be applied to the net rental income from an investment property to provide a guide on its capital value as follows.

$$YP \text{ in perp.} \times \text{net annual income} = \text{Capital value}$$

To identify the yield and the YP relationship in any particular market, a cluster of recent property transactions could be analysed to reveal what property investors were willing to accept as the yield on their investment purchases. The example could be a cluster of prime office blocks in the central business district of a city each of which has sustainability credentials in the form of a BREEAM rating. It could be assumed that these buildings have been let recently at a market rent to reliable tenants. Of course these idealized circumstances are unlikely to be found in reality but for the purpose of illustrating the principles involved the schedule arising from this scenario might look as shown in Table 4.2 below.

Table 4.2 A schedule of office purchases

Property	Net annual rental income	Sale price achieved	Date	Yield	YP in perp. (1/yield)
Office Block A	£600,000	£9,231,000	April 2011	6.5%	15.385
Office Block B	£400,000	£6,400,000	August 2011	6.25%	16
Office Block C	£350,000	£5,833,000	November 2011	6%	16.667
Office Block D	£250,000	£4,000,000	February 2012	6.25%	16

The information in Table 4.2 lends itself to a number of interpretations one of which is that in current market conditions investors are willing to accept a yield of around 6.25 per cent on their investment purchases and over the last 10 months that position has shown some consistency and consolidation. Thus a valuer who was trying to place a capital value on the next office block of similar specification and location and which had been recently been let at a market rent to produce an annual income of £500,000 would have some justification in capitalizing the income at a 6.25 per cent yield as follows:

Capital value = £500,000 × (1/0.0625) Capital value therefore: £8,000,000

The capitalization principle applies beyond office investment property and for example Armatys et al. (2009: 128) provide an example involving industrial units to reveal the yield and YP in perp. relationship based upon comparable data.

In reality the yields for different classes of property asset move around as they are influenced by the interplay of a variety of factors such as the demand from occupiers, the supply pipeline of new offices, the yields obtainable in other investment markets and the market sentiment expressed by major property investors.

The research departments of leading firms of chartered surveyors keep these factors under review so that they are in the best position to be able to advise their investment clients on movements in capital values. For example Jones Lang LaSalle (2010: 6) were able to report that at the end of 2010 the yield for prime offices in London's West End stood at 4 per cent having been compressed from 4.75 per cent at the beginning of that year. In the City of London several miles away, the yield for prime offices at the end of 2010 stood at 5.25 per cent having been compressed from 5.75 per cent over that year. By May 2011 similar figures were reported in Estates Gazette (2011) to show that the market had not changed for some time.

The yield compression mentioned above, arises when property investors are in competition with one another to purchase a limited number of prime property assets available in a market, revealing that they are convinced by the longer-term financial performance of these assets. When yields slacken the opposite is true in that investors are showing a diminished appetite for investing in the particular asset class, perhaps believing that returns are weakening. An example of the mathematics involved is contained in Chapter 8.

4.7 Comparison and development land

Given particular circumstances the comparison method can be used to value land which has development potential confirmed by the existence of a planning consent. The RICS comment that:

> Typically, comparison may be appropriate where there is an active market and a relatively straightforward low density form of development is proposed (for example, if the land is greenfield within a rural economy where infrastructure costs are consistent and not excessive, or small residential developments, and small industrial estates), and it is likely that density, form and unit cost of the development will be similar. Less frequently, it may be possible to compare large sites for housing developments on this basis. (2008: 7)

This advice does not exclude edge-of-town and city land where the development of similar housing types at similar densities is envisaged. Thus the recent sale of 2 hectares of land on the edge of a city with planning consent for three and four bedroom semi-detached houses at a density of 40 dwellings per hectare for £4 million, provides an obvious guide for the value of this type of land per hectare. If similarly consented sites were also changing hands for around £2 million per hectare there would be strong evidence to justify the valuation of the next available site on that basis.

Shapiro *et al.* (2009: 53) confirm that in these situations, the unit of comparison could be expressed as value per hectare (around £2 million in this example) or value per plot (around £50,000) or value per square metre gross internal area (floor plans would be needed for this) or value per habitable room. The latter is the bedrooms plus the main living room and so for example if one hectare of land were to be developed for twenty-five three bedroom houses and fifteen four bedroom houses there would be 175 habitable rooms per hectare, producing a value per habitable room of £2,000,000/175 = £26,667. There is something to be said for disaggregating down to this unit of comparison, as it would enable the build-up of value on a neighbouring site which might have planning consent for various house types including some low rise flats.

Helpfully the Valuation Office Agency (VOA) produces an annual property market report which summarizes data arising from transactions in various sectors of the property market. For example the VOA (2011: 12) reported that the year leading up to January 2011 the market for suburban housing sites of 0.5 hectares and above had seen very little change in values. A selection of locations and their housing land values reported upon by the VOA are shown in Table 4.3.

Even where there is potential to make what appears to be a straightforward comparison, no site is exactly the same as another and adjustments would need to be made. One of the adjustments might be to account for the timing of the valuation, as the pattern of previous sales might reveal a gradually rising market at a small percentage per annum for example. The subject site might not be as close to schools, shops and the railways station, there might be an electricity pylon crossing one corner of it and it might be subject to a section 106 agreement requiring infrastructure payments and the transfer of a proportion of affordable housing to a housing association.

Table 4.3 Value of suburban land for residential development at January 2011

Location	£ per hectare	£ per habitable room	£ per m² GIA
Bristol	2,100,000	13,270	580
Cardiff	2,750,000	17,400	765
Croydon	4,700,000	20,690	930
Manchester	1,350,000	8,500	375
Nottingham	1,200,000	6,430	280
Oxford	4,000,000	25,250	1,100

All sites will be subject to constraints like this and they will have been taken account of in previous transactions. It is for the valuer to determine whether the bundle of constraints encountered on a site is generally comparable with those encountered on other sites. If the bundle of constraints was materially different, a valuer would form a judgement on the extent to which the particular combination of constraints had coalesced on a site to affect its value.

As the necessity to make adjustments and assumptions increases the further a comparison based valuation is drawn away from the underlying principle of comparing like with like. Thus in the discussion above the value per habitable room for a suburban housing site was identified at £26,667 but it would be dangerous to transpose that onto a town centre riverside site which was to be developed for high rise housing including studio, one, two and three bed flats which reflected a density of 150 dwellings per hectare. The comparison would have been stretched too far at this point and the residual method of valuation (discussed in Chapter 7) would take over.

Even when a more specialized valuation method such as the residual method is the most appropriate choice, comparison can still play a useful supporting role by providing a broad check on the value arrived at using the more specialized technique. Thus for the high-density flatted development discussed above, a valuer having conducted a residual valuation, would look at similar high density riverside schemes to ascertain the value per unit or value per habitable room which applied on those schemes.

4.8 Summary

This chapter has explored the use of the comparison method of valuation as it applies in different property sectors. There is no escaping the fact that comparison lies at the heart of the valuation process because prices arrived at in the market are irrefutable evidence that somebody was willing to pay whatever it was to acquire a particular interest in property.

Comparison works particularly well in residential property markets and where very similar interests in property are being marketed such as hectares of agricultural land of the same quality or large plots of suburban residential development land. However, even in these apparently straightforward settings a valuer still has to adjust the comparable market evidence to suit the peculiarities of the subject property. For example, despite appearances, no two flats or houses are exactly the same and a valuer will need to adjust comparable data to suit the condition, location and characteristics of the subject property.

There comes a point where the principle of comparing like with like can become stretched too far and other more specialized valuation techniques (discussed in the following chapters) will need to be used. However even in those circumstances it is likely that comparison will play a role in calibrating the variables in those calculations. Comparison can also play a useful supporting role as a reality check against the value identified using more specialist methods.

References

Armatys, J., Askham, P. and Green, M. (2009) *Principles of Valuation* (London: EG Books).

Bond, P. and Brown, P. (2006) *Rating Valuation: Principles and Practice* (2nd edn, London: EG Books).

Estates Gazette (2011) 'Growth Slows as Yields Plateau', 1119, 14 May, p. 49.

Jones Lang LaSalle (2010) *The Central London Office market Q4 2010* (Available in e-format at: www.joneslanglasalle.co.uk).

Mackmin, D. (2008) *Valuation and Sale of Residential Property* (3rd edn, London: EG Books).

RICS (2006) *The Analysis of Commercial Lease Transactions: Valuation Information Paper No. 8* (London: Royal Institution of Chartered Surveyors).

RICS (2008) *Valuation of development land: Valuation Information Paper 12* (London: RICS).

Shapiro, E., Davies, K. and Mackmin, D. (2009) *Modern Methods of Valuation* (10th edn, London: EG Books).

Valuation Office Agency (2011) *Property Market Report 2011.* Available in e-format at: www.voa.gov.uk

Self-assessment questions for Chapter 4

1 The freehold of an investment property is to be sold. The property is market rented to a tenant on a long lease and it is generating a net annual income of £125,000 per annum. Comparison suggests that other investors are willing to accept an initial yield of 7 per cent for this type of asset. On that basis what might therefore be the capital value of the property?

2 A rental valuation is required for a high street shop whose frontage is 6 metres and whose depth is 16 metres. Market evidence suggests that the rental value per square metre in terms of Zone A in this high street is £550. Value the shop.

3 What are the usual outgoings and who is liable for them in the context of an FRI lease?

4 It what circumstances might it be appropriate to use the comparison method as the principal valuation method and in what circumstances might it fulfil a secondary role?

5 Although there might be a wealth of recent comparable market data to support a valuation what other factors would a valuer need consider?

Outline answers are included at the back of the book.

5

The profits method of valuation

5.1 Introduction
5.2 Principles, definitions and
    assumptions
5.3 Maintaining the wider perspective
5.4 Illustrating the process
5.5 The divisible balance, tenant's bid
    and turnover rents

5.6 Discounted cash flow and the
    profits method
5.7 Summary
    References
    Self-assessment questions

Aims

This chapter explores the concept and application of the profits method of valuation which is based upon the turnover generated by a business in the hands of a reasonably efficient operator. The profits method is often used to value properties which have a degree of uniqueness, making it difficult to identify market comparables and thus precluding valuation by a more conventional method.

The chapter will explain that the types of properties that are appraised using the profits method include hotels, golf courses, country clubs, pubs, marinas and casinos. While these types of properties are sometimes categorized as leisure properties, the chapter will explain that the profits method is not entirely restricted to that context and may for example be used to value petrol filling stations or car parks.

Key terms

>> **Reasonably efficient operator** – a hypothetical concept which a valuer adopts when trying to ascertain the trading potential of a business. The reasonably efficient operator is assumed to be able to run the particular business in an efficient manner and the hypothetical turnover arising is used to value the business and the premises.

>> **Fair maintainable turnover** – a valuer has to from a judgement on the sustainable turnover which could be achieved from a business which was properly equipped and operated by a reasonably efficient operator. The word 'fair' is important as it would be unfair to benchmark potential turnover against unreasonable expectations. For example it would be unfair to expect that a business's best day's trading could be sustained every day

as this would require super-human performance to be sustained through-out the year by the reasonably efficient operator. Credibility must not be stretched too far regarding expectations on turnover, as this will only serve to distort the valuation process giving rise to an unfeasible capital value.

>> **EBITDA** – the abbreviation which describes that part of the net profit which remains for a business before deductions are made for interest, tax, depreciation and amortization of any loans which the business may be carrying. EBITDA is sometimes capitalized to identify the capital value of a business as distinct from the value of the land and buildings used by the business. The latter is found by capitalizing the annual rent which the business pays.

5.1 Introduction

The profits method of valuation, which is sometimes referred to as the income or accounts method, is used where the value of a property is based on the profit-generating potential of a business operating in the premises. The profits method is normally used where the uniqueness of the property makes it diffi-cult to identify direct comparisons which are regularly traded in the market. The uniqueness may come about because there is only one such property in a partic-ular location, or that the property holds something of a monopoly because of the grant of a licence to operate, or because the design of the building is only applicable to a specific use.

Examples of properties where the valuer might legitimately choose to use the profits method are hotels, casinos, marinas, golf courses, pubs and nightclubs. While these properties could be categorized as leisure properties, this does not mean that the profits method is only applicable to that sector. The profits method can also be used to evaluate petrol stations and motorway service outlets and Saunders (2010: 187–217) illustrates how the method may be used to evaluate car parks, managed workspaces, student halls of residence and self-storage warehouses.

5.2 Principles, definitions and assumptions

The profits method, as Scarrett (2008: 10) confirms, is often used where there is an element of monopoly and where it is the operation of the business which is driving value rather than the premises occupied. Greyhound stadia, speedway tracks and racecourses are examples of leisure properties where it is the business which generates the income and where site values might otherwise be relatively low in the absence of that type of business activity.

Other types of property which could legitimately be assessed using the profits method derive their uniqueness from a site or location which enables the operation to dominate the particular type of trade or activity in the local-ity. For example, a city centre may only boast one opera house and one casino, while a town may only have one cinema or bingo hall or bowling alley. Motorway service areas provide a monopolistic setting for petrol filling stations, restaurants and other facilities such as overnight budget hotels. Railway stations and airports provide a quasi-monopolistic environment for some types of trader.

A degree of monopoly may also be enjoyed by a business because of the grant of a licence or franchise, hence one post office per village or one extended licence for a bar or nightclub or casino in a particular location. These types of licence-related monopolies generate income which can legitimately be valued using the profits method. In these circumstances it would be legitimate for a valuer to make an explicit assumption in a valuation report that the licence upon which the business depends would be renewed.

Where a valuer decides that the profits method is appropriate, the properly audited business accounts need to be analysed for at least the preceding three years. This will ensure that no aberrations or extraordinary items have distorted the true picture of a business's average profitability. The analysis of the accounts should give a picture as to whether the business is being run efficiently and some aspects of the evaluation could be compared on a local or regional basis. For example the industry benchmark for average profit per budget hotel room in a city or region could be ascertained. While that comparison figure might not map directly onto the specific subject property, it would provide a guide for a valuer when assessing the accounts of a budget hotel. There is therefore a degree of comparison which comes into play upon which the RICS comment that:

The actual trading performance should be compared with similar trade related property types and styles of operation. Therefore a proper under-standing of the profit potential of those property types and how they compare with one another is essential. (2011: 88)

Figure 5.1 Hotels such as this are candidates for valuation using the profits method

Figure 5.2 Bingo halls which can be found in most towns are considered to be part of the leisure sector where a profits-method approach to valuation is applicable

Enever *et al.* (2010: 66) comment that a valuer who uses the profits method will need to be a specialist who is capable of interpreting business accounts to arrive at a reliable valuation. This is reinforced by the RICS which advise that:

> It is important that the valuer is regularly involved in the relevant market for the class of property, as practical knowledge of the factors affecting the particular market is required. (2011: 86)

The expressions and definitions which are part of the profits method include the concept of a *fair maintainable turnover.* The RICS (2011: 84) explain that the latter is the level of trade which a reasonably competent operator could achieve assuming that the subject premises are properly equipped, repaired, maintained and decorated.

Following the deduction of all costs which a reasonable efficient operator would incur to run a business, there will remain what the RICS (2011: 84) term a *fair maintainable operating profit.* The adjusted net profit is also referred to as the *divisible balance* as it is divided between the business and the property, normally on a 50/50 basis. The 50 per cent share to the business represents its annual returns for operating the enterprise and the remaining 50 per cent represents the annual rental income.

When trading businesses are discussed, the concept of *goodwill* surfaces which is an intangible asset associated with a business and not the property. The value of the goodwill reflected in enhanced business turnover stems from customer loyalty towards a particular proprietor, company name, brand or

Figure 5.3 A profits-method valuation of a pub would look at the accounts to identify the *fair maintainable turnover* assuming the pub is managed by a *reasonably competent operator*

franchise. Thus a restaurant which is owned by a celebrity TV chef is likely to attract significantly more custom than a very similar restaurant which does not have a famous proprietor. Similarly a sports and leisure franchise associated with a famous sports personality and where there are positive lifestyle associations, is likely to attract more business than a similar facility which does not have the brand association.

In a profits valuation the additional income which could be attributed to goodwill should be discounted, because the method is assuming that the business is being operated by a hypothetical reasonably efficient operator. This implies an effective average performer rather than an operator buoyed up by celebrity kudos or a special brand association. The logic is that it would be unfair to encumber the average business with the unreasonable expectation that they could generate revenue in the same way that a few top performing brands are capable of. The valuer is not therefore valuing the real business but is using the real accounts as a guide to what an average well run business could reasonably achieve in the circumstances. In many cases the real accounts will reflect what an average well-run business could achieve and so no adjustment is needed.

5.3 Maintaining the wider perspective

When undertaking an assessment of the accounts, a valuer should not lose sight of the wider perspective, as with all types of business operation there is an opportunity cost represented by foregoing a return on risk free investments such as bonds or a savings account. For example, if a return of 5 per cent could be earned from a building society savings account, there would have to be a special reason to justify a 4 per cent return on capital invested in a restaurant. The special reason could be that the 4 per cent return represented the early performance of a start-up business and that low initial returns could be tolerated because they might lead to significantly increased earnings in the longer term. The analysis of the accounts will provide key profitability ratios which will help maintain a wider perspective and enable general comparison with other investments. Key ratios include:

- Trading profit as a percentage of turnover.
- Profit before interest and tax as a percentage of average capital employed.

The wider perspective must also be considered by the valuer in terms of the arrival of competition which obviously reduces the degree of monopoly previously enjoyed by the entity. Thus the development of a new five-star hotel in a city centre will make it harder for the existing five-star hotel to maintain the same level of profits going forward. Most will be familiar with the demise of the traditional high street cinema when the new generation of edge of town multiplexes with ample car parking became established. Valuers have to be able to detect and reflect this kind of trend in their valuation work if it is to be credible.

Valuers who work in this specialized field will also be sensitive to the volatility in spending that can affect particularly leisure-related businesses. The latter can appear to be trading particularly well during periods when the economy is thriving and when there is virtually full employment. However, during recessionary periods, non-essential expenditure on things such as golf club, health club and gym memberships can quickly become seen as unnecessary expenditure and thus the profitability of leisure-related businesses can be erratic.

While the profits method may be a logical choice for a valuer when evaluating a trade-related property, it may become obvious that the conversion of the site to another use, perhaps through redevelopment, would give rise to a higher value. While it might not be explicitly referred to in a client's instructions, the RICS (2011: 83) expects valuers to draw attention to alternative use or development potential. However, if not instructed to do so, there is no obligation to undertake a detailed appraisal of that other use as that would fall within the remit of what would probably be a follow-on instruction from a client.

5.4 Illustrating the process

The following example of a profits-method calculation is based upon a hypothetical city centre hotel with 60 rooms. Scott (2008: 471) confirms that for hotels the core component of gross income arises from the interplay between the number of rooms available over a year multiplied by the room rate net of VAT multiplied by the occupancy rate. Thus for the hypothetical hotel a schedule could be worked up to model the income attributable to its rooms as follows.

No. of rooms available per year	Average overall occupancy rate	Single occupancy rate @ 75%	Average single net room rate per night: £55	Double occupancy rate @ 25%	Average double net room rate per night: £75	Total room revenue	Room yield
60 × 365 nights = 21,900	65% × 21,900 = 14,235	75% × 14,235 = 10,676	£55 × 10,676 = £587,180	25% × 14,235 = 3,559	£75 × 3,559 = £266,925	£587,180 + £266,925 = £854,105	£854,105/ 21,900 = £39.00

An experienced valuer having assessed the accounts, might deduce that the sustainable annual income (net of VAT) which a reasonably competent operator could earn from the hotel rooms over the year might represent 75 per cent of the hotel's overall income. Other hotel services would then account for the balance of the hotel's income as shown at the top of the calculation which follows.

The calculation below reveals that the hotel is grossing £1,138,807 per annum. From that sum, all of the costs incurred in running the hotel for a year in order to generate the income need to be deducted to identify the net profit. The expenditures incurred by the business are grouped under two main budget headings, the first of which is the *purchases* of necessities required to keep the business functioning and which in this example include food, beverages and room laundry.

The second budget heading for expenditure is *operating costs*, which could be thought of as the necessary overheads to run the business. The latter is a longer list of items beginning with staff wages and national insurance contributions, followed by items such as utility bills (gas, electricity, water rates), business rates, insurance premiums of various sorts, telephone bills, hospitality, postage and the various other costs shown in the calculation below.

The operating costs would not normally include the property rent, as the profits-method calculation works towards identifying that variable. Ground rents would not normally be deducted nor any property loan costs and if the valuation was for the purposes of identifying the rateable value of the property, business rates would also be excluded.

As shown below an allowance is normally made for the interest forgone on the business owner's investment in furniture, fixtures and fittings, stock and cash. The business owner's or manager's salary is also a legitimate cost to be borne by the business.

After the deduction of the various costs, an adjusted net profit emerges which is also referred to as the *divisible balance*, because it is shared (usually on an equal basis) between the owner of the business and the landlord. The return to the business is sometimes referred to as EBITDA (earnings before interest, tax, depreciation and amortization) which is what the business receives out of the enterprise after the rent and all other costs (including the manager's salary) have been paid. In the example below this figure is £63,404.

Gross income (turnover)

Rooms income @ 75% of hotel's total income	£854,105
Food and beverage income @ 20% of hotel's total income	£227,761
Other income @ 5% of hotel's total income	£56,941
Total income	£1,138,807

Less purchases

Costs of food, beverages, laundry etc	£350,000
Gross profit (total income less purchases) therefore	£788,807

Deduct operating costs

Staff costs (wages and National Insurance)	£250,000
Manager's salary	£85,000
Repairs, maintenance and redecoration	£30,000
Business rates	£10,000
Utility bills	£15,000
Telephone	£8,000
Postage and stationery	£2,000
Insurance	£10,000
Solicitors, accountants and other fees	£10,000
Advertising, marketing and hospitality	£25,000
Bank charges	£1,000
Vehicle servicing, insurance and fuel	£10,000
Cleaning	£5,000
Renewal of licences, satellite TV subscriptions, etc.	£5,000
Sundry expenses	£3,000
Bad debts	£5,000
Total operating costs	£474,000
Net profit (gross profit less total operating costs)	314,807

Less interest on tenant's capital		
Furniture, fixtures and fittings	£50,000	
Stock in hand	£15,000	
Cash in hand	£10,000	
Total	£75,000	
Interest @ 8%	£6,000	
Adjusted net profit (divisible balance)		£308,807
50% of divisible balance to the business:		£154,404
Less managers salary and interest on tenant's capital		£91,000
Annual business profits therefore		£63,404
Capital value of business @ 3 × annual profits =		£190,212

50% of divisible balance to the landlord as annual rent	<u>£154,403</u>
Capitalized at a market derived yield of 8%, YP 12.5	£1,930,038

Total capital value of the enterprise as a going concern	
Value of land and building	£1,930,038
Capital value of business	£190,212
Value of fixtures, fittings stock and cash at hand	<u>£75,000</u>
Going concern value	£2,195,250

At the conclusion of the valuation the going concern value of the business is shown, which comprises of the value of the property plus the value of the business plus the value of fixtures and fitting, etc. Thus if another hotel operator wanted to take over the enterprise 'lock, stock and barrel' a price of around £2.2 million might in be expected in this example.

5.5 The divisible balance, tenant's bid and turnover rents

Bond and Brown (2006: 298) discuss the use of the profits method for identifying the rateable value of a golf course where the divisible balance is shared 45 per cent to the tenant and 55 per cent to the landlord. It is the latter which forms the basis for the rateable value of the property. Where the business entity is also the freehold owner, the division is notional and only serves the purpose of identifying the annual rent that a hypothetical tenant would pay to use the premises to operate the particular business. As illustrated in the example above, that figure can be capitalized to identify a capital value for the premises if required.

There are differing opinions on how the divisible balance should be shared between the landlord and (sometimes notional) tenant in any particular circumstance. The crux of the matter lies in what a hypothetical tenant would be prepared to pay as an annual rent to occupy the premises in order to operate a business to earn the types of returns that it is capable of achieving. Thus the portion of the divisible balance attributed to the landlord (the rent) is sometimes referred to as the *tenant's bid*.

In the context of pubs which are commonly valued by the profits method Crocker (2008: 455) reports that for popular pubs in good locations, the landlords share i.e. the tenant's bid, could be 60 per cent. For less attractive tenancies which will require a lot of expenditure to upgrade the premises to attract clientele, the tenant's bid could be as low as 30 per cent.

In some circumstances therefore an arbitrary application of a 50/50 split in the divisible balance could give rise to an unreasonable rental value, while in other circumstances the return to the property might be insufficient. This is one of those areas where the valuer must be trusted to make a reasoned judgement in the light of the circumstances prevailing. While it is possible to delve into the case law to examine different scenarios and splits in the divisible balance, this is not necessary at this level of engagement with the subject and thus a 50/50 split can be assumed to apply for practical purposes.

In recent years the concept of 'turnover rents' has become more accepted amongst the business community and commercial property landlords. The concept is a logical development from the business and the landlord sharing in the divisible balance as described above. Thus the annual rent payable is harmonized with annual business performance rather than fixed in a standard lease under which the rent will not change between rent reviews.

For a business tenant, turnover based rents provide some flexibility in that during difficult trading years one of the key overheads (the rent) will be less of a burden and this might mean the difference between a business being able to continue or failing completely. From a landlord's perspective, turnover rents create some uncertainty and therefore additional risk exposure, however there is also the prospect of increased income when trading is buoyant. It may also be preferable for a landlord to receive a lower income during difficult economic periods than to see a tenant go into liquidation which raises other sorts of difficulties.

5.6 Discounted cash flow and the profits method

In contrast to the portrait style of presenting and working through a profits-method valuation illustrated above, Saunders (2010: 194–5) and Scott (2008: 476–7) both show how it is possible to use discounted cash flows (DCFs) to identify the capital value of a business using the profits-method principle. The concept of DCF will be explored in Chapter 9 of this book but at this point a simple DCF example is included to illustrate its potential for profits-method evaluation.

The scenario envisages a greyhound stadium and a valuer who has examined the accounts has concluded that the fair maintainable turnover for the business is £5 million per annum. One of the benefits of using a DCF approach is that it enables the explicit modelling of assumptions about growth and in this example a 5 per cent per annum growth rate in income is felt to be appropriate.

The valuer has ascertained that for this business, the net income reflects 30 per cent of the gross income after all expenses and costs have been deducted. However in years 2 and 3 an allowance has been made for additional expenditure to upgrade and modernize the facilities at the venue as in the scenario it is felt that this will be necessary to sustain its ability to attract a wide range of customers. The effect in these two years is that the net income will reduce to 20 per cent. This is also one of the strengths of the DCF approach in that it can absorb 'lumpy' rather than perfectly linear expenditure and income profiles going forward.

The discount rate of 13 per cent used in the example, reflects an allowance for an investor's cost of capital, inflation and risk. The discount rate could be thought of as the minimum rate of return sought by an investor relative to the risks of investing in the particular asset (this aspect is considered more fully in Chapter 10). Thus if the buildings and the business were to be sold as one entity to a leisure operator who required a 13 per cent annual return on this type of venture, then the maximum that such as an operator would pay to acquire the asset is £15,476,825.

Year	Gross income £	Net income £	PV of £1 @ 13%	DCF £
1	5,000,000	1,500,000	0.8850	1,327,500
2	5,250,000	1,050,000	0.7831	822,255
3	5,512,500	1,102,500	0.6931	764,143
4	5,788,125	1,736,438	0.6133	1,064,957
5	6,077,531	1,823,259	0.5428	989,665
6	6,381,408	1,914,422	0.4803	919,497
7	6,700,478	2,010,143	0.4251	854,512
8	7,035,502	2,110,651	0.3762	794,027
Net present value of the income stream				7,536,556

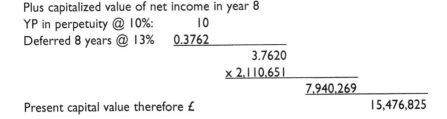

Plus capitalized value of net income in year 8
YP in perpetuity @ 10%:   10
Deferred 8 years @ 13%   0.3762
                                              3.7620
                                          x 2,110,651
                                                           7,940,269
Present capital value therefore £   15,476,825

The greyhound racing business and the stadium are therefore worth close to
£15.5 million. The stadium and associated car parking areas occupy 5 hectares
of land in a suburban area where housing sites are worth £1,250,000 per
hectare. Thus the value of the current use of the site easily exceeds the value
of the alternative which in this case is assumed to be redevelopment for housing and which would attract bids from house builders of around £6.25
million.

5.7 Summary

This chapter considered the profits method of valuation which, because it relies
upon the analysis of business accounts, is sometimes referred to as the *accounts*
or *income* method. The profits method is used to evaluate trade-related properties which are a diverse category including hotels, holiday villages, nightclubs
and bowling alleys. These properties are traded on the basis of their earnings
potential. What distinguishes these properties and makes them candidates for
evaluation by the profits method, is that they are difficult to value by comparison because they have a degree of uniqueness. This uniqueness might be
because the particular business dominates the local market, enjoying a form of
monopoly and/or that the building has been specially designed for a specific
purpose and/or because there are a limited number of licences or franchises
granted for the particular activity.

As for all valuation methods judgements are required of the valuer and in
particular a view has to be taken on what the sustainable profit levels might be
from the business under the management of a hypothetical reasonably efficient
operator. This kind of judgement and the ability to read and interpret business

accounts requires a valuation specialist who is familiar with the type of property and the operating context.

A profits-method valuation can identify the divisible balance which is the net profit remaining after normal business costs have been deducted from the annual income generated by the business. The divisible balance is shared (usually equally) between the business and the landlord and the latter's share is deemed to be the annual rent for the property. In many cases the business will also be the freehold owner of the property from which it operates and so the rental value is notional, perhaps fulfilling a valuation role for accounting purposes or to determine the rateable value.

References

Bond, P. and Brown, P. (2006) *Rating Valuation: Principles and Practice* (2nd edn, London: EG Books).

Crocker, S. (2008) 'Public Houses', in R. Hayward (ed.), *Valuation: Principles into Practice* (6th edn, London: EG Books).

Enever, N., Isaac, D. and Daley, M. (2010) *The Valuation of Property Investments* (7th edn, London: EG Books).

RICS (2011) 'The Valuation of Individual Trade Related Properties: Guidance Note 2', in *RICS Valuation Standards – Global and UK* (7th edn, London: RICS).

Saunders, O. (2010) *Valuation calculations: 101 worked examples* (London: RICS).

Scarrett, D. (2008) *Property Valuation: the Five Methods* (2nd edn, Abingdon: Routledge).

Scott, B. (2008) 'Hotels', in R. Hayward (ed.), *Valuation: Principles into Practice* (6th edn, London: EG Books).

Self-assessment questions for Chapter 5

1 Summarize the circumstances in which a valuer might choose to use the profits method to value a property.

2 An 80 bedroom hotel has an average annual room occupancy rate of 67 per cent. Single occupancy is 70 per cent and the average net room rate on that basis is £50 while for double occupancy the net room rate is £70. Given these figures, complete the schedule below to identify the total revenue and the room yield for this hotel.

No. of rooms available per year	Average overall occupancy rate	Single occupancy rate @ 70%	Average single net room rate per night: £50	Double occupancy rate @ 30%	Average double net room rate per night: £70	Total room revenue	Room yield
80 × 365 nights = 29,200							

3 The room income identified above for the 80 bed hotel can be assumed to account for 70 per cent of the hotel's total income. Calculate the total hotel income and then deduct all expenses and operating costs which amount to 80 per cent of the total income to leave an adjusted net profit or divisible balance. Capitalize the landlord's

share of the divisible balance using a yield of 8.5 per cent to identify the capital value of the property.

4 What are some of the special qualities required of a valuer to produce a competent profits-method valuation?

5 Outline the advantages of adopting the discounted cash flow format for a profits-method appraisal?

Outline answers are included at the back of the book.

6

The contractor's method of valuation

6.1 Introduction
6.2 The theory and stages in the DRC method
6.3 Applications of the DRC method
6.4 Fire insurance
6.5 Summary
References
Self-assessment questions

Aims

This chapter explores the contractor's method of valuation whose proper title is the depreciated replacement cost (DRC) method. It will be explained that this specialized cost-based approach to valuation is used for a wide but disparate group of properties including hospitals, schools, public buildings and football stadia which are seldom, if ever, traded on the open market.

Because there is no market information and no rental income stream to capitalize, the chapter will explain how the DRC method relies upon the creation of a hypothetical asset which is then depreciated to arrive at a value for the subject property. The chapter will outline the stages involved in this delicate process and how reliance must inevitably be placed on judgements made by a valuer. Worked examples are included towards the end of the chapter to illustrate the valuation calculation.

Key terms

>> **Depreciated replacement cost (DRC)** – the correct title for the contractor's method which approaches the valuation of specialized properties from a cost basis. The method is used for specialized properties such as fire-stations, schools and libraries which are seldom traded on the market.

>> **Decapitalization rate** – the percentage rate used to convert a capital value arrived at using the DRC method into an annual rental value where that is required for rating purposes. The decapitalization rates are provided and periodically reviewed by government and at the time of writing these are 3.33 per cent for healthcare, education and defence properties and 5 per cent for all other properties.

6.1 Introduction

The contractor's method of valuation takes its name from building contractors who notionally provide an overall cost to construct a building. The contractor's method has become the familiar term which is often used, although technically the method should be referred to by its official title which is the Depreciated Replacement Cost (DRC) method. Given that the valuer's professional body: the RICS, prefers the DRC label, this chapter will henceforth refer to DRC despite having used the familiar title in the chapter heading.

The DRC method is a specialized cost-based approach to property valuation which is sometimes referred to as the method of last resort. The method is used to value specialized properties which are not ordinarily traded in the market and for which there are therefore no comparables. Another distinguishing feature of these properties is that there is no rental income stream which could be used to produce a capital value. This applies to a surprising number of property types including hospitals, schools, churches, university buildings, libraries, police stations, fire and ambulance stations, prisons, army barracks, football stadia, infrastructure facilities such as pumping stations, airports, power stations and steel works. These specialized properties are predominantly found in the public sector, although they can also be found in the private and voluntary sectors.

Although the specialized properties described above are seldom traded, a valuation is often needed either for accounts purposes or for rating purposes or for compulsory purchase. A variant of the method is sometimes used for insurance purposes and that topic is revisited towards the end of this chapter at section 6.4.

Given that there is no actual market for these specialized properties but that they obviously have some value, the DRC method has evolved to try to capture that value. The DRC method does this by creating a fictional market based upon what a hypothetical tenant would pay a hypothetical landlord to use the subject building. The logic underpinning the method is that if the hypothetical landlord were to ask for an unreasonable rent, the hypothetical tenant would have the option of borrowing money to acquire a site and develop it for a building which met the intended purpose. In comparison to an exorbitant rent, that option would be the most rational for a hypothetical tenant and it is this principle which lies at the heart of the DRC method which will now be expanded upon.

6.2 The theory and stages in the DRC method

As discussed above DRC is a cost based method used to value specialized properties for which there are no market comparables. One of the contexts in which DRC is used is when properties are valued for rating purposes by the Valuation Office Agency. The majority of these valuations can be done on a more conventional comparison basis but as Healey (2009) the then Minister for Local Government confirmed, approximately 11 per cent of non-domestic buildings in the UK are valued using the DRC method because there is no relevant comparable evidence. The DRC method is also used to identify the capital values of specialized properties in the public and private sectors for accounts

Figure 6.1 The British Library, a candidate for evaluation using the DRC method

purposes or when specialized properties are to be acquired by compulsory purchase.

As well as having quite wide application the DRC method has been in use and has evolved over a very long period of time. Bond and Brown (2006: 159–88) for example are able to cite cases as early as 1831, confirming that the method has been shaped and arguably strengthened by numerous decisions which have been handed down at various times by the courts or Lands Tribunal.

The DRC method has surfaced periodically in the courts and tribunals because it has some subtle theoretical aspects and it relies upon a number of valuer produced assumptions which can occasionally provoke challenge. It is not necessary to review the cases here as the focus is upon how the method works. Figure 6.2 summarizes the five stages in the method which as Shapiro *et al.* (2009: 480) confirm have now become accepted practice.

In stage 1, the land is specifically excluded as the focus is upon the cost to produce the building only. Even given that focus, Bond and Brown (2006: 166) explain that it is sometimes possible to draw a distinction between a 'substitute' building and 'replacement' building. A substitute building might be very expensive to replicate because the subject building might have a special design which is an intrinsic part of its identity, reinforcing the building's function, status and historical significance. This situation could apply where the subject property was listed because of its architectural or historic interest and where it would be unrealistic to benchmark construction costs against a 'no-frills' modern replacement.

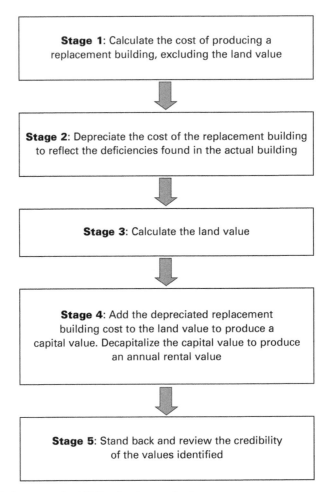

Figure 6.2 Stages in the DRC valuation method

It is not always possible or necessary to replicate every ornate embellishment or to match all of the original materials used on a historic building and so some modern alternatives could be transposed for practical purposes. However in many instances where DRC is used and for the remainder of the chapter, it is assumed that a modern replacement building rather than a historic replica can suffice as the equivalent building.

The modern equivalent building need not necessarily be the same size and shape as the subject building but it must have the same functional capacity. Given that modern layouts can be more efficient, it is possible for the modern equivalent building to have a smaller floorspace than the actual subject building, although any adjustment made by the valuer must be seen to be credible. In essence the modern replacement building envisaged must be fit for purpose.

The costs to produce the modern equivalent building can be obtained from reputable sources such as the Building Cost Information Service. Bond and Brown (2006: 165) confirm that in addition to the construction costs an allowance should also be made for ancillaries such as laying out car parking areas, landscaping work and connecting-up services. Other legitimate costs to add in at stage 1 are professional fees, a contingency allowance and the cost of finance. The combination of all of these costs produces the gross replacement cost as shown in examples later in the chapter.

Stage 2 of the process is perhaps the most creative and contentious as it requires the judgement of a valuer to depreciate the costs identified at stage 1 to produce a net replacement cost. The depreciation factor is derived from the degree of obsolescence found in the actual building. Obsolescence in this context could arise from a combination of factors:

- Physical deterioration through wear and tear which has not been entirely arrested by maintenance.
- Functional obsolescence due to layout or building configuration.
- Technical obsolescence because the industry or function for which the building was originally designed has evolved further to leave the building behind.
- Market or external obsolescence where the original requirement for the particular use in the particular location no longer exists.

It should not be assumed however that just because a building is old that it must therefore be partially or fully obsolete. For example there are many examples of Victorian buildings which have been maintained adequately and which are still providing good service. These buildings could also continue to provide service into the future having already exceeded their original design life. However, most buildings which have existed for some time will have begun to exhibit a degree of obsolescence on one or all of the dimensions listed above and so some attempt needs to be made to capture that deprecation in monetary terms.

Because there are practical difficulties in trying to identify a precise depreciation rate in each case, it is not surprising that valuers have tended to adopt a straight line depreciation approach sometimes used by accountants when depreciating other types of asset. Thus for a 20-year-old building which had a design life of 80 years it could be assumed that it had depreciated 25 per cent, i.e. 20/80.

The RICS (2007: 16) confirm that the straight-line approach to depreciation is perfectly acceptable in a DRC valuation although it is not the only permissible method open to a valuer. The latter could decide that the circumstances warranted an S-curve or reducing-balance approach which are both non-linear approaches to asset depreciation.

It is also recognized that different parts of complex buildings might depreciate at different rates. Thus because of technological advances the services within a building might depreciate at a faster rate than the physical fabric of the building. Even then the walls and superstructure of a building might have a longer life ahead of them than say the roof which may have depreciated rapidly and which might need early replacement. It is beyond the scope of this chapter to explore disaggregated approaches to the depreciation of different building elements, however those who are interested in this topic could examine worked examples of the genre in Saunders (2010: 226–31) or in Shapiro *et al.* (2009: 479–80).

Figure 6.3 Lee Green Fire Station, built in 1906

At stage 3 of the DRC process the value of the land is brought into the equation. However, it is important to stress that the land value is for the current use of the subject property and not for an alternative use which may or may not have a higher value. This raises a dilemma because the DRC method is used precisely because there is no market in the particular type of property, so it is also very unlikely that there will be an active market in sites for the particular type of use. A number of assumptions are therefore required to create a proxy land value which can be attributed to the site value for the specialist property being valued.

For example it is highly unlikely that there would anywhere be an active market for fire stations such as shown in Figure 6.3.

A valuer could however reasonably deduce that a modern equivalent fire station might require 0.3 hectares of land in a strategic location such as on a town's ring road system so that fire tender journey times to emergencies were optimized. The valuer might then identify that light industrial sites along the town's ring road were changing hands for £1 million per hectare and so there was evidence that landowners in that vicinity would sell a 0.3 hectare plot on a pro rata basis for £300,000. That figure would then be adopted as the land value for the modern equivalent fire station. It is not perfect substitution but it is practical and connects with reality.

At stage 3 of the process the valuer is able to form a view on the size of the site and does not have to replicate the size of the plot on which the existing building sits if a modern equivalent building could function perfectly adequately on a smaller site. The valuer is also not constrained by the location of the current site, as for example it would be very unlikely that a hypothetical fire service would purchase a cramped town centre site (where the real property may be) which was next to congested traffic and which made access and egress of fire tenders in emergencies problematic if not dangerous.

A DRC valuation may apply in situations where clients may have inherited buildings and their locations which were the product of decisions taken many years ago. From a modern perspective it may be obvious that subject to planning consent, such sites could be redeveloped for something more valuable than the existing use. The RICS (2007: 18) advises valuers that while the development potential should not form part of the DRC valuation, it should separately be reported to the client to enable comparison of the two figures.

Stage 4 combines the net building replacement cost with the land value to produce a capital value for the subject property on a DRC basis. For some types of valuation there is no requirement to produce an annual rental equivalent of the capital value, although for valuations for rating purposes, an annual rental value is required. At that point the government's decapitalization rates come into play and which are currently 3.33 per cent for healthcare, education and defence properties and 5 per cent for all other properties. As Scarret (2008: 168–72) explains prior to the relatively recent imposition of statutory decapitalization rates, the issue had periodically surfaced in the courts where a 'fair rate' was sought in various cases. To put an end to this arguably wasteful process the government stepped in to create certainty and consistency on the matter.

When applied to a DRC valuation of a university building which was found to have a capital value of say £2,000,000, the decapitalized rate of 3.33 per cent will generate an annual rental equivalent of £66,600. Similarly a police station which when valued on DRC terms was found to have a capital value of £750,000 would be decapitalized at 5 per cent to provide an annual rental value for rating purposes of £37,500.

The RICS (2007: 19) and Bond and Brown (2006: 182) confirm that in stage 5 the valuer should stand back and look at the outcome of the DRC valuation. This advice implicitly acknowledges that a number of value judgements have by that stage been made and there is potential for error and double counting. In this situation a valuer might for example look at the rental value identified under a DRC valuation for a suburban police station and then to look at the rental value being achieved for second-hand suburban office space of the same size. Although they are not directly comparable, neither are they so different that there should be an enormous gulf between the two values.

6.3 Applications of the DRC method

Having considered the theory and stages followed in a DRC valuation, the following examples provide a guide on how the calculations are constructed. The first example envisages a town centre library which is 20 years old but which has a total design life or 80 years. A valuer could deduce that because this is a specialized building for which there is no market that the DRC method is the most appropriate method to use to value the building. A valuer might then begin by assessing the cost to produce a modern equivalent library as follows:

Cost to build a modern equivalent library

Floorspace: 1,200 m² @ £1,600 per m²	£1,920,000	
Fees @ 12% of building costs	£230,400	
Ancillaries @ 5% of building costs plus fees	£107,520	
Contingency @ 5% of building costs, ancillaries and fees	£112,896	
Finance @ 8% of total over ½ × 2 years	£189,665	
Gross replacement costs		£2,560,481
Depreciate for age and obsolescence @ 25%	£640,120	
Net replacement cost		£1,920,361
Land cost 0.2 hectares @ £2,000,000 per hectare	£400,000	
Finance on land @ 8% for 2 years	£66,560	
		£466,560
Capital value on a DRC basis therefore		£2,386,921
Decapitalize @ 5% to identify the annual rental value		£119,346

In the above scenario the valuer would consider whether a hypothetical tenant who wished to operate a library would source a smaller building or move to where land was cheaper on the outskirts of the town. Because this building is part of the town's civic apparatus, it is expected that it would occupy a prominent, central and accessible location and a move to a peripheral location is rejected. Library floorspace is also a function of the size of the collection and the population served and so the valuer also decides that the current building size of 1,200 m² is fit for purpose and no adjustment is made.

Readers who are not clear about how finance has been calculated above could add the construction costs, fees, ancillaries and contingency which should come to £2,370,816. In these calculations that sum is assumed to be gradually borrowed from a bank at the best interest rate obtainable at the time and which is assumed in this case to be 8 per cent. However a prudent borrower would not need to take all of the money out at the beginning of the two-year development programme but would gradually draw the loan down in instalments to pay the construction contractor and professional team and to meet ancillary costs and contingencies as they arose. The gradual drawdown of the loan facility over two years is approximated to the equivalent of borrowing all of the money but for one year, hence the finance charges above are the product of 8% × £2,370,816 = £189,665.

The second point at which a finance charge occurs in the above calculation relates to the land cost where £400,000 is paid to acquire the site at the beginning of a two year period. Interest therefore accumulates on that sum over two years and the finance calculation is based on the compound interest formula $(1 + i)^n$ and which in this situation appears as follows:

$$((1 + 0.08)^2 \times £400,000) - £400,000 = £66,560$$

The second example of a DRC valuation which follows envisages a primary school which was built in 1950 and which is thought to have another 20 years of useful life ahead of it. The space standards provided in the 1950s were generous and allow for classroom supported activities now required by the curriculum. However it is evident from an inspection of the building fabric and services that 60 years of an intended 80-year lifespan have been consumed and so the valuer feels justified in adopting a linear approach to depreciation which results in a 75 per cent depreciation rate.

Although considered, the valuer has dismissed the idea of relocating the school to an area where land is cheaper because the school does need to be at the hub of the neighbourhood. The site area of 0.3 hectares includes a playground and is felt to be sufficient. The school is assumed to benefit from access to neighbouring playing fields which are part of a middle school also owned by the education authority but those facilities do not form part of the calculation below.

On the subject of playing fields Saunders (2010: 224) comments that particularly for secondary schools and universities the playing fields could be relocated to the edge of town where land is less expensive while the main buildings can remain in the accessible town or city centre. This mimics what a prudent education authority would do if faced with the need to provide a replacement facility and it is consistent with advice given by the RICS (2007: 8) to valuers on this issue.

Cost to build a modern equivalent school

Floorspace 1,200 m² @ £1,300 per m²	£1,560,000	
Fees @ 12% of building costs	£187,200	
Ancillaries @ 5% of building costs plus fees	£87,360	
Contingency @ 5% of building costs, ancillaries and fees	£91,728	
Finance @ 8% of total over ½ × 2 years	£154,103	
Gross replacement costs		£2,080,391
Depreciate to reflect age and obsolescence @ 75%	£1,560,293	
Net replacement cost		£520,098
Land cost 0.3 hectares @ £1,500,000 per hectare	£450,000	
Finance on land @ 8% for 2 years	£74,880	
		£524,880
Capital value on a DRC basis therefore		£1,044,978
Decapitalize @ 3.33% to identify the annual rental value		£34,798

The third example is a 100-year-old fire station in a high street location. Because of regular maintenance over the years by the fire brigade, the property has outlived its design life and could continue to play a role for the brigade for at least the next 10 years. However the modern needs of the brigade are not entirely met in the current building where the relationship between equipment storage, yard space, training and office space is not optimal. There is also conflict with heavy traffic passing the site which hampers fire tender response times to emergencies. The valuer decides that a site on the town's recently completed ring road system where there are high capacity roads would be more sensible and so has based the site value on industrial land values at those locations.

In addition the valuer also reported to the client that the existing site had development potential for a mixed use scheme of retail on the ground floor with offices and some residential above. If planning consent could be obtained for such a scheme, the site value would be of the order of £800,000 which is obviously higher than the DRC valuation of £660,366 under existing use terms. This comparison would help the client make more informed decisions on the overall estate management strategy to be pursued.

Cost to build a modern equivalent fire station

Floorspace 850 m² @ £1,700 per m²	£1,445,000	
Fees @ 12% of building costs	£173,400	
Ancillaries @ 10% of building costs plus fees	£161,840	
Contingency @ 5% of building costs, ancillaries and fees	£89,012	
Finance @ 8% of total over ½ × 2 years	£149,540	
Gross replacement costs		£2,018,792
Depreciate for age and obsolescence @ 80%	£1,615,034	
Net replacement cost		£403,758
Land cost 0.2 hectares @ £1,100,000 per hectare	£220,000	
Finance on land @ 8% for 2 years	£36,608	
		£256,608
Capital value on a DRC basis therefore		£660,366
Decapitalize @ 5% to identify the annual rental value		£33,018

The three examples provided above provide a general demonstration of the application of this valuation method. For those who wish to pursue the subject further, examples of DRC calculations have been provided by Saunders (2010: 219–33) Scarrett (2008: 173–84) and Thorne (2008: 431–8).

6.4 Fire insurance

The contractor's method is used to assess the reinstatement value of premises in case of destruction by fire and other perils. However note the change in terminology at this point to 'contractor's method' rather than DRC. This is because an insurance policy holder would expect a serviceable building to replace the one that was lost to fire and would not want to be financially compensated against the value of a depreciated building. The value of the latter might not be sufficient to replace a building lost to fire.

The loss of a building to fire would not eradicate the site and so a fire insurance valuation is based upon the building reinstatement costs prevailing at the time of the reinstatement. The property is measured on a gross internal area basis and a cost per square metre for the particular building type is applied. Other incidental costs would be added to the construction costs and these include professional fees, the loss of income to a landlord during the rebuilding period (if applicable) and the cost of alternative accommodation.

6.5 Summary

The contractor's method is more formally known as the depreciated replacement cost (DRC) method of property valuation. Whichever term is preferred, it is a specialized cost based approach to valuation which is sometimes referred to as a method of last resort. This is because if there is a simpler alternative method such as direct comparison or the investment method, the courts and the valuers' professional body the RICS have shown their preferences for those methods to be used. However because of the specialized nature of the properties involved and which includes infrastructure facilities and public buildings, it is seldom possible to use a conventional valuation technique. This is because there is no rental income passing to capitalize and neither is there an active market from which to analyse rental or capital sales data.

At a fundamental level cost is not necessarily a good guide to value. For this reason a number of assumptions and adjustments have to be made in the DRC method so that the cost of producing a modern equivalent building can be converted into the value of the subject building as it stands. Because the subject building may be many years old it is unlikely to have the same value as the modern replacement. This presents challenges and the need for judgements to be made at every stage. It is not surprising therefore that the DRC method has featured in court and tribunal cases over the years when various principles have been tested. Rather than the DRC method withering away under these challenges, what has emerged is a five-stage process that is now widely accepted as a way of valuing specialist properties which do not have a market. It seems that there is continuing merit in creating a fiction involving a hypothetical landlord and a hypothetical tenant who notionally interact around a property to determine its value.

References

Bond, P. and Brown, P. (2006) *Rating Valuation: Principles and Practice* (2nd edn, London: EG Books).

Healey, J. Rt. Hon. (2009) *Rates: Non-Domestic Valuations, House of Lords Written Ministerial Statement on 19.1.09* (London: Hansard).

RICS (2007) *The Depreciated Replacement Cost Method of Valuation for Financial Reporting: Valuation Information Paper 10* (London: RICS).

Saunders, O. (2010) *Valuation Calculations: 101 Worked Examples* (London: RICS).

Scarrett, D. (2008) *Property Valuation: The Five Methods* (2nd edn, Abingdon: Routledge).

Shapiro, E., Davies, K. and Mackmin, D. (2009) *Modern Methods of Valuation* (10th edn, London: EG Books).

Thorne, C. (2008) 'Valuations for Financial Statements', in R. Hayward (ed.), *Valuation: Principles into Practice* (6th edn, London: EG Books).

Self-assessment questions for Chapter 6

1 What is the unofficial but often used alternative name for the depreciated replacement cost (DRC) method of valuation and why has that name emerged?

2 What types of properties lend themselves to appraisal using the DRC method and why is that method most appropriate for those types of property?

3 Which element in a DRC valuation is not normally depreciated and why is that?

4 Apart from construction and land costs what other costs are admissible in a DRC calculation?

5 What is decapitalizing which takes place at the end of a DRC valuation and what purpose does it serve? Demonstrate that you can decapitalize @ 3.33 per cent in the context of a property whose capital value is £800,000.

Outline answers are included at the back of the book.

7

The residual method of valuation

7.1 Introduction
7.2 The basic residual valuation model
7.3 Headings in the residual valuation
7.4 Adding detail to the residual valuation model
7.5 Factoring in affordable housing and infrastructure costs
7.6 Risk and change in variables
7.7 Sensitivity testing

7.8 Comparing refurbishment with redevelopment
7.9 Development potential and existing use value
7.10 A critique of the residual valuation method
7.11 Summary
References
Self-assessment questions

Aims

This chapter discusses the principles underpinning the residual method of valuation as well as examining the detailed elements found in this type of appraisal. The chapter will explain how this type of valuation can be used to determine the viability of development or if necessary how it can be used to determine whether refurbishment of existing buildings is viable.

The chapter will explain how a residual valuation can identify the site value or the development profit where the land value is already known. Because a residual valuation relies upon assumptions and the interplay of a number of variables, the chapter explains that although the outcome is a spot figure, it should best be thought of as one value among an array of possible outcomes. The role of sensitivity analysis to explore a range of values is important in this respect and thus the chapter explains how this type of analysis can supplement the residual valuation method.

Key terms

>> **Residual valuation** – one of the five valuation methods, this method is sometimes referred to as a development appraisal. Residual valuations can be used to identify the site value or, where the land value is already known, it can be used to identify the developer's profit.

>> **Gross development value** (GDV) – the capital value of a completed development.

>> **Existing use value** (EUV) – refers to the value of a site in its current use before development. The EUV is often used as a benchmark to see if development proposals will result in a higher site value, as this will determine whether the site will be made available for development.

>> **Planning agreements** – interchangeably referred to as section 106 agreements (from the Town and Country Planning Act 1990) or planning obligations or planning gain. Essentially these are agreements brokered between a local authority and a developer and which require the developer to pay money or carry out works to the same value, as contributions to affordable housing and/or infrastructure.

>> **Sensitivity analysis** – a supplementary process to the residual valuation which explores variations in the calibration of variables and the effects of those changes on the residual outcome. A sensitivity analysis will normally focus upon change to 'big ticket' variables in the valuation, such as build costs, rents and capital values.

7.1 Introduction

This chapter will discuss the residual method of valuation which is sometimes referred to as a development appraisal. The residual valuation is a calculation that estimates the completed development value and deducts costs and developer's profit to arrive at a residual land value. This method of valuation is prone to error and can result in a wide range of answers depending on the assumptions made, the quality of inputs and the calibration of the many variables which make up the valuation.

Wherever possible, valuers will use the direct comparison method of valuation as outlined in Chapter 4 of this book. However, because developments are by their nature unique, there is a limit to the extent to which genuinely comparable developments are available. The RICS (2008: 7) advises valuers that the comparison method may be applicable for simple forms of development, such as low density housing development on suburban sites. However the RICS confirm that the comparison method will seldom be applicable for high-density or complex development or where existing buildings are being appraised for their development potential. In those situations the residual method comes into its own.

The residual valuation is therefore used by valuers in cases where existing buildings or sites are being explored for their development potential. Given government policy ambitions to promote sustainable development, most of these types of appraisals will be focused on brownfield sites such as that shown below in Figure 7.1 below rather than greenfield sites.

In simple terms a brownfield site is one which has been developed before and will typically contain existing buildings or structures which may require demolition. In the above case the old swimming pool needed to be demolished (a modern replacement was built nearby) and a residual valuation would factor in those costs. The method can also be used where some or all of the buildings will be retained and improved.

Figure 7.1 The site of the former Eltham swimming pool being redeveloped for housing

7.2 The basic residual valuation model

A residual calculation works backwards by envisaging a completed development and ascribing a capital value to it, which is referred to as the gross development value (GDV). From the GDV the totals costs of development (except the land cost) are deducted. In this connection the developer's profit is considered to be one of the costs. The bottom line or outcome of the valuation is the residual land value and the basis of calculation is:

- value of completed development
- *less* cost of carrying out the development including profit
- *equals* amount available to pay for the land.

If the land value is already known because it has been purchased or is already owned, then it may be included in the total development costs which, when they are deducted from the GDV, will identify the profit arising from a project. The calculation in that case would be:

- value of completed development
- *less* cost of land and carrying out development excluding profit
- *equals* profit remaining.

The prevailing use of the residual model however is to identify the land value, so in simplified form, the calculation which is more usually encountered would appear as follows:

Gross development value

Net lettable area m^2 @ 80% of 10,000 m^2 gross	8,000
Rental value £ per m^2	380
Annual rental income	3,040,000
Yield @ 8% = YP	12.5
	38,000,000

Development costs

Building costs: 10,000m^2 × £1,400 per m^2	14,000,000	
Ancillary cost @ 5% of building costs	700,000	
Contingencies @ 5% of building and ancillary costs	735,000	
Professional fees @ 13% of building costs	1,820,000	
Interest on half combined costs above @ 8% over 1½ years	1,035,300	
Total development costs	18,290,300	
Profit @ 20% of development costs	3,658,060	
Total costs plus profit		21,948,360
Residual amount for land		16,051,640

Before considering how the various budget headings in a residual valuation are calibrated by a valuer, it might be noted at this point that the residual valuation relies on the other valuation methods. For example, a residual valuation for a commercial development utilizes the investment method to determine the gross development value (GDV). If the development being examined is a housing scheme, it would rely upon comparison of recent residential sales to determine the scheme's GDV. The building costs used in a residual are derived from comparison with costs arising on similar projects. Depending on the type of property, the profits method may also be used to determine the gross development value. The residual method therefore draws upon a number of different techniques to produce its numerous variables.

7.3 Headings in the residual valuation

In the simplified example of a residual valuation above it can be seen that there are a number of budget headings which combine to produce a residual sum which can be used to acquire the land. The first of these headings is the GDV because a residual works backwards from assessing the value of the completed scheme.

Gross development value (GDV)

For commercial property developments such as offices, shops, warehousing or industrial units the GDV is an investment valuation based upon the net annual rental income expected from the completed development multiplied by a Years' Purchase (YP) generated from the development yield. The convention is that appraisals are based on today's rental values and yields without allowing for inflation over the period of the development.

The valuer will identify an appropriate rental value for the scheme by analysing comparable market evidence from lettings and rent reviews before forming a view on a realistic rental value. In the example above it is £380 per m^2 and which is multiplied by the net lettable area of the scheme. Because the scheme has not yet been built, this calculation is dependent upon the planning consent which confirms what could be built on the site.

Although some development sites will change hands with the benefit of planning consent, other sites will require planning permission for the development envisaged. In the latter case, discussions with the planning authority will be necessary leading up to a planning application comprising drawings and supporting documents. Once these have been lodged with the local authority, it can begin a statutory process of consultation with various stakeholders.

Obtaining planning consent for a development of any magnitude is seldom straightforward and where the quantum of floorspace in a scheme had not been confirmed by a planning consent, the valuer would have to make it very clear that a special assumption was being made regarding the development potential of a site. The assumption would have to be realistic and justifiable, as a valuer could face a charge of professional negligence if a residual valuation was undertaken on a site which had no prospect of securing planning consent for development.

In the calculation above, there is a consented scheme which permits 10,000 m^2 of gross office floorspace to be built. The net floorspace has been calculated at 80 per cent of the gross floorspace and that figure has been multiplied by the market rent per m^2 to produce the annual rental income of £3,040,000. The annual rent has been capitalized at a YP of 12.5 which is the reciprocal of the yield of 8 per cent. The yield is determined by the valuer based upon an analysis of market evidence and which reflects property investors' perception of the value of this type of asset in the particular location.

For residential developments the GDV is the sum of the sales values of the units in the scheme based upon comparable evidence. In most local authority

Figure 7.2 An opportunity site in Dartford town centre with potential for a multi-storey mixed use development the gross development value of which could be estimated against the planning consent and local market comparables

areas, housing developments over 15 units will normally be required to contain a proportion of affordable units which are normally sold to a housing association under a section 106 agreement. In such a scheme the GDV will therefore be the total of open market sales plus the receipts received from a housing association for the affordable units. An example of how this issue might be tackled by a valuer is provided later in the chapter.

Whether the development is a housing, mixed use or commercial development, the GDV is a monetary estimate of the value of the completed scheme. When assessing GDV, the valuer will consider not only the market evidence and planning consent but will also factor in judgements about the demand for the particular use and how the density, design, layout and surrounding infrastructure might have a bearing upon the value of the development. Thus there will be some explicit and implicit assumptions made by the valuer when framing the GDV in a valuation and this is one of the reasons why the whole process is more of an art than a science.

Building costs

There are a number of sources which help a valuer to calibrate the building costs, which will always be a major cost element in a residual valuation. One of the most popular sources is the Building Cost Information Service (BCIS) which provides building costs expressed in £ per m^2 for the gross internal floorspace for virtually all building types. The data is collected and averaged from recent contracts involving work of the same type. Average UK figures are provided but these can be weighted for particular regions if necessary. BCIS is an online subscription service which is updated quarterly and examples of building costs from the first quarter of 2011 are shown below in Table 7.1.

The costs per square metre shown are for construction work and exclude the costs of external works, contingencies, professional fees and VAT. The latter is payable on new contracts, except housing, and on refurbishment

Table 7.1 Examples of building costs for the first quarter of 2011 provided by BCIS

Building type	Average £/m^2 gross internal floor area
Offices, general	1,213
Offices, with air conditioning	1,341
Offices, 6+ storey with air conditioning	1,824
Shops, general	755
Supermarkets	1,047
Retail warehouses	558
Factories, general	683
Warehouses	529
Estate housing semi-detached	802
Estate housing terraced	814
Flats, generally	969

contracts, but can be recovered where developers/builders are registered for VAT.

The costs are apportioned to the gross internal area of the proposed buildings which the RICS Code of Measuring Practice (2007) defines as the area of a building measured to the internal face of the perimeter walls at each floor level. There are a number of detailed exclusions such as external open-sided balconies, covered ways and fire escapes. This measurement contrasts with other measures used in the development process. Planning matters are dealt with on gross external areas while rentals are normally dealt with on a net internal basis where common parts, services and access ways are excluded. A rule of thumb guide for converting gross to net floorspace may be 0 per cent for new industrial/warehouses, 10 per cent for industrial property generally and up to 20 per cent for shops, offices and older industrial units.

Although the building costs derived from an averaging process of contracts provides a useful guide for valuers, it is recognized that bespoke building designs will generate specific cost implications as will the type of construction contract used. Thus for very large-value developments, valuers would go further in calibrating building costs and they would almost certainly consult a quantity surveyor who has access to more detail on building costs.

Ancillary costs

Apart from the direct building costs there will inevitably be additional activities which attract costs for the developer. For example the building will need to be connected to infrastructure such as water and gas mains, the electricity supply and highways network. The building will thus face connection charges of one sort or another and sometimes mains have to be moved or on site substations relocated. Depending on the site and its characteristics these can be very expensive but necessary operations for a developer and which would need to be factored in to an appraisal.

For expansive developments such as business parks or retail warehouse parks there is normally a requirement for extensive landscaping and surface car parking. The latter might for example necessitate the installation of oil interceptors to prevent ground and water course pollution from on-site spillages. Some sites might need flood attenuation works. This budget heading could therefore be significant and could well exceed the modest allowance of 5 per cent benchmarked against the building costs in the simplified example above, and which would reflect the development of a relatively unproblematic site.

The ancillary costs might well encompass obligations on the developer arising from section 106 planning agreements, which in many areas are calculated from tariffs designed to secure both affordable housing and funding for infrastructure. Thus for a large housing development a tariff would be used by a local authority to seek payments from the developer against a number of budget headings. The latter would include affordable housing and payments for school places, open space, community safety and local health care facilities.

Although payments arising under planning obligations stem from formulas in tariffs, there is still scope for negotiation on the degree to which particular obligations might apply to a particular site. Not surprisingly, developers will normally try to negotiate down their contributions against the backdrop of a 'necessity test' provided by the government (Department for Communities, 2005). The necessity test tries to provide some boundaries on planning agreements in order to prevent them from becoming extortionate and from corrupting the decision-making process.

The bargaining process which takes place around section 106 agreements has attracted debate and research regarding fairness, consistency and the overall value of obligations secured (see for example University of Sheffield, 2010). The outcome has been that the government supports the continued use by local authorities of section 106 agreements to secure affordable housing. However, regarding infrastructure, the government (Department for Communities, 2010) would like local authorities to move, on a voluntary basis, from negotiated section 106 agreements to the Community Infrastructure Levy (CIL).

The CIL is a provision under the Planning Act 2008 which, in summary, starts from the basis that the cost of infrastructure needed to support development must first be estimated. Once the cost of providing infrastructure is known then existing budgets are assessed to see if they are able to meet the expected costs. Assuming that costs are found to exceed existing budgets, then the local authority is empowered to secure the gap funding required by deploying a charging schedule. The latter will essentially capture on a pro rata basis, payments from developers when they commence their schemes.

The government feel that the CIL will be a fairer and more transparent method for securing payments towards infrastructure, as the revenue capture will be spread across a wider range of schemes in a more consistent manner. Where a local authority chooses to adopt the CIL, most developments of any magnitude will make some kind of contribution to increasing the infrastructure capacity in the area. The government hope that the randomness of section 106 agreements identified in research such as that carried out by De Montford University (2008) and the problem of the 'free rider' will largely be removed.

A debate on the merits of CIL or indeed section 106 agreements is beyond the scope of this book. The key point is that whether in the guise of section 106 agreements or the CIL, developments of any magnitude will almost certainly have to contribute towards local infrastructure provision. It is important therefore that developers factor in the expected infrastructure costs into their appraisals, as not to do so may leave them financially exposed. Later in the chapter there are examples of how this can be done using explicit budget headings which distinguish these costs from the more conventional ancillary costs discussed above.

Contingencies

Given that development is a risky activity, there are bound to be unexpected costs or marginal cost over-runs of one sort or another, even though the main building contract may be on the basis of a fixed price. The inclusion of a contingency sum acts like a buffer to prevent the erosion of the profit element which has been embedded in the residual appraisal. If however the project does not go particularly smoothly or that the contingency allowance is too thin from the outset, then it will soon be consumed and subsequent unforeseen costs will begin to eat into the developer's profit. Valuers will therefore form judgements about the scheme and its propensity to generate unexpected costs before fixing the contingency allowance. Typically this will be within a range of 3 to 5 per cent benchmarked against the building and ancillary costs, although the allowance could be higher where the development is non-standard and contains a number of uncertain elements.

Professional fees

In addition to the costs of construction, the residual valuation includes an allowance for professional fees. The bulk of these fees will go to the architectural practice, structural engineers and quantity surveying firm working on the project for the developer. These consultants will do most of the design, specification and project management work for the client to ensure that it progresses satisfactorily. For larger and more complicated projects there might in addition be an independent project manager who will be busy on the project for most of its duration. There are numerous other professional specialists such as planning consultants and landscape architects who will make discrete but important inputs at various stages of a project.

The calibration of professional fees in a residual valuation is normally set against the estimated building costs, although this could also encompass ancillary costs were these are significant and require management by one or other of the professional team. The scale of fees charged by professional practices is built up against the time commitment made to a particular project by different types of professional at different levels of seniority. The presence of other equally competent professional practices willing and able to undertake the work, ensures that professional practices keep their fee charges within reasonable limits. Professional practices are also keen to retain developer clients for subsequent projects and so it would be counterproductive for them to try to overcharge their clients for professional services.

The outcome of market forces and the desire to retain clients is that an average pattern has established itself as shown in the simplified example above and where the 13 per cent sum is benchmarked against the building costs. An indicative build-up of this figure is shown below.

Architect	6%
Quantity surveyor	4%
Engineer	2%
Other professional inputs	1%
Total	13%

Complex schemes on difficult sites will tend to require a wider range of professional inputs and more professional time to tackle site specific challenges. Thus there might need to be more input needed from landscape architects and ecological consultants on sensitive greenfield sites and there might need to be additional civil engineering inputs to overcome access, drainage, flood risk and ground condition problems on some sites.

Most major schemes will require a planning consultant to negotiate planning consents and obligations arising from section 106 agreements. For controversial schemes this could extend to representing a client's scheme at public inquiry. Given that the concept of sustainability will continue to gain momentum in the development process, there will need to be inputs from sustainability consultants, which will increase the developer's bill for professional fees. Conversely for repetitive types of development on easy to develop sites where all consents have already been obtained, the professional fees bill for the developer could well less than the 13 per cent example shown above.

Interest on costs

An allowance for finance charges is customarily included in a residual valuation on the assumption that the developer will be borrowing all of the money for the scheme. In reality this will seldom be the case, as a developer will probably be contributing some equity alongside borrowed money. This issue is discussed further later in the chapter, however a simplifying assumption is made in a residual valuation that the borrowing rate be applied to all of the money regardless of whether it is debt or equity.

A realistic borrowing rate of interest is then used to calculate interest on half the total building cost for the building period. This approximation represents the fact that not all the money to fund the development will be required at the beginning but that money will be progressively drawn down from a loan facility as work proceeds.

The professional fees are front-end loaded reflecting the fact that a lot of design, planning, cost estimation and site survey work are undertaken before construction work can start. The interest on professional fees in a residual appraisal is therefore weighted at between three quarters and two thirds of the fees over the total building period. While the professional fees element has not been separated out for interest calculation in the simplified residual calculation considered earlier, they have been in the more detailed examples which follow below in this chapter.

Following construction it is customary in a residual valuation to allow for a void period to reflect that fact that only on rare occasions will a scheme be completely pre-let or pre sold. During the void period interest is charged on the total costs as shown in Table 7.2. The void period reflects time set aside to allow completed buildings to be marketed for letting or sale. The allowance that a valuer makes for a void period depends on the particular scheme and market conditions in the locality. In Table 7.2 an optimistic 3 months has been allowed but in difficult market conditions, it is not unknown for newly built commercial developments to take several years before they are fully let and then sold on as investments.

Table 7.2 depicts the pre-construction, construction and post construction stages and links this to the interest charges which could be assumed to accrue during these stages. The relatively short construction period of nine months would reflect a simple project such as the levelling of a site and then the building of single storey steel frame retail warehouses. This type of construction relies upon a number of standard prefabricated elements which are assembled on site and this type of approach is particularly appropriate for standard no-frills projects where speed is of the essence.

The construction contractor is paid monthly by the developer but the bank may assess interest on outstanding amounts on a monthly or quarterly basis,

Table 7.2 Interest charging on debt over the development period

Total development period of 18 months																	
1	2	3	4	5	6	7	8	9	10	11	12	13	14	15	16	17	18
Panning period of 6 months						Construction over 9 months									Void period of 3 months		
Interest charges on land costs for whole 18 months																	
						Interest on one-half of building cost over 9 months											
						Interest on two-thirds professional fees over 9 months											
															Interest on total costs for 3 months		

thus interest should be compounded on the same basis. In the residual example earlier in the chapter, simple interest has been used so that the building, ancillary costs, contingencies and professional fees have been summed to £ 17,255,000 and interest charged at 8 per cent on half that figure over the building period of 1.5 years. Thus the interest of £1,035,300 arises from the calculation: 8 per cent × 1.5 × (0.5 × £17,255,000). Later in the chapter there are more detailed examples of the residual valuation which show how interest charges are calculated on a compound basis.

Where a loan agreement has not been brokered and the interest rate is not known, it could be established by adopting an interest rate which reflects a lender's margin over the rate in the interbank market from which lenders source their money. The interbank rate is in turn influenced by the prevailing base rate set by the Bank of England Monetary Policy Committee. Thus if the base rate were 3 per cent and the interbank rate 4 per cent then a developer might be able to source a loan for a speculative development at say a 3 per cent margin over the inter-bank rate. The loan would therefore have an interest rate of 7 per cent.

The risk profile of a scheme and the credit rating of the developer will have a bearing on the rate offered by lenders and so for an unknown developer embarking on a speculative venture, the loan rate is likely to be in excess of that offered to an established developer who is borrowing against a pre-let scheme. Some developers will have been fortunate enough to have secured a pre-sale agreement with a financial institution, which comes with finance at below market rates. For very large schemes where there is a high degree of risk, the developer might use a financial intermediary to source the best possible finance deal in the money markets. This could be a syndicated loan provided by a number of banks who are diversifying their own risks by not seeking full exposure to a scheme.

Profit

In a residual valuation the developer's profit is normally expressed as a percentage rate which is supposed to represent the reward for bearing risk. The profit expectation is thus a variable which each developer will 'fix' to reflect the perceived risk of the project against the backdrop of rates of return on other perhaps less risky ventures. Profit expectations will thus vary over time depending on the economic context and the risks and scale of the project. Thus a relatively modest percentage rate of return might be accepted by a developer on a very high-value project which is pre-let and pre-sold (and thereby has low risk) because that relatively modest percentage return might equate to many millions of pounds.

The percentage profit expectation may be benchmarked against a scheme's GDV or its total costs and examples of both approaches can be found practice and in academic books. Wilkinson and Reed (2008: 104–5) show an example where the developer's profit is benchmarked as 20 per cent of development costs while Scarrett (2008: 129) includes a residual where the developer's profit is 15 per cent of GDV. Havard (2008: 127) and Blackledge (2009: 277) show that there is no contradiction in reporting profit as both a percentage of cost and as a percentage of GDV in the same valuation. This approach is illustrated in Figure 7.3 where the profit of £1.5 million is expressed as representing either 15 per cent of the GDV or 20 per cent of the development costs.

There is arguably more justification for benchmarking the profit rate against a scheme's GDV rather than its costs, as to do the latter implies that ineffective project management which allowed costs to increase would reward the developer

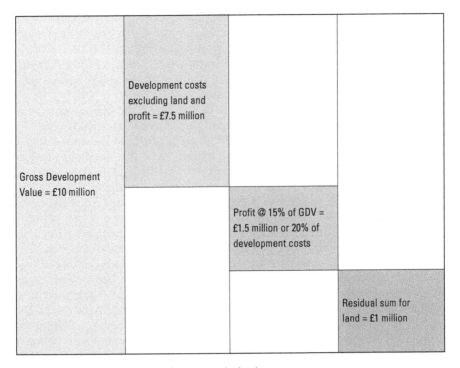

Figure 7.3 Benchmarking profit in a residual valuation

with more profit. In contrast, a profit rate benchmarked against a scheme's GDV implies a degree of incentive in that if a high-quality scheme is produced, then the developer will probably be rewarded above expectation for the additional effort and value added.

The significant point is that profit is a cost extracted from a scheme and if the profit expectation is excessive, regardless of whether it is benchmarked against development costs or GDV, there will be insufficient money remaining for a developer to make a competitive site bid. Thus in the above example, if a developer expected 20 per cent profit on GDV which is £2 million, there would remain only £0.5 million to bid for the site. Where other developers bidding for the site were satisfied with a profit of around 15 per cent of GDV, i.e. £1.5 million they would have the ability to make superior bids in the region of £1 million for the site. Thus a developer who expects too much from a scheme will not be able to secure the site if there is competition to purchase it (which is normally the case).

It was noted above in this chapter that the residual valuation formula is:

GDV less (Building Costs plus Profit) equals Residual for Land

This can be transposed to identify the profit as the residual element where the land value is already known, so that the formula becomes:

GDV less Total Cost (which includes the Land Cost) equals Profit

From the residual example above the profit as a percentage of total cost would therefore be:

$$\frac{£3,658,060}{£18,290,300 + £16,051,640} = 10.65\%$$

There is yet a further way to depict profit and this occurs where a development is retained by a developer because the annual rental income from the scheme exceeds the cost of carrying the debt at a rate of interest. Using the figures from the calculation considered earlier, by the end of the development the developer would have purchased the land for £16,051,640 and paid all of the development costs of £18,290,300 but importantly would not have taken a profit. The developer would therefore have a debt against the development of £34,341,940.

One of the options open to the developer at that point is to refinance the debt at an interest rate lower than 8 per cent because the scheme had been completed and was income producing. The banks would perceive the asset as a far lower risk than when it was in its development phase and when 8 per cent was the appropriate loan rate. The debt could then be refinance at a lower rate of say 6.5 per cent and so the annual repayments on an interest-only loan, on the debt of £34,341,940 would be £2,232,226. The annual rental income from the scheme would be £3,040,000 leaving a net income for the developer (who by that stage would be cast in the role of property investor) of £807,774 which reflects a 1.5 per cent margin above the cost of capital.

There are a number of scenarios going forward from that point, one of which is that the developer could refinance using a commercial capital and interest repayment mortgage at 6.5 per cent. The latter would gradually erode the debt to a point where at some point in the future (dependent upon the term of the loan) the developer would become the outright owner of a very valuable development. There would be higher annual repayments and thus a lower annual net income, but the incentive would be to achieve outright ownership. Alternatively the developer could gradually build up a portfolio of similar schemes to generate a significant income stream by using debt financing. The exploration of these different scenarios is beyond the scope of this book but readers who are particularly interested in the mechanics of property investment appraisal could consult Enever *et al.* (2010).

Regarding profit margins, there has been speculation and rumour that developers such as volume housebuilders have sometimes colluded to manipulate site bids. This type of anti-competitive practice would produce lower than expected site bids and thereby sustain artificially high profit margins. However no hard evidence has emerged to substantiate these claims. It is difficult to subscribe to the conspiracy theory given that development sites are normally subject to marketing and are thus open to bidding from a wide variety of capable organizations from both within the UK and overseas.

Residual amount for the land

The simple residual valuation depicted earlier suggests that up to £16,051,640 could be used to purchase the site for the hypothetical scheme. However there are two important caveats regarding this sum of money. The first is that the sum represents the site value at the end of a development period lasting 1.5 years. The residual amount therefore needs to be adjusted to its present value equivalent to account for the interest charges of holding the land over 1.5 years when it is being developed. This would be true of any capital asset which was purchased now but whose value was crystallized at some future date. The calculation employs the Present Value of £1 formula which is:

$$\frac{1}{(1 + i)^n}$$

In this example *i* is 8 per cent and *n* is 1.5 years, producing 0.890973 which is the present value of £1 in 1.5 years at 8 per cent. When this value is multiplied by £16,051,640 it produces the present value of the residual sum: £14,301,578. The theory is that if £14,301,578 had been borrowed at 8 per cent to purchase the site, by the end of 1.5 years compound interest would have increased the total debt to £16,051,640. This of course can be proved by using the compound interest formula: $(1 + i)^n$ to work the process in reverse. Thus $1.08^{1.5} = 1.122369 \times £14,301,578 = £16,051,648$. The difference of £8 is due to rounding to 6 decimal places for legibility.

The present amount available to purchase the land: £14,301,578 must also take account of the purchaser's costs as well as the land cost itself. Thus a transaction of this magnitude will attract 4 per cent stamp duty land tax. There is normally an additional 1 per cent allowance for agents' fees and solicitors' fees given that they will handle the conveyancing process for the purchaser. Thus in total the land purchase costs are 5 per cent of the land value and which is not the same as calculating 5 per cent of £14,301,578 (which would come to £715,079).

The calculation to find the purchase costs is: £14,301,578 − (£14,301,578/1.05) = 681,028. To put it another way, the net land value is £13,620,550 which when the 5 per cent purchaser's costs are added to it: 1.05 × £13,620,550 produces the gross figure of £14,301,578. This may seem a trifle pedantic but to follow the incorrect method would have seen the purchaser lose £34,051 in this case.

The above of course assumes that the vendor is offering the site with vacant possession and an unencumbered freehold title. In reality there may be constraints of one kind or another which will typically generate costs to achieve a 'clean site' and these would need to be assessed and then deducted from the present value of the land before a purchase price is arrived at.

7.4 Adding detail to the residual valuation model

The simplified residual model considered earlier in the chapter has now served its purpose as an example against which there could be some discussion on some of the main elements in this type of valuation. Because it was a simplified example, it omitted some of the specialized headings which can appear in this type of valuation and it dealt with the finance costs in a simplistic manner. A more detailed example of a residual valuation is now provided in the calculation below as a basis to explore these issues.

Gross Development Value			
Gross office floorspace m^2	5,400		
Net floorspace m^2 @ 85% of gross	4,590		
Rental value £ per m^2	350		
Annual rental value £	1,606,500		
Yield in perpetuity @ 7.5%	13.3333		
		21,419,946	
Less purchaser's costs @ 5.75%		1,164,678	
Net Development Value			20,255,268
Less Costs			
Demolition and site clearance costs		200,000	
Building costs 5,400 m^2 offices @ £1,400 per m^2		7,560,000	
Ancillary costs @ 3% of building costs		226,800	
Contingency @ 5% of demolition, building and ancillary costs		399,340	
Letting fees @ 15% of annual rental value		240,975	
Marketing and advertising fees @ 1.5% of NDV		303,829	
Interest on half of total costs above for 18 months @ 9%	616,206		
Professional fees @ 12.5% of building and ancillary costs	973,350		
Interest on two-thirds fees for 18 months @ 9%		89,535	
Costs subtotal			10,610,035

Interest on costs subtotal for a void of 3 months @ 9%	231,067	
Developer's profit @ 15% of NDV	3,038,290	
Total costs plus profit		13,879,392
Value of site in $1\frac{3}{4}$ years		6,375,876
PV of £1 in $1\frac{3}{4}$ years @ 9%	0.8600	
Present value of the site therefore		5,483,253
Land acquisition costs of 5% (stamp duty @ 4% plus legal fees @ 1%)		
Acquisition costs = present site value − (present site value × 1/1.05)		261,107
Site value therefore		5,222,146

In the above residual the interest charges have been compounded using the $(1 + i)^n$ formula so that interest at 9 per cent has been charged on half of the total of demolition, building, ancillary, contingency, letting and marketing fees. The calculation in full would look as follows:

$$((1.09^{1.5}) \times (0.5 \times £8,930,944)) - (0.5 \times £8,930,944) = £616,206$$

A similar process has been undertaken for the professional fees so the compound interest charge calculation there would look as follows:

$$((1.09^{1.5}) \times (0.6666 \times £973,350)) - (0.6666 \times £973,350) = £89,535$$

Finally a compound interest calculation has been carried out on the costs subtotal for the three-month void period and which would look as follows:

$$((1.09^{0.25}) \times £10,610,035) - £10,610,035 = £231,067$$

As well as compounding interest charges, some new headings have also appeared in the residual valuation above and these are discussed as follows.

Purchaser's costs

In a similar way to the adjustment to land value to allow for the purchaser's costs of stamp duty and solicitors' fees, there is conventionally an adjustment made to the GDV to allow for the purchaser's costs of the completed scheme. This is based on the principle that a large corporate property investor, such as a financial institution, requires a rate of return against investment which is inclusive of the costs of the transaction.

In the residual valuation, a purchaser is paying the developer £20,255,268 (the net development value) because that purchaser is also meeting stamp duty, agents and solicitors fees amounting to an additional 5.75 per cent. The figures are based upon the calculation: $1.0575 \times £20,255,268 = £21,419,946$ and which is the scheme's GDV. By accepting the net development value, the developer has absorbed the purchaser's costs and while the merits of this practice may be debated, these valuations are conducted on that basis.

Letting agents' fees

The letting of a speculative commercial development such as an office block or retail warehouse or industrial unit to business tenants, is critical to the financial viability of a development. The letting agent therefore plays a key role in the development process and this is reflected in a residual valuation by benchmarking the letting agent's fees at 10 per cent of the annual rental income secured in a letting. If joint agents are used, the convention is to allow for 15 per cent of the annual rental income as the letting fees.

Marketing and advertising costs

The cost of marketing a development will include setting up a web site, preparing and distributing property particulars and undertaking marketing by placing advertisements in the property press. Large commercial developments will also gain exposure through invitations to agents and property investors to attend topping out ceremonies, open days and conducted tours. For housing schemes there could be a permanent staff presence on site in a show home in order to meet and greet prospective purchasers and to provide them with the inevitable glossy brochure.

The degree of promotion needed for a scheme will depend on a variety of factors such as the type of development, the locality and market factors. Some developments will simply 'sell themselves' and for example it may be possible to sell a proportion of the units in well located housing schemes 'off plan', i.e. before construction has even started on site. Even where concerted marketing is required, the advertising budget is unlikely to make a serious impact upon the overall viability of a scheme and in a residual valuation an allowance benchmarked at between 0.5 and 1.5 per cent of the development value.

7.5 Factoring in affordable housing and infrastructure costs

The residual examples discussed so far have focused upon hypothetical office developments, but the model can of course be used to assess housing development or mixed use developments. There follows an example of a residual valuation for the development 87 flats on a brownfield site where a 25 per cent affordable housing policy and a section 106 planning obligation have been applied.

Gross Development Value (GDV)

Open Market Housing	No.	Unit Value £	£	£
1 bed flats – open market sales	20	150,000	3,000,000	
2 bed flats – open market sales	30	195,000	5,850,000	
3 bed flats – open market sales	15	220,000	3,300,000	
Affordable housing				
1 bed flats – affordable	7	68,400	478,800	
2 bed flats – affordable	10	82,080	820,800	
3 bed flats – affordable	5	103,968	519,840	
Total no. of flats =	87			13,969,440

Less costs

	£m²	Net m²	Gross m²	
Demolition and site clearance costs:				150,000
Building costs	£m²	Net m²	Gross m²	
I bed flats each 50m² @	950	1,350	1,688	1,603,125
2 bed flats each 60m² @	950	2,400	3,000	2,850,000
3 bed flats each 76m² @	950	1,520	1,900	1,805,000
Ancillary costs @ 3% of building costs				187,744
Contingency @ 5% of demolition, building and ancillary costs				329,793
Marketing costs @ 1.5% of GDV				209,542
Cost of obligations under a Section 106 agreement				250,000
Interest on half the total costs above over 18 months @ 9%				509,555
Professional fees @ 12.5% of building and ancillary costs				805,734
Interest on two-thirds professional fees for 18 months @ 9%				74,117
Costs subtotal				8,774,610
Interest on total for sales period of 3 months @ 9%			191,095	
Profit @ 15% of GDV			2,095,416	
Total costs plus profit =				11,061,121
Site value in 1¾ years time = GDV – Total Costs =				2,908,319
PV of £1 @ 9% for 1¾ years			0.8600	
Present value of the site therefore				2,501,154
Acquisition costs of 5% (stamp duty @ 4% plus legal fees @ 1%)				
Acquisition costs = present site value – (present site value × 1/1.05)				119,103
Site value therefore				2,382,051

The inclusion of the affordable housing policy and section 106 payments for infrastructure in schemes such as those shown above, are at the behest of local authorities. In the absence of these policies it is unlikely that even a developer with a corporate social responsibility would volunteer them. Whatever developers may think of these policies they are applied to these types of sites and valuers working for developers have a duty to respond to this reality in their work. The government supports this approach by local authorities because it is not expected that tax payers contribute all of the costs of meeting affordable housing objectives or infrastructure improvements.

The value of the affordable units will vary from scheme to scheme and will be contingent upon a number of factors, such as whether the affordable housing is social rented, intermediate rented or shared ownership (or other forms of affordable housing). The funding package which the acquiring housing association puts together can also be a factor.

In the example above the value of the affordable units has been simplified to reflect 120 per cent of the cost to build plus an allowance for the common areas in the blocks of flats. In reality placing a value on the affordable units in a scheme is a specialized valuation task involving a discounted cash flow of future net rental income and tranches of shared ownership sales. This degree of complexity is beyond the scope of this book, but should readers want to find out more about the process, the RICS (2010) has provided guidelines for valuers on how to account for the affordable housing element in a development appraisal.

The principal financial effect of applying these policies is upon the residual land value. This is revealed by comparing the land value in the residual valuation above with that generated by the same valuation below, but in which the affordable housing policy and section 106 obligations have been removed. There is also some effect on the developer's profit but it is not of the same order of magnitude as for the change in the land value.

Gross development value (GDV)

Open market housing	No.	Unit Value £	£	£
I bed flats – open market sales	27	150,000	4,050,000	
2 bed flats – open market sales	40	195,000	7,800,000	
3 bed flats – open market sales	20	220,000	4,400,000	
Total No. of flats =	87			16,250,000

Less costs

	£m²	Net m²	Gross m²		
Demolition and site clearance costs:				150,000	
Building costs					
I bed flats each 50m² @	950	1,350	1,688	1,603,125	
2 bed flats each 60m² @	950	2,400	3,000	2,850,000	
3 bed flats each 76m² @	950	1,520	1,900	1,805,000	
Ancillary costs @ 3% of building costs				187,744	
Contingency @ 5% of demolition, building and ancillary costs				329,793	
Marketing costs @ 1.5% of GDV				243,750	
Cost of obligations under a section 106 agreement				0	
Interest on half the total costs above over 18 months @ 9%				494,666	
Professional fees @ 12.5% of building and ancillary costs				805,734	
Interest on two-thirds professional fees for 18 months @ 9%				74,117	
Costs subtotal					8,543,929
Interest on total for sales period of 3 months @ 9%				186,071	
Profit @ 15% of GDV				2,437,500	
Total costs plus profit =					11,167,500
Site value in 1¾ years time = GDV – total costs =					5,082,500
PV of £1 @ 9% for 1¾ years				0.8600	
Present value of the site therefore					4,370,950
Acquisition costs of 5% (stamp duty @ 4% plus legal fees @ 1%)					
Acquisition costs = present site value – (present site value × 1/1.05)					208,140
Site value therefore					4,162,810

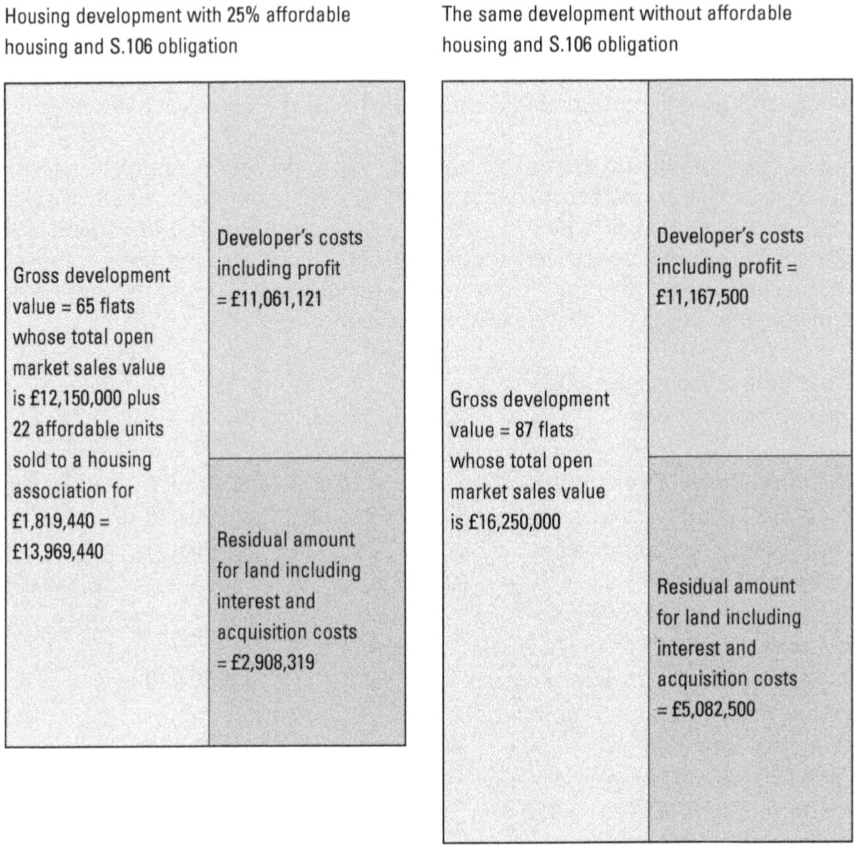

Housing development with 25% affordable housing and S.106 obligation

The same development without affordable housing and S.106 obligation

Gross development value = 65 flats whose total open market sales value is £12,150,000 plus 22 affordable units sold to a housing association for £1,819,440 = £13,969,440

Developer's costs including profit = £11,061,121

Residual amount for land including interest and acquisition costs = £2,908,319

Gross development value = 87 flats whose total open market sales value is £16,250,000

Developer's costs including profit = £11,167,500

Residual amount for land including interest and acquisition costs = £5,082,500

Figure 7.4 Comparing the effects on land value of applying policy

Figure 7.4 summarizes the comparisons between the two versions of the residual valuations to highlight the effects of a development carrying the affordable housing and section 106 obligations.

7.6 Risk and change in variables

The number of variables in a residual valuation and the way that they interact makes the method prone to inaccuracy. Relatively modest changes to particularly the large-value items in a residual valuation can lead to proportionately larger changes in the residual answer. This movement can be critical in regeneration situations or where the property market is fragile and where a development proposal is only marginally viable. Experienced developers are realistic enough to accept that as a development progresses, the value attributed to each and every variable at the outset is likely to change at the margin. Valuers can therefore alter the variables to determine the outcome as a form of sensitivity analysis, a process which is discussed later.

Although a contingency sum is built in to the residual to provide a reserve which can be used to meet unforeseen cost increases, it is also prudent to model likely movements in the key variables in a residual such as the building costs, the market rent, yield or sales values. Sensitivity testing enables a developer to assess the implications arising from the likely direction and magnitude of change to key variables. The RICS acknowledges the reality of change to elements in a residual valuation and suggest that in particular circumstances it is valid for valuers to agree with clients that a range of site values be reported:

> It may be appropriate to present an appraisal based on provable values along-side a sensitivity analysis to show the effect on the land value of differing assumptions as to the future rent and yield. The aim is to assist the client in assessing the likely land value by reference to present and future market trends, and the likely shifts in supply and demand. Wherever possible, the treatment and presentation of these issues is to be discussed with the client. (2008: 17)

A simple example of a sensitivity test is provided below at Table 7.3, but before considering that, the discussion now explores the types of change that can happen in the development process and which affect the variables in a residual.

Potential for change in land costs

As discussed earlier in this chapter, most residual valuations focus upon trying to identify a realistic land value because developers will normally be in competition with one another to acquire sites. However where a vendor has a fixed asking price for a site (or a site has already been purchased) then that price can be put into the residual appraisal to identity whether a satisfactory profit can be achieved. If the appraisal suggests that an acceptable developer's profit is not possible, then either the scheme would have to be abandoned or some means found to reduce development costs. In some situations the asking price for the land could well be open to negotiation and would thus be a variable in which change could be explored.

Potential for change in the quantum of development

There will normally be a planning consent confirming the floorspace for a commercial scheme or the number of housing units which can be built on a site. Some projects can be renegotiated with the local authority and an amended planning application submitted if there is a realistic prospect of consent for a different and perhaps larger scheme. However, for many developments the planning consent is the end result of a period of negotiation and an iterative process from which the optimum scheme has emerged. Sometimes there is scope to improve the internal gross to net floorspace ratio in commercial projects, as by increasing this efficiency ratio by a few per cent, the overall viability of a project can improve considerably.

Potential change in building costs

The estimate of the cost of construction is a major element which may be affected by inflation. The overall rate of increase in the building costs is made up of the increase in the cost of building materials and in the cost of labour. It is usual to allow foreseeable increases in wages and material costs that can be reasonably estimated for perhaps six months or so ahead. During recessionary periods when there are fewer construction contracts being tendered, then construction costs may deflate, as contractors put in lower than normal bids just to secure the work and remain economically active.

Potential change in the rental value

The rental value for a commercial development which appears in a residual valuation is an estimate of the rent that the development will achieve when it is completed and let. Experience, independence and judgement are required on the part of the valuer to gauge the rental value, as it is a volatile variable in commercial schemes. Because the rental value largely determines the capital value and ultimately the viability of a scheme, it is usually a prime candidate for sensitivity testing. Apart from the minority of schemes which are pre-let and where there is some guarantee that a particular rent will ultimately be realized, rental values are dynamic and subject to market forces. For this reason change in this variable is largely beyond the control of any single developer.

Potential change in the investor's yield

The capital value of a commercial development is arrived at by capitalizing the rental income at the appropriate investor's yield. The yield adopted by the valuer is subject to analysis of comparable market transactions set against the economic backdrop and the characteristics of the scheme. Essentially the valuer will marginally increase a yield relative to a property asset's peer group to reflect higher risk, while the yield will be reduced to reflect lower risk.

If a development has been pre-sold to a property investor prior to the start of the development, the yield will be lower than if the scheme is entirely speculative. There are more risks in the latter scenario with the likelihood of a void period before a scheme is fully let to business tenants. As for the rental value, the yield is also a highly sensitive variable in a residual valuation as change in it will have a significant effect on the capital value of a scheme. The yield will therefore normally be a candidate for sensitivity testing.

For housing schemes, the GDV will be based upon prevailing sales values which reflect the capital value of the housing units. In appraisals of those schemes, there would also be sensitivity modelling of the expected housing values to gauge the effect on the viability of the scheme.

Potential change in the duration of development

A residual valuation tries to take account of the time dimension in a development because time affects the cost of holding the land and the cost of finance used to meet all other development costs. There can be delays in the development process because even when the freehold of a site can be secured there might be continuing issues around obtaining vacant possession in order to start development. This might be because some of the existing buildings might be subject to occupational leases and it is not unknown for disputes to arise which can take several months to resolve.

On the assumption that planning consent is in place, the developer can draft construction contracts and where a traditional procurement route is being followed, a bill of quantities can be prepared by the quantity surveyor. The valuer will also be busy providing updated values and rents. Assuming a site is not in a conservation area and that there are no listed buildings involved, demolition, site clearance and ground condition surveys can take place to prepare the ground for construction. There would then follow a lengthy time horizon over which the development was realized and for speculative schemes there might follow a void period for letting or sales.

Development timelines therefore involve a number of stages each of which involve complex exchanges which come with a degree of uncertainty in terms of the time required. It is not therefore surprising that assumptions about the delivery time of a project can slip. Given the implications for additional interest charges on accumulating debt, it is therefore legitimate in a sensitivity test to vary assumptions on the timeline of a project to explore the extent to which delay will threaten overall viability.

7.7 Sensitivity testing

Having discussed how some of the variables in a residual might change, Table 7.3 contains a simple two variable sensitivity test to illustrate the principles at work. The example uses the residual site value of £5,222,146 from the earlier residual calculation for an office development. In the sensitivity test below, +/– 5 per cent and +/– 10 per cent changes are explored in two large-value variables with are the building costs and the rental value. Large-value items like this are deemed to be sensitive variables, because relatively small changes in them will tend to exert a disproportionate effect on the residual outcome.

Only two variables have been used in this example for clarity, but in reality prudent developers and their appraisers would almost certainly explore combinations of changes in a number of the key variables discussed earlier in the chapter. Fundamentally the modelling process is seeking to identify whether the financial characteristics of a scheme are robust enough to withstand a worst case scenario in which changes to a number of variables conspired against a scheme. Thus a 'what if' analysis would consider the combined effects of added costs, lower than expected values and lengthier void periods when interest costs were accumulating. A scheme which remained viable despite these adverse changes could be thought of as a robust proposition, providing some comfort for a developer and the institutions funding the developer.

Some of the variables in a residual valuation can be controlled to some extent. This applies mainly to the cost elements where construction and professional fees contracts can be agreed up front and where effective project management can prevent costs from increasing. However the value elements in a residual are more capricious, as they result from an interplay between factors such as market sentiment, economic conditions, business confidence, interest rates and fiscal policy. Developers will therefore seldom be able to influence the value side of the equation and while they would prefer to secure pre-lets and pre-sales on their schemes to create certainty, those idealistic conditions are seldom found in reality. This is why development is inherently risky and why the rate of return should be commensurate with bearing the risks.

Table 7.3 A two-variable sensitivity test

		Variation in rental value £ per m²				
		−10%	−5%	0%	5%	10%
Variation in building costs £ per m²	−10%	4,681,146 (−10.36%)	5,361,850 (2.68%)	6,042,557 (15.71%)	6,723,265 (28.75%)	7,403,970 (41.78%)
	−5%	4,270,940 (−18.21%)	4,951,645 (−5.18%)	5,632,351 (7.86%)	6,313,058 (20.89%)	6,993,765 (33.93%)
	0%	3,860,733 (−26.07%)	4,541,439 (−13.04%)	5,222,146	5,902,853 (13.04%)	6,583,558 (26.07%)
	5%	3,450,528 (−33.93%)	4,131,233 (−20.89%)	4,811,940 (−7.86%)	5,492,648 (5.18%)	6,173,353 (18.21%)
	10%	3,040,324 (−41.78%)	3,721,029 (−28.75%)	4,401,735 (−15.71%)	5,082,442 (−2.68%)	5,763,149 (10.36%)

There are a number of interpretations of the two dimensional sensitivity test in Table 7.3. From the perspective of a risk-averse developer, perhaps the worst-case scenario in the bottom left hand corner would catch the eye and it would be disconcerting. The site value shown there has fallen by nearly 42 per cent as a result of building costs increasing by 10 per cent and rental values falling back by 10 per cent. If the developer had already paid the core value of £5,222,146 for the land at the outset of the scheme, the worst case scenario would see £2,181,822 lost from the scheme and which is the product of £5,222,146 − £3,040,324. A look back at the original valuation confirms that in unchanged circumstances the developer stood to make a profit of just over £3 million, however in the worst-case scenario the developer's profit would have been dramatically reduced to around £800,000.

As discussed earlier the developer can do something about the costs side of the equation and if it was felt that more certainty were required around the building costs then some form of fixed price procurement method would be used. In that way the risks of any subsequent changes in labour or materials costs would be passed on to the building contractor. The developer could do little about changes in rental values, although could commission market research to assess the likelihood of positive or negative change in rents in the short term.

7.8 Comparing refurbishment with redevelopment

The residual method can be used to compare the profit arising from refurbishing existing buildings with the profit arising from completely redeveloping a site. The refurbishment option will normally involve a lower capital outlay than for complete redevelopment. Both options will see an increase in the quality of space provided but the redevelopment option may also see an increase in the quantity of floorspace provided on a site.

Table 7.4 Comparing refurbishment with redevelopment

Refurbishment Activity	Cost/value £	Redevelopment Activity	Cost/value £
Purchase vacant offices	1,500,000	Purchase vacant offices	1,500,000
Refurbish offices	1,000,000	Redevelop site	2,000,000
Total costs	2,500,000	Total costs	3,500,000
Let and sell offices	3,000,000	Let and sell offices	4,300,000
Return to developer	500,000	Return to developer	800,000
Percentage return on costs	20%	Percentage return on costs	22.8%

Table 7.4 sets out a summary example in which a vacant 30-year-old office building has become available on the market for £1.5 million. The £1.5 million could also reflect the existing book value of an asset if the property were already owned. A developer (or current owner) has the option of buying the building and then spending an additional £1 million refurbishing it before letting it and then disposing of it for an estimated £3million. The developer's alternative option is to buy and redevelop the site, which is a more expensive and riskier option. However this strategy would produce more floorspace and a more valuable asset, as the development could be let and sold to property investors for an estimated £4,300,000.

Although the table above shows that the absolute and percentage return is superior for the redevelopment option, the developer would have to consider whether the additional profit made by pursuing that option would provide adequate compensation for the additional risks involved. The developer would also compare the time required to reach the end objective in each case.

7.9 Development potential and existing use value

Development value exists where land or buildings can increase in value by the application of capital. It may be that this arises from a change of use of the land permitted by planning permission but the property development process usually implies the application of capital in the form of construction work.

The simplified example above regarding refurbishment and redevelopment options brings into view the concept of existing use value (EUV) which is sometimes overlooked when the residual valuation is discussed. In the example it could be assumed that the asking price for the empty office building of £1.5 million reflects its valuation as a potentially lettable office building which would generate a rental income. Although the rental income would need to be deferred to reflect a realistic void period, the deferred income when capitalized by an appropriate yield, would produce a capital value of £1.5 million. Thus the site could be bought and sold for around that figure based upon its existing use.

One potential purchaser of the site and the office building on it could be the developer, who in the above example has calculated that following purchase at £1.5 million, a new scheme could be built on the site at a cost of £2,000,000. The end result would be an asset which could be sold for £4,300,000 enabling the developer to pay off all costs and retain a profit of £800,000. There would in this scenario be sufficient incentive for the developer to try to acquire the site at its asking price, thus meeting the current owner's expectation. The vendor is assumed to be indifferent as to whether a future owner continues with the present use or takes on the risk of trying to obtain planning consent in order to redevelop the site. The key point is that the existing use value can be matched by the developer's evaluation of the situation and in all probability the site would come forward for development.

However, if the developer's scheme had an end value of £4,000,000 with costs of £2,000,000 and a profit expectation of £800,000, the best bid that the developer could make would be £1,200,000 which is £300,000 less that the existing use value. The vendor's expectations would thus not be met by the developer. In that scenario the site would probably not come forward for development but would remain in its existing use for the foreseeable future or until the existing use value depreciated to the point where the site in its present use was £1,200,000 or less.

Where the developer's end value was considerably higher than £4,300,000 the developer could afford to bid beyond £1.5 million and in that scenario the site would almost certainly come forward for development. Conversely if the developer was fortunate enough to negotiate the land purchase at a price lower than the EUV, then assuming the other costs remain static, an abnormal profit would be achieved.

7.10 A critique of the residual valuation method

Having considered the basis for the residual valuation, the context in which it is used and how some of the key variables are calibrated, this part of the chapter explores some of the strengths and weaknesses of the technique.

The outcome from a residual valuation whether expressed as the land value or developer's profit, can be very susceptible to small changes in variables such as the rent, initial yield, construction costs, finance rate and building period. This issue has been explored a number of times by the Lands Tribunal in cases as far back as *First Garden City Ltd* v. *Letchworth Garden City Group* in 1966. The outcome from these cases has been that the Lands Tribunal felt that the residual method should only be used as a last resort when direct comparison was not an option.

The rather scathing verdict on the residual technique by the Lands Tribunal has not deterred valuers from using it in practice, simply because it is often the only realistic way to assess bespoke developments. There seldom are directly comparable projects for many mixed use developments or those containing different combinations of housing tenures or which may simply be unique architectural designs which defy comparison.

The RICS (2008) acknowledges that the increasing diversity of developments justifies the use of the residual method, although valuers are reminded that they must have sufficient expertise and experience to use the method in the particular market context. Where there are grey areas regarding the calibration of variables in an appraisal, valuers are asked to consult suitably qualified experts. When these quality control issues have been addressed, then a broad background comparison might be undertaken to see if the residual valuation outcome makes sense in terms of the general pattern of land values in a particular setting. If the outcome of the residual looks credible, then a sensitivity analysis could be undertaken to explore how change in key variables might affect the residual outcome.

One of the weaknesses in the residual valuation process is that despite the development timelines involved, the variables are calibrated to reflect values at the point when the appraisal is undertaken. Although the GDV of a scheme might actually be realized by the developer several years after the initial appraisal, the GDV is calculated upon the sales values or rents gathered from comparables at the time of the appraisal. In all probability the sales values or rents will move around over the development period and could end up being substantially higher or lower than when the appraisal was undertaken.

Conventionally it was assumed that any change in the end value of a project would be positive and would therefore be of benefit to a developer. There was also an implied trade off in that while values could be expected to change marginally then so would costs, so that the overall effect would broadly be a cancelling out process. Thus a small increase in value would compensate for a small increase in costs. However, the credit crunch which began in 2007 and which had dramatic effects on property values over the ensuing two years, challenged this assumption and had the effect of making developers far more cautious in their land acquisition and development programmes.

While it is possible to factor in a forecast of inflation into a residual valuation, the orthodoxy has been not to, unless as part of an explicit sensitivity test. Generally therefore, inflation in costs or values is not factored into the residual calculation because to do so would probably lead to even greater inaccuracy.

Another problematic aspect in the residual valuation concerns the finance rate used, which is based upon prevailing market interest rates and which assumes that the developer is borrowing 100 per cent of the costs. In combination these two assumptions place a higher price on the finance costs than might in fact be the case.

Most developments are funded by a combination of debt in the form of borrowing and equity from the developer's own funds and/or from capital provided by shareholders. Funding development therefore bears some similarities to purchasing a house, where typically around 20 per cent of the money is equity in the form of the purchaser's deposit, while the remaining 80 per cent is debt in the form of borrowed money. For a developer, the interest rate which could be earned on equity (and is therefore its opportunity cost) will be less than the interest rate payable on debt and thus the overall rate (known as the weighted average cost of capital) should be less than the market rate of interest. However it is the latter which is commonly used in a residual valuation.

The residual valuation also employs broad brush proportions to approximate the consumption of fees and costs over the timeline of a development. This is another criticism of the method in that it will tend to overestimate finance costs arising on a project. In reality the progressive consumption of money during a project is more likely to bear some relationship to an S curve as depicted in Table 7.5 and which has produced Figure 7.5.

Table 7.5 Quarterly cumulative costs and interest charges

Quarter	Quarterly spend %	Amount (£)	Cumulative construction spend (£)	Cumulative %	Quarterly interest payments (£)	Total quarterly expenditure	Brought forward
1	3%	600,000	600,000	3%		600,000	600,000
2	5%	1,000,000	1,600,000	8%	11,658	1,011,658	1,611,658
3	15%	3,000,000	4,600,000	23%	31,315	3,031,315	4,642,973
4	17%	3,400,000	8,000,000	40%	90,213	3,490,213	8,133,186
5	18%	3,600,000	11,600,000	58%	158,028	3,758,028	11,891,214
6	20%	4,000,000	15,600,000	78%	231,046	4,231,046	16,122,260
7	14%	2,800,000	18,400,000	92%	313,256	3,113,256	19,235,516
8	8%	1,600,000	20,000,000	100%	373,746	1,973,746	21,209,262
Totals	100%	20,000,000			1,209,262		

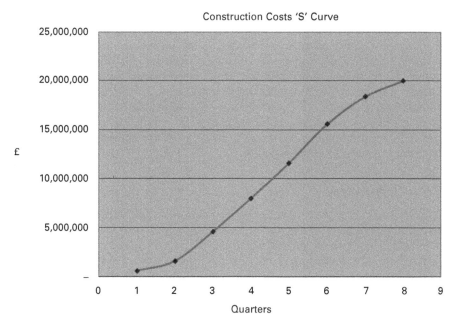

Figure 7.5 An S curve representing the cumulative building costs

Annual Interest =	8%
Quarterly equivalent =	1.943%
Construction Cost =	£20,000,000
Interest calculated by the traditional method =	£1,664,000
Interest calculated by the S curve method below =	£1,209,262
Difference between the two methods =	£454,738

In the above example the residual valuation method of calculating the interest on the basis of the half the costs multiplied by the interest rate over the period, would generate an interest cost of £1,664,000. However if a more forensic S curve approach was adopted, the interest charges would be £1,209,262 suggesting that the traditional method is overcalculating the interest charges by just over £450,000.

The discussion above on how greater accuracy is possible in modelling the anticipated flow of costs over time, confirms that while the residual technique does have its merits, it is not adequate to deal with more complex development situations. This is particularly true where expenditure and income are being made and received at different times over a long project time scale.

Greater accuracy can be achieved by supplementing a residual valuation with a period by period cash flow on a quarterly basis as illustrated by Isaac *et al.* (2010: 110–12) or on a monthly basis as illustrated by Isaac and Steley (2000: 164–9). Alternatively a valuer might decide to use the discounted cash flow (DCF) technique in which future cash flows are discounted back to the present. When that type of appraisal is applied to development projects, the developer's profit expectation and cost of capital are together subsumed into the discount rate adopted in the DCF.

Cash flow approaches do not solve all the difficulties encountered when using the residual method in that changes in the value of the elements in an appraisal can still have a significant effect on the final site value. Sensitivity analysis is therefore just as applicable to cash flows. For example, explicit change can be made to variables in a cash flow, such as adjusting future costs and values to reflect inflation forecasts. This type of exercise can identify where change will most affect profitability and thought can be given to whether it is possible to take steps to reduce the uncertainty.

7.11 Summary

This chapter has explored the residual valuation technique which, among the five methods of valuation, is the method used by valuers to identify the value of sites which have development potential. The residual method is sometimes referred to as a development appraisal. As well as being able to identify site values, it can also be used to determine a developer's profit where the land value is already known.

The residual method is selected by the valuer when the use of the comparative method is no longer tenable. This is because developments are unique and it is often difficult to find directly comparative schemes. However the residual method does rely on comparison to the extent that the variables in the valuation, such as building costs, rents and yields, are calibrated by reference to comparable market data. Thus while a commercial or housing development might be unique it will not be entirely independent from market trends in rents or housing values prevailing in an area.

The residual valuation works from the interplay of a number of variables over the envisaged development timeline. Given that it might take several years to complete a development, it is inevitable that change will occur in the values ascribed to variables at the outset when the valuation is undertaken. It is not surprising therefore that there is scope for variance between what the valuation suggests to be the site value and what actually transpires on a site. The word 'error' does not quite describe the conundrum but perhaps the word 'tolerance' does, in that the site value or profit identified by a residual will always be subject to a plus or minus tolerance.

To try to deal with this uncertainty, valuers will usually undertake a sensitivity analysis for schemes of any value. The principles underpinning this type of exercise were discussed in the chapter where it was found that a range of outcomes emerged from stepped changes in key variables. This type of exercise is educative in that it can reveal how susceptible a scheme might be to marginal changes in variables. Developers can then take a view on the expected parameters of change and whether the outcomes in any particular combination can be tolerated. The exercise also helps a developer to identify whether any of the key variables might be controlled or, if that is not possible, whether the remaining risk is adequately compensated for in the rate of return expected from the scheme.

References

Blackledge, M. (2009) *Introducing Property Valuation* (Abingdon: Routledge).

Building Cost Information Service. An online subscription service at: www.bcis.co.uk.

De Montford University (2008) *Review of Practice in the Use of Section 106 Agreements to Facilitate the Delivery of Affordable Housing in the East Midlands* (Leicester: De Montford University, Centre for Comparative Housing Research).

Department for Communities (2005) *Circular 05/2005: Planning Obligations* (London: Department for Communities and Local Government). Originally published by the Office of the Deputy Prime Minister. Available in e-format at: www.communities.gov.uk

Department for Communities (2010) *The Community Infrastructure Levy: An Overview* (London: Department for Communities and Local Government). Available in e-format at: www.communities.gov.uk

Enever, N., Isaac, D. and Daley, M. (2010) *The Valuation of Property Investments* (7th edn, London: EG Books).

Havard, T. (2008) *Contemporary Property Development* (2nd edn, London: RIBA Publishing).

Isaac, D., O'Leary, J. and Daley, M. (2010) *Property Development, Appraisal and Finance* (2nd edn, Basingstoke: Palgrave).

Isaac, D. and Steley, T. (2000) *Property Valuation Techniques* (London: Macmillan).

RICS (2007) *Code of Measuring Practice* (6th edn, London: RICS).

RICS (2008) *Valuation of Development Land, Valuation Information Paper 12* (London: RICS).

RICS (2010) *Valuation of Land for Affordable Housing* (London: RICS).

Scarrett, D. (2008) *Property Valuation: The Five Methods* (2nd edn, Abingdon: Routledge).

University of Sheffield (2010) *The Incidence, Value and Delivery of Planning Obligations in England in 2007–08* (London: Department for Communities and Local Government). Available in e-format at: www.communities.gov.uk

Wilkinson, S. and Reed, R. (2008) *Property Development* (5th edn, Abingdon: Routledge).

Self-assessment questions for Chapter 7

1 Summarize the purpose and context in which the residual valuation method might be used.

2 Explain some of the limitations associated with the residual method.

3 A 1 hectare site with planning consent for 15 two bedroom houses, 20 three bedroom houses and 10 four bedroom houses is for sale at a fixed price of £2.2 million. A developer will purchase the site if a profit margin equivalent to 15 per cent of the scheme's gross development value (GDV) can be realized. Market comparables suggest that new two bedroom houses will sell for £180,000 in this location while the three bedroom houses will sell for £250,000 and the four bedroom houses for £320,000. The total costs to complete the scheme including construction costs, fees, contingencies and finance (but excluding profit) are estimated to be £7,500,000. Using a simple residual approach in which there is no need to adjust for present value, calculate whether such as scheme would meet the developer's profit expectations.

4 Using the housing site scenario described above, the site value is now the unknown variable to be identified after the developer has included an allowance for 15 per cent profit benchmarked against the scheme's GDV. However the GDV is now affected by an affordable housing policy under which 25 per cent of each of the three types of houses will be

sold to a housing association for 65 per cent of their market value. Thus for the 15 two bedroom houses, 4 will be sold to a housing association for £117,000 each and the remaining 11 will be sold for their market value of £180,000 each. For the 20 three bedroom houses, 5 will be sold to the housing association for £162,500 while the remaining 15 will be sold for their open market value of £250,000 each. For the four bedroom houses the same pro rata arrangement applies. Identify the site value.

5 (a) The site value identified in answer to question 4 can now be assumed to be realizable in two years' time. On the basis that the developer's cost of finance is 8 per cent calculate the present value of the site

  (b) Having identified the present value of the site deduct the purchase costs which are the solicitor's and agent's fees which together amount to 1 per cent of the present value of the site plus stamp duty land tax in accordance with the following thresholds.

Property value	Stamp duty tax rate
Up to £150,000	Nil
£150,001 to £250,000	1%
£250,001 to £500,000	3%
Over £500,000	4%

Outline answers are included at the back of the book.

8

The investment method – traditional approach

8.1 Introduction
8.2 Capitalizing using a yield
8.3 Freehold investment properties
8.4 Identifying the net rent
8.5 Term and reversion
8.6 The layer method
8.7 The equivalent yield
8.8 Over-rented property

8.9 Leaseholds and profit rents
8.10 Premiums
8.11 A critique of traditional
     investment methods
8.12 Summary
     References
     Self-assessment questions

Aims

This chapter investigates the traditional investment method of property valuation which capitalizes the net rental income from an investment property by using a multiplier called the Years' Purchase (YP). It will be explained that the YP is the reciprocal of a yield which is sometimes referred to as the 'all risks yield' and which is normally derived from comparable market evidence. The discussion will explain that the yield reflects what rational investors are willing to pay to acquire properties within the particular asset class.

Using examples, the chapter will show how the traditional investment method can be used to identify the capital value of investment properties. The method can also assess the rents passing on a property in combination with the anticipated rent which will arise on review at a future point in time. This type of valuation is concerned with what are called reversionary properties and it will be seen that there are a number of ways this type of valuation can be conducted. The chapter also shows how this type of valuation can be adapted to appraise properties which are over-rented relative to the current estimated rental value which might reasonably be achieved. The chapter also considers the value of profit rents and the role played by premiums.

Key terms

>> **Investment method** – the capitalization of the net income arising from an investment property using a multiplier called the Years' Purchase (YP).

>> **Years' Purchase (YP)** – a capitalizer based on the yield appropriate for the particular property investment. The YP can be for a specific term of years which may be the unexpired term on a lease or the term leading up to a rent review. The YP may also be used to capitalize an income which is assumed to continue into the future without interruption in which case the expression 'YP in perpetuity' is used.

>> **Net income** – rental income from a property less outgoings such as expenditure for repairs and building insurance premiums. The lease terms will determine whether it is the landlord or tenant who pays for these outgoings. Regardless of who is responsible, it is the net income which is capitalized in the investment method.

>> **Reversionary property** – when a property has been let for some time and there has not been a recent rent review, the rent passing will be historic and unlikely to be the same as the market rent. The latter is sometimes referred to (and is the same as) the estimated rental value (ERV) and at the next rent review or upon lease expiry there will normally be a reversion to the ERV.

>> **Term and reversion** – the term is the period up until the next rent review or lease expiry on an investment property during which an agreed annual rent will be paid by a tenant to a landlord. The reversion is the period following the term and when it is likely, although not guaranteed, that the rent will change. The reversionary rent will normally increase to reflect inflation but see comments below on over-rented property.

>> **Layer method** – depicts the rental income from an investment property as if it were two horizontal layers going forward in time. The lower layer is often referred to as the hardcore rent and it is assumed to continue from the date of a valuation into perpetuity. Following a rent review a top slice of rent may be added to reflect the uplift in rental value at that time. The hardcore rent is thought to be at less risk than the top slice and so the two layers of income are customarily valued using a different yield for each layer.

>> **Over-rented property** – this is where the rent passing is based upon historic market levels which have subsequently fallen. Thus on the expiry of a lease or at the next rent review, it is unlikely that the rent will increase and may fall depending on the terms of the lease.

8.1 Introduction

The traditional investment method of valuation evolved as a way to determine the capital value of a property by capitalizing its actual or anticipated rental income. In its simplest form, the investment method assumes that a property investor will look at the annual rental income from a tenanted property and will pay a multiple of that income to acquire the freehold in order to receive the rental income. Thus the property investor's interest in identifying the capital value of the property is not so that it can be purchased for occupation but for the financial performance of the property in both the flow of rental income and the future potential for capital growth.

If a property is well located, in a good condition and has a reliable tenant it probably has good growth prospects and thus it will be sought after by investors

Figure 8.1 Retail warehouses such as these at Crayford are typical examples of commercial investment properties

who may be willing to pay many times the annual rental income in order to acquire the property. The actual number of times is referred to as the Years' Purchase (YP). Alternatively if a property is in a poor condition in a secondary location and leased to a tenant who might be in financial difficulties, then investors will be willing to pay fewer multiples of the income to acquire the property. The examples in the chapter will explore the mathematics which captures these types of trade-offs and which in essence represent investors' perceptions of the risks and rewards for investing in different property assets.

The investment method is used most widely in the commercial property sector to determine the capital value of properties such as shops, retail warehouses, offices, factories and warehouses. These properties will typically have business tenants who have agreed to pay rents in return for occupational leases of varying lengths and which would normally contain provision for periodic rent reviews.

The investment method can also be applied to private rented housing where buy-to-let investors will be interested in the relationship between the cost to acquire a house or flat and its actual or potential rental income. Indeed it is now quite common for residential estate agents to promote particular residential properties to investors on the basis of their actual or predicted income yield. The discussion in this chapter however will focus mainly upon commercial property because it is in that field where these techniques are most often used.

8.2 Capitalizing using a yield

Rational investors seek a return on their investments either as an annual income or a capital gain or a combination of both. The investment method of valuation tries to identify the return for investing in properties which are let to business or residential tenants and thus producing a rental income. The investment method therefore begins by trying to identify the relationship between the income from an investment property and its capital value. This can be made easier where the investor has a predetermined minimum rate of return, as this can be factored into the equation to assess whether the investment would meet the investor's expectations as follows:

$$\text{Rental income} = \text{Capital value} \times \frac{i}{100} \text{ where } i \text{ is the investor's required rate of return.}$$

For example if £1,000,000 is to be paid for an investment property by an investor who requires an 8 per cent return, the annual rental income from the property would need to be:

$$£1,000,000 \times \frac{8}{100} = £80,000 \text{ per annum}$$

In the example above, the capital value and investor's rate of return were the given variables and from their interplay it was possible to calculate the required income. In most property situations however, the rental income will be a known variable, either because the rent is actually passing under a lease or it is estimated from the letting of comparable properties. In that situation the capital value may be calculated by transposing the formula so that the capital value becomes the subject as follows.

$$\text{Capital value} = \text{Rental income} \times \frac{100}{i}$$

Thus the capital value of a property producing an annual rent of £80,000 can be calculated for an investor requiring an 8 per cent return as follows:

$$\text{Capital value} = £80,000 \times \frac{100}{8} = £1,000,000$$

This process capitalizes the annual income to produce a capital sum. It is essential that the income being capitalized is net income which is clear of any expenses incurred by the investor under the lease. A more precise representation of the formula is therefore.

$$\text{Capital value} = \text{Net rental income} \times \frac{100}{i}$$

Table 8.1 Selected yields and their YP in perpetuity counterparts

Rate of return	100/i
7%	14.29
8%	12.50
9%	11.11
10%	10.00
11%	9.09
12%	8.33

For given rates of return $100/i$ will be constant as shown by the examples in Table 8.1.

The constant $100/i$ in the right-hand column above is referred to as the Years' Purchase in perpetuity (abbreviated to YP in perp.). The YP in perp. is effectively a multiplier of the rent to identify the capital value and thus the formula can finally be modified to:

Capital value = Net rental income × YP in perp.

The YP in perp., calculated by using $100/i$ applies to freehold properties let at a market rent where the income is assumed to be receivable without interruption into the future, hence the expression 'in perpetuity'. Incomes to be received for specific periods of years can also be capitalized but must use the YP for a given term. The formal name for this multiplier in *Parry's Valuation and Investment Tables* (Davidson, 2002) is the Present Value of £1 per annum, the formula for which is used in examples later in the chapter.

Investment method valuations have traditionally been conducted on the basis that the rental income from properties is received annually in arrears. This is a simplification which has made the calculations easier and compatible with one another, but it does not reflect reality as most commercial leases require the tenant to pay rent quarterly in advance. There has been a gradual shift towards conducting these valuations on a quarterly in advance basis and later editions of Parry's Tables now contain both annual in arrears and quarterly in advance tables.

In this introductory text it is not intended to explore the intricacies of applying the quarterly in advance approach, but rather to promote a good understanding of the principles and application of capitalization in different property contexts. Given that ambition, the annual in arrears principle has been adhered to in the examples which follow. Once these principles are understood, those readers who want to go further by factoring in quarterly in advance assumptions could examine applications of that approach in Isaac and O'Leary (2011: 182–6) or in Banfield (2009) where the topic is explored in some depth.

To consolidate key points arising from the discussion so far, the estimation of the capital value of an investment property using the traditional investment method requires clarification of three variables:

- The annual net rental income to be received or actually passing on a property.
- Whether the net income is to be received in perpetuity or for a specific term of years.
- The yield associated with the particular investment.

Clarification on the first two points can be obtained by inspecting the lease of the subject property. If the property is unlet, then an estimate of its rental value can be derived by analysing the lettings of comparable properties and an assumption made that the income will be receivable in perpetuity. The yield can be obtained from analysing sales of comparable property investments. To calibrate these variables a valuer must therefore have an understanding of both the lettings and investment markets applicable to the particular property.

8.3 Freehold investment properties

Having set out the basic principles underpinning the investment method, a simple example follows which illustrates the straightforward capitalization of an income assumed to be receivable in perpetuity. The scenario is that a modern industrial unit with sufficient parking spaces and convenient motorway access has recently been let on a long lease with five-year rent reviews to a reliable industrial firm for an annual net rent of £60,000. Recent comparable market evidence suggests that this type of investment property is purchased by corporate property investors for capital sums which reflect a yield of 5 per cent. A valuer might therefore reasonably produce the following calculation to identify the capital value of the property.

Annual net rental income	£60,000
Years' Purchase in perpetuity @ 5%	x 20
Capital value therefore	£1,200,000

Scarrett (2008: 85) suggests that this straightforward application of the investment method is often used at the commencement of a lease or soon after, when the rent agreed under the lease is the same as the market rent. The purchaser is buying an asset whose income, it is assumed, will keep pace with inflation because there are periodic rent reviews written into the lease. The tenant is assumed to be a reliable business which is able to meet rental obligations.

Saunders (2010: 5) and Scarrett (2008: 86) confirm that a purchaser of this type of investment property would normally have to meet purchaser's costs which are an amalgam of stamp duty at 4 per cent (where the property has a value of at least £500,000) plus solicitor's and other fees surrounding the transaction. In total these costs amount to around 5.75 per cent of the value of a property. Thus in the example above if an investor wanted to preserve the relationship between the capital value paid and the rental income so that it represented a 5 per cent yield, then the purchaser's costs would have to be inclusive of the £1,200,000 paid.

An error can occur at this stage, as it is sometimes assumed that this is just a matter of calculating 5.75 per cent of £1,200,000 and deducting that figure: £69,000 from £1,200,000 to arrive at the net value of £1,131,000. This is not however correct, as the calculation should identify the figure which if 5.75 per cent is added to it will produce £1,200,000. The correct calculation is therefore £1,200,000/1.0575 = £1,134,752 which is the net cost and which if 5.75 per cent (65,248) purchaser's costs are added the result will be a total spend of £1,200,000.

Because this chapter is more concerned with discussing the principles underpinning the traditional investment method of valuation, the requirement to find the net value after purchaser's costs have been deducted will henceforth be relaxed so that attention is not drawn away from the main objective. Those readers who will go on to study property valuations at a more advanced level will however come across the concept of net value following deduction of purchaser's costs.

The yield used to capitalize the income from properties is sometimes referred to as the capitalization rate and sometimes the 'all risks yield'. This is because in calibrating the yield against the backdrop of market evidence and the characteristics of the property, the valuer is implicitly taking into account the trade-off between the risks posed to the financial performance of the property against the potential for rental and capital growth. The 5 per cent yield in the example above suggests that the valuer is confident that there will be some sort of combination of rental and capital growth in future and that the growth potential of the asset is felt to outstrip the threats.

The all risks yield in this type of valuation may also confusingly coincide with and share the same numerical value as the *initial yield*, which describes the relationship between the rental income and capital value at the point of purchase. However later on in the chapter when the valuation of reversionary properties is explored it will become evident that there is a distinction to be drawn between the all risks yield and the initial yield in that they do not always share the same numerical value. This is essentially because the dynamics of the property market will see rents and capital values change over time.

In the example above if the investor pays £1,200,000 for the property investment (inclusive of purchaser's costs) a return of 5 per cent (£60,000) on the capital invested will be received at the outset. However, over the longer term, the return is likely to be much better than 5 per cent when capital and rental growth are taken together. The valuation does not however specify what the level of performance above 5 per cent might be and this is a characteristic of this type of valuation which has attracted legitimate criticism from authors such as Scarrett (2008: 85–6).

One of the reasons that the yield will be different when re-visited a number of years later and when it will be referred to as the 'running yield', is that inflation will have taken effect. This normally means that rents have increased and there may also be some capital growth. However the rate of growth in the rental value might not be the same as the rate of growth in the capital value. As the RICS (2010: 6) confirm, the tendency towards inflation induced growth can also be counteracted in many commercial buildings by a degree of obsolescence. This is especially true when new and probably more sustainable buildings are developed which have lower running costs and which present stiff competition for the stock of existing buildings.

As well as interim changes in the relationship between income and capital value, the expression 'exit yield' may be used when referring to the sale of what have become second-hand buildings a number of years after they were first purchased. At the point of disposal the relationship between the rent and capital value will have changed significantly from when a building was first acquired.

It is not possible to be definitive or to suggest a formula to quantify the relationship between the initial yield and the exit yield for a property because the duration to the point of disposal will vary considerably between investors. Properties will also perform differently due to their location and characteristics. For example, prime high street shops enjoy something of a monopoly position and so the ongoing financial performance of these assets is closely tied to the overall popularity and attractiveness of the town centre and the economic strength of the economy as a whole. A relaxation of hitherto strict retail planning policy which allowed the development of an out of town regional shopping centre nearby would of course have a significant detrimental effect on the financial performance of high street shops nearby.

For offices, the appearance in a central business district of new office towers with advanced sustainability credentials, will have a significant effect on the financial performance of neighbouring second-hand office towers. Unless second hand buildings have some special characteristics or iconic status, they could well have become obsolete in 20 years. The options in that scenario are to refurbish and rebadge such buildings so that they have a new lease of life or to redevelop the site to provide typically larger and higher specification buildings.

A complex interplay of factors will thus affect the value of property assets going forward and which is difficult to unravel and forecast with any great certainty. Hence the use of the all risks yield to produce a capital value. The calibration of the all risks yield relies upon the instinct and judgement exercised by a valuer who tries to encapsulate in one figure, the way that these countervailing forces will play out for the particular property under analysis. At a fundamental level the more risks perceived by the valuer the higher will be the all risks yield, following the basic maxim that as risks increase so must rewards. Conversely where the growth potential of the property is felt to significantly outweigh the risks, the added sense of security is reflected in a lower yield.

It is probably unwise to be too prescriptive regarding the all risk yields associated with different types of property, simply because it is in the nature of markets to change over time. There are also inevitable quality differences within broad property categories and especially between prime and non-prime properties. This is reflected in the quite wide parameters suggested by authors such as Shapiro *et al.* (2009: 96–100) who cite yield ranges for shops of between 4 to 15 per cent, for offices the range is 6 to 12 per cent, for factories and warehouses the range is 8 to 15 percent, for houses between 5 and 15 percent and for flats the range is between 8 and 10 per cent.

While it is helpful to know the broad yield parameters for property asset classes, an experienced valuer will identity comparables from sources such as internal corporate records and/or Focusnet and/or EGi which in essence are regularly updated online databases containing (among other things) market information on investment deals. The IPD (Investment Property Databank) monitors the financial performance of a representative sample of commercial and residential investment properties and is able to report yields for broad property classes such as retail, offices and industrial. The IPD can also be commissioned to undertake bespoke analysis and forecasting where the transaction and scale of investment warrants a more forensic approach.

The type of valuation being discussed here is normally carried out for the property investment market where investment properties are bought and sold. However, the techniques also enable the calculation of the capital value of owner-occupied premises by assuming that a notional rent equivalent to a market rent is passing. Thus a capital value can still be assessed and which might be needed for accounting purposes, even though no actual rent is passing.

In valuation parlance and in some academic books, the market rent is sometimes referred to as the 'rack rent' which is a historical reference to stretching something out on a rack to its maximum extent. Thus a rack rent is the best that could possibly be achieved for a property given its characteristics and the economic circumstances prevailing. However the term which is recognized in the RICS (2011: 31) and which valuers should therefore use is *market rent.* Just to confuse matters further there is sometimes references made in text books and elsewhere to the *estimated rental value* (ERV) which is an equivalent unofficial term. There is obviously scope here for some consolidation and consistency in the use of valuation terminology.

The letting terms are an important consideration in investment valuations because if a tenant is responsible for all repairs and insurance then the rent will be less than if the landlord is responsible. The usual situation is that a business tenant agrees to take a lease under which they become responsible for repairs and insurance. By covering these outgoings the tenant will have taken a full repairing and insuring (FRI) lease. The landlord therefore does not have any outgoings and the rent received is the net income. The discussion in the following section explores how these obligations which arise under a lease are accounted for.

8.4 Identifying the net rent

The capitalization method discussed so far assumes that the rent arising is net of any outgoings, implying that the property has been let on full repairing and insuring terms under which the tenants is responsible for all the repairs and insurance premiums. Where this is not the case some adjustments have to be made to the rent to convert it into net income which can then be capitalized. This process of adjustment is illustrated below in examples 8.1 and 8.2.

Example 8.1 An investment valuation of a business park office unit to be let on FRI terms

A valuer has been instructed to value the freehold interest in Unit 9 which is a new office building on a successful business park. Unit 9 has 1,600 m^2 of lettable floorspace and is available for letting to business tenants on full repairing and insuring terms. Market evidence suggests that when this type of property is purchased by property investors the transaction reflects a yield of 7 per cent. Unit 7 is also a new office building on the business park with the same specification as Unit 9 but is larger with 2,250 m^2 of lettable space. Unit 7 was recently let for an annual rent of £450,000 on internal repairing terms, leaving the landlord responsible for external repairs and insurance.

Approach

Given that the subject property, Unit 9 has not yet been let, it relies on the comparable, Unit 7 which was recently let to provide the estimate rental value. Some adjustment would need to be made to the rent passing on Unit 7 to identify the net income which can then be expressed as a rent per square metre and applied to Unit 9 as follows.

Analysis of Unit 7

Annual rent passing		£450,000
Less		
External repairs @ 10%	£45,000	
Insurance @ 2.5%	£11,250	
Management @ 2.5%	£11,250	
Total outgoings		£67,500
Net rent therefore		£382,500

Net income per m^2 (£382,500/2,250 m^2) = £170

Valuation of Unit 9

Net annual income: £170 × 1,600 m^2	£272,000	
YP in perp. @ 7%	14.2857	
Capital value		£3,885,710

If Unit 7 had been sold to investors for £5,880,000, then this could alter the valuation for Unit 9 because a valuer would conduct analysis on that transaction to ascertain whether the assumed yield of 7 per cent was now being challenged by more recent investment deals. The valuer would be aware of the possibility of *yield compression* where investors are sometimes willing to pay more for properties because they believe that there is additional growth potential. In this scenario, a summary of the analysis of the investment deal on Unit 7 might be as follows:

Net annual income	£382,500	
YP in perpetuity	X	
Capital value		£5,880,000
YP in perp. (X) = 5,880,000/382,500 =	15.3725	

Yield = 1/YP in perp. = 1/15.3725 = 6.5% (rounded up)

If the valuer felt that the evidence suggested that yield compression was taking place, the capitalization of the net income for Unit 9 might then be undertaken to reflect a yield of 6.5 per cent as follows:

Net annual income for Unit 9:	£272,000	
YP in perpetuity @ 6.5%	15.3846	
Capital value		£4,184,611

Because the yield has reduced by 0.5 per cent (from 7 to 6.5 per cent) the capital value for Unit 9 has increased by £298,901 (a product of £4,184,611 – £3,885,710). This is one of the aspects of the traditional investment method which is not always fully grasped by those coming into contact with it for the first time. This is understandable as it is counter-intuitive that the capital value will rise when the yield reduces.

The process works in reverse, so that if investors begin to believe that a particular investment has limited growth potential, they will tend to pay fewer multiples of the annual income to acquire the asset. Thus the capital value will fall but the yield will rise, which is sometimes referred to as a slackening yield.

Before moving on to consider Example 8.2, those whose understanding of this relationship is fragile might want to consolidate their knowledge at this point by assuming that the yield for Unit 9 is now 7.5 per cent to see what effect that would have on the capital value.

Example 8.2 An investment valuation of offices to be let on internal repairing terms

An office building containing 2,500 m^2 of lettable space, has recently been let on fully repairing and insuring terms (FRI) at an annual rent of £462,500. The building was then sold to a property investor for £6,600,000. A valuer has been asked to value the freehold interest in a nearby office building of similar specification which has 1,750 m^2 of lettable space and which is to be let on internal repairing terms.

Approach

The comparable can be analysed to identify the market rent per square metre and the yield which can be used to value the subject property, although the rent will have to be adjusted to reflect the different lease terms as follows.

Analysis of comparable

$$\text{Rent per m}^2 = £462,500/2,500 \text{ m}^2 = £185 \text{ per m}^2$$

$$\text{Yield} = (\text{Net income/Capital value}) \times 100\% = (462,500/6,600,000) \times 100\% = 7\%$$

Valuing the subject property

The valuer could well decide to adjust the yield to 7.5 per cent as the lease terms are not quite as favourable as for the comparable property because the subject property's external repairs and insurance obligations fall on the freehold owner. Before finalizing the yield, the valuer would also look at the quality of the covenant, i.e. the corporate credit rating and general reliability of the prospective business tenant to meet rental payments in comparison to the tenant in the comparable property.

The comparable property has been let on FRI terms and so its rent is already the net rental income which can be applied to the subject property to determine the capital value as follows:

Net annual income: 1,750 m^2 × £185 per m^2 £323,750
YP in perp. @ 7.50%   13.3333
Capital value   £4,316,656

However, the subject property is to be let on internal repairing terms only and so an uplift in the rent which will pass is justified because the landlord will have to pay for external repairs, insurance and some management costs. The gross rent received by the landlord will therefore need to include an allowance for these outgoings as shown below.

Valuation

Net annual income if let on FRI terms:		£323,750
Add allowance for landlord's outgoings:		
External repairs @ 10% of rent	£32,375	
Insurance @ 2.5% of rent	£8,094	
Management @ 2.5%	£8,094	
Total outgoings		£48,563
Gross annual rental income therefore:		£372,313

8.5 Term and reversion

Sayce *et al.* (2006: 108) confirm that the term a reversion method is one of two traditional ways of evaluating reversionary investment properties. The other method is the layer approach and it will be discussed later in this chapter. Term and reversion describes a situation where a freehold property is valued subject to a lease under which the rent passing is not the same as the market rent. For example, the rent paid by the tenant to the landlord might have been agreed at the commencement of a lease several years earlier and may be significantly lower than the present market rent.

The effect of inflation over time normally means that historically determined rents which have not been reviewed recently, will tend to be lower than prevailing market rents. In those situations the expectation is that at the next rent review, the rent would be increased to the market rent. This uplift is the *reversion* and the period preceding it is the *term*, hence the expressions: term rent and reversionary rent. The approach taken in a term and reversion valuation illustrated below in Figure 8.2 is to capitalize the block of income arising during the term and then to add it to the capitalized block of income arising on reversion.

At pre-agreed stages during a commercial lease it is normal for the rent to be reviewed. In the past, a typical commercial lease might be for 25 years with provision for rent reviews every five years. However in recent years the average lease length for commercial properties has reduced mainly because business tenants have sought more flexibility. In many cases businesses quite understandably do not wish to commit to the same premises for 25-year terms. Although shorter leases are now the norm, there would still typically be provision for rent reviews at three- or five-year intervals.

The rent review process creates tension between a landlord and tenant because the landlord expects the rent to increase so that its real value is not eroded by inflation. Conversely the tenant would probably prefer the rent to

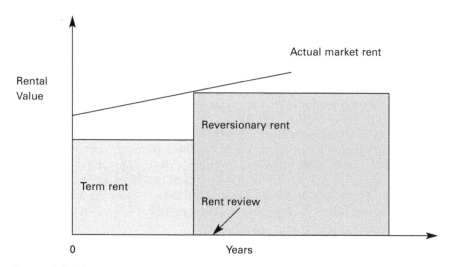

Figure 8.2 The term and reversion concept

remain unchanged or to increase only marginally, for the obvious reason that property rents are a significant overhead for many businesses. It is not surprising therefore that for high value properties, the rent review process can become adversarial. Even where there is goodwill between the parties, the process is best handled by specialist firms of surveyors acting for landlord and tenant.

In the context of rent reviews, surveyors will try to identify the market rent for the subject property by making comparisons with rents recently agreed for new leases and rent reviews on similar properties. Adjustments are made to take account of the specific characteristics of the subject property and the passage of time between the valuation and the comparable transactions.

Market transactions are normally reduced to a unit of comparison, such as the rent per square metre of lettable space in commercial premises. However for shops the rent per square metre in terms of Zone A is identified in order to take account of the proportion of frontage relative to the depth of the shop (that type of calculation was illustrated in Chapter 4 which looked at the comparison method of valuation). The surveyors involved will usually base their calculations on the net income to the landlord after outgoings have been paid.

Before exploring term and reversion further, it should not be forgotten that periodic banking crises and over-speculation in property can coincide to significantly weaken property markets, and thus a term rent passing on a property may sometimes be higher than the market rent. In that scenario, the rent may fall at the next rent review assuming the lease terms allow this to happen. This is still a reversion to the market rent but in an over-rented context which requires a different approach which is discussed later in the chapter.

At this point an example of a term and reversion valuation is introduced to illustrate the approach, which begins by assessing the capital value of the term before adding to it the capital value of the reversion to produce an overall capital value for the property.

Example 8.3 Term and reversion

A freehold retail warehouse was let three years ago to an established retail company on a full repairing and insuring lease for a period of 10 years with a rent review after five years. The annual rent agreed at the commencement of the lease was £35,000 and this is now passing between the tenant and landlord, although current market evidence suggests that the market rent is now £40,000.

In this scenario there are three different periods going forward and logically it might be supposed that there might be three different rents to capitalize which would then be added together to produce the overall capital value for the property. As Figure 8.3 shows, there is a term of two years up to the first rent review, following that a five-year term up until the expiry of the lease and then a period beyond when in all probability the building will be re-let to generate an income.

However one of the characteristics of the traditional investment method of valuation is that it does not explicitly engage in forecasting what rents might be in future but uses current passing rents and market rents. These rental values are capitalized by a valuer who exercises judgement to calibrate the yield for the respective blocks of income. While there are really three periods of time in the example, a valuer using this method might justifiably decide to merge the second term and the period beyond the expiration of the lease into one future period. The valuer would then form a judgement around the appropriate yield to use to capitalize income expected for that period.

The rationale for the approach described above is that that there are a number of uncertainties at the point when the lease expires in seven years' time. It would not be clear to the valuer or indeed any other party, whether the current tenant would seek to extend the lease. If the current tenant decided not to extend the lease it is not clear seven years ahead of the event whether the property could be re-let and whether such a re-letting would be instantaneous or would follow a void period.

After seven years the landlord might also decide to upgrade the property to enhance its competitiveness and this would result in a void period before the building was re-let. Alternatively the landlord might decide that the site was more valuable in another use and might then seek planning consent in order to

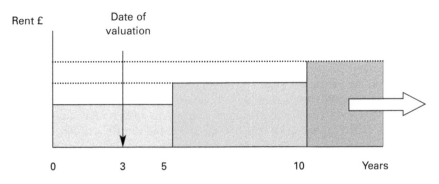

Figure 8.3 The term and reversion format applied to example 8.3

redevelop the site for something else. Thus there are a number of scenarios which could plausibly apply seven years hence although they are suppositions, each of which will have different value implications.

The speculation about what might happen to the property when the lease expires is a dilemma which could easily lead to a very inaccurate assessment of the property's capital value. For example although the stepped diagram above implies that the rent beyond the expiration of the lease would rise there can be no guarantee seven years ahead of the event that the rent will increase. Even if it were to increase, there is no firm evidence about the margin of that increase. Although historical time series data could give an indication of how rents have performed in the past there is no guarantee that rents will perform that way in future. Property markets are notoriously volatile and forecasting in this field is hazardous.

Defenders of the traditional investment method point to its simplicity and its avoidance of forecasting. These attributes could be thought of as a safety mechanism which prevents overspeculation, acting as a subliminal restraint on overestimating the value of properties. There is therefore an inherent conservatism in the traditional investment method which could be seen as a strength, depending on the perspective taken.

Returning to example 8.3 it was noted that it was very likely that a valuer would condense the three future stages in the life of the property into two periods as follows:

- A term of two years up until the rent review when the annual rent passing on the property will be £35,000. The income in this period seems reasonably certain as the tenant has already demonstrated that this obligation can be met and may also be aware that the rent is less than would have to be paid if a new lease were to be taken on a similar property.
- A reversionary period comprising five years until the lease expires plus the period beyond into perpetuity. Following the rent review and until the expiration of the lease it is highly likely that that a rent of at least £40,000 will apply. Note that this is not a forecast of what the rent will be in two years' time but is based upon market evidence at the time of the valuation.

As discussed above, what happens beyond the expiry of the lease is uncertain and lends itself to a number of competing scenarios. Given the maxim 'simple is best' in such a situation, the valuer could reasonably decide that the property has some sort of income producing future at least as good as the last five years remaining on the lease. The valuer would then look at market evidence to see how other investors have behaved when faced with similar situations.

Unfortunately it is not always possible to find directly comparable market data which mimics the characteristics and circumstances of the property being valued. Valuers are therefore sometimes faced with the challenge of analysing scant or tenuous market information from which to adjust the key variables so that they can be credibly applied to the subject property. Experience and judgement is therefore required.

In the example it might be that market evidence showed that fully rented properties with less risky futures represented by lengthy leases with rent reviews, had changed hands to reflect an all risks yield of 7 per cent. Armed with that information the valuer would then at least have a benchmark against which to adjust the yields in a term and reversion valuation (as shown below) to reflect the greater risk and uncertainty in the scenario.

The RICS (2010: 9) confirm that reversionary property investments will always be riskier propositions than those that are let at the market rent, simply because more of the value is tied up in the less certain reversionary period. Thus in the scenario and without a directly comparable reversionary property transaction to analyse, the valuer might deduce that the reversionary yield for the subject property would need to be 8 per cent, i.e. a 1 per cent uplift on the all risks yield for a market rented property. This uplift is not scientific or derived from a formula but would reflect the judgement by the valuer in the particular circumstances.

By now it will be apparent that a lot of thought and judgement has been exercised by the valuer to frame what appears to be a relatively straightforward calculation as follows.

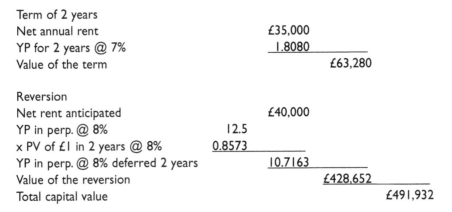

Term of 2 years		
Net annual rent	£35,000	
YP for 2 years @ 7%	1.8080	
Value of the term		£63,280
Reversion		
Net rent anticipated	£40,000	
YP in perp. @ 8%	12.5	
x PV of £1 in 2 years @ 8%	0.8573	
YP in perp. @ 8% deferred 2 years	10.7163	
Value of the reversion		£428,652
Total capital value		£491,932

The yield for the term has been reduced to 7 per cent, i.e. 1 per cent below the yield for the reversion to reflect the risk and security attributable to the term income. This is because three years into the lease, the rent passing is below the market rent and thus the occupying retail firm is unlikely to relinquish this position easily. Even if that tenant were to disappear for whatever reason, the property could reasonably be expected to re-let for a rent of at least £35,000. These factors reduce the risk and have led the valuer to reduce the yield to 7 per cent to capitalize the term income.

Sayce *et al.* (2006: 109) confirm that reductions of between 0.5 and 2 per cent are commonly applied to the yield used to capitalize the term income in this type of situation. Although the precise reduction relies upon the valuer's judgement in the light of the particular circumstances, the overall principle is that as the gap widens between the rent passing in the term relative to the market rent, the tenant is deemed to be enjoying more of a bargain and thus the income becomes more and more secure. Thus a very secure income represents reduced risk and the valuer might then adjust the yield down by a full 2 per cent relative to the reversionary yield.

Blackledge (2009: 209) also confirms this phenomenon but articulates what many feel when they first encounter this principle in that it is to some extent counter-intuitive. It could be argued that because the term rent is lower than the market rent, an investor is effectively making a loss for that period and should not therefore reduce the yield for the term, as this has the effect of increasing its capital value. Following this line of argument the yield for the term should instead be increased to reduce its capital value. There are therefore a number of conundrums which surface when navigating through the intricacies of the traditional investment method and which will be commented upon towards the end of this chapter.

In the scenario above, a property investor would recognize a degree of uncertainty regarding the reversion which includes the period up to and beyond lease expiry. It would not be apparent seven years ahead of the event, how difficult it might be to re-let the subject property if the current tenant decided not to seek a lease renewal. The uncertainty increases the risk above that for a fully rented property let on a long lease. In the latter case the market evidence suggested an all risk yield of 7 per cent but a prudent investor would want a higher rate of return to compensate for the additional risks in the scenario.

If the valuer felt that the risks were escalating, then the yield adopted for valuing the reversionary period might justifiably be raised beyond the 8 per cent shown in the example to perhaps 8.5 or 9 per cent or beyond. As the perceived degree of risk increases, the yield will also normally be increased which has the knock on effect of reducing the YP capitalizer which in turn deflates the capital value of the income stream.

Adjustments to the yield in these circumstances require experience, expertise and judgement to be exercised by the valuer and it is another aspect of the traditional investment method of valuation which is an art rather than a science. As the example shows, the reversionary income is capitalized by multiplying it by the deferred Years' Purchase in perpetuity at 8 per cent deferred two years and when it is added to the value of the term the overall capital value for the property is found to be £491,932. As for other examples in this chapter it is recognized that this type of valuation cannot be accurate to the nearest £2 and so of course in practice this outcome would be rounded up to £492,000.

The term and reversion approach can also be used where it is anticipated that there may be breaks in the income stream, perhaps at the end of a lease when a property needs to be re-let and when a void period is expected. Even if no money is spent on the building at that point there will be business rates to pay and re-letting fees and so a void period is not costless from a landlord's perspective.

Depending on the age and quality of the building, the landlord may realize that in order to attract a competitive rent or to strengthen re-letting prospects, some investment would need to be made to upgrade the building. Increasingly for some commercial buildings refurbishment and improvements will be carried out to attract a recognized sustainability rating in order for the building to remain competitive and to attract tenants who are looking for buildings which are efficient to operate.

In the scenario below there are two years remaining on a 20-year lease on a small office unit on a business park. The tenant is planning to relocate when the lease expires and so the prospect of a void is seen by the landlord as an opportunity to upgrade what will then be a 20-year-old building.

As shown in Figure 8.4, the rent passing in the term is £45,000 although following upgrading work it is anticipated that the unit could attract a rental

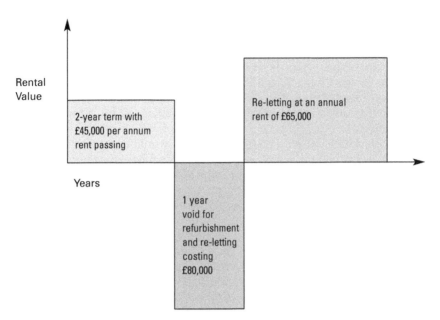

Figure 8.4 Term and reversion format depicting a refurbishment and re-letting scenario

value similar to market rented new properties on the business park and for this unit that would equate £65,000 net per annum. However there will be a one-year void period when refurbishment work will be carried out during which there will be business rates and letting fees to pay. It is anticipated that these costs will amount to £80,000.

The calculation accompanying the above scenario is as follows.

Term of 2 years		
Net annual rent	£45,000	
YP for 2 years @ 7%	1.8080	
Value of the term		£81,360
1-year period for refurbishment and re-letting		
Cost of work, letting fees and business rates	£80,000	
PV of £1 in 2 years @ 6%	0.8900	
Present value of the costs		£71,200
Reversion		
Net rent anticipated	£65,000	
YP in perp. @ 8%	12.5	
x PV of £1 in 3 years @ 8%	0.7938	
YP in perp. @ 8% deferred 3 years	9.9225	
Value of the reversion		£644,963
Total capital value having deducted costs of £71,200		£655,123

The yield of 7 per cent for the relatively secure term income is benchmarked against the yield on similarly secure incomes. The discount rate of 6 per cent applied to the refurbishment costs represents the cost of capital which does not need to be increased above that threshold as it is not risk prone income. The yield of 8 per cent for the reversionary income represents a modest increase in risk tempered by the fact that the newly refurbished building with its sustainability credentials should be competitive in letting terms.

8.6 The layer method

The layer method is an alternative to the term and reversion valuation approach for assessing the capital value of a reversionary property. As Figure 8.5 illustrates, the layer method capitalizes the present rent which is referred to as the hardcore rent, into perpetuity. This sum is then added to the capitalised uplift in the rent: the top slice, which will commence from reversion.

A key feature of the layer method is that it focuses upon the increase in rental value expected on reversion and attaches to this top slice income a specific yield to reflect the differential risk posed to it in comparison to the less risky hardcore rent. In volatile markets there may be some merit in separating the two elements of rent in this way. The layer method also lends itself to valuing turnover rents, where a relatively certain core rent may be supplemented by a relatively uncertain top slice which will depend on the actual turnover generated by the tenant.

During fragile or falling markets when the prospect of any top slice income at rent review could evaporate entirely, the layer method does provide the

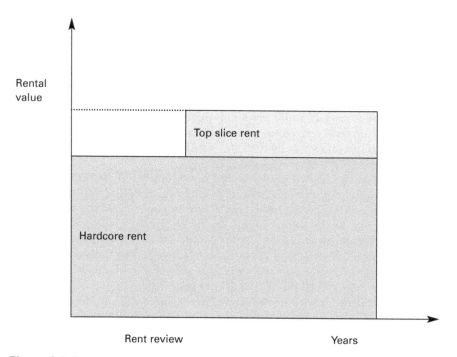

Figure 8.5 The layer method of valuing reversionary properties

valuer with the option of attaching a high yield to the top slice. This would effectively devalue the top slice significantly in contrast to the more certain hardcore income. The layer method also identifies the capital value of the hardcore in isolation from the top slice, and that could be useful information where market conditions suggest that it is unlikely that any top slice income will materialize.

As with all valuation approaches, the layer method does have some conceptual weaknesses, one of which is that it is artificial to divide the income into two elements as if they were from different sources. In reality the security of the reversionary income is not divisible, because if a tenant defaults or exercises a break clause, then the whole rental income ceases and not just the top slice. It is also difficult to value using comparables from the market, as these will provide an overall yield which is not disaggregated into a yield for the hardcore rent and another for the top slice.

The calculation below uses the layer method to value the property described in example 8.3 above.

Hardcore annual rent passing		£35,000	
YP in perp. @ 7%		14.2857	
Value of core income			£500,000
Top slice rent anticipated in 2 years		£5,000	
YP in perp. @ 8%	12.5		
PV £1 in 2 years @ 8%	0.8573		
YP in perp. @ 8% deferred 2 years		10.7163	
Value of the top slice			£53,581
Total capital value			£553,581

In the above example the yield for the hardcore rent has been set at 7 per cent to reflect the security of the tenant enjoying a lower than market rent for the next two years. Beyond that point and into perpetuity, there is every prospect that a rent of at least £35,000 per annum could be achieved. However as for the term and reversion valuation, there is some uncertainty in the reversionary period and so the valuer has uplifted the yield for the top slice to 8 per cent to reflect the perceived risks.

When adjusting yields, a valuer would have considered factors such as the trading strength of the tenant, the economic environment for this type of retailer, the lease terms, the characteristics of the property and the retail park it is located upon. As for the term and reversion approach, there is contextual knowledge brought to bear in this type of valuation as well as interpretation of comparable deals. If the set of circumstances suggested to the valuer that the risks to the top slice income were significant then the yield could be increased beyond 8 per cent and could be 9 or 10 per cent for example.

As the calculation above reveals, the capital value using the layer method is £553,581 while that produced using the term and reversion method with the same rental values and yields was £491,932. This is a difference of more than 10 per cent in the values arrived at using each method. It is reasonable for readers to ponder on which figure and which method should be relied upon and these questions bring the discussion to a consideration of what is known as the equivalent yield.

8.7 The equivalent yield

The term and reversion and layer methods discussed above both rely upon a valuer's judgement to set different yields for the term and reversionary or core and top slice incomes to reflect differential risk. The two yields arrived at may be defensible from the perspective of an experienced valuer but they appear subjective as they are not calibrated against a formula or systematic process. For this reason there has been some academic criticism of this approach which will be considered later in this chapter. However at this point the focus is on whether it might be logical to apply the same or *equivalent yield* to the different income tranches to reflect the overall trade off between risk and reward suggested by the investment.

Earlier in the chapter the term and reversion approach was used in example 8.3 to identify a capital value of £491,932 and that example can now be used to calculate the equivalent yield. A distinction should be drawn at this point between the equivalent yield and the *initial yield*. The latter was discussed earlier in the chapter where it was confirmed that it is simply a reflection of the relationship between the capital value and the initial term rent. Thus the initial yield in the example would be £35,000/£491,932 = 7.1 per cent. However this figure places the investment too close to the yield for market rented properties with more certain futures and which it may be recalled from the scenario was reflecting an all risks yield of 7 per cent.

The initial yield of 7.1 per cent does not take into account the reversion expected to a market rent in two years' time which will change the relationship between the property's capital value and its income stream. What is required is the calculation of the equivalent yield, which is also the internal rate of return (IRR), which when applied to both the term and reversion income will produce £491,932. There are a number of ways to calculate the equivalent yield, one of which, as Blackledge (2009: 213) explains is to use interpolation between two trial rates. In the context of the example the two trial rates could be 7 and 8 per cent and which would produce the following calculations.

Term and reversion with a trial rate of 7%
Term of 2 years
Net annual rent	£35,000	
YP for 2 years @ 7%	1.8080	
Value of the term		£63,280

Reversion
Net rent anticipated		£40,000	
YP in perp. @ 7%	14.2857		
x PV of £1 in 2 years @ 7%	0.8734		
YP in perp. @ 7% deferred 2 years		12.4771	
Value of the reversion			£499,084
Total capital value			£562,364

Term and reversion with a trial rate of 8%
Term of 2 years

Net annual rent	£35,000	
YP for 2 years @ 8%	1.7833	
Value of the term		£62,416

Reversion

Net rent anticipated		£40,000	
YP in perp. @ 8%	12.5		
x PV of £1 in 2 years @ 8%	0.8573		
YP in perp. @ 8% deferred 2 years		10.7163	
Value of the reversion			£428,652
Total capital value			£491,068

The interpolation formula used to identify the equivalent yield is as follows:

$$\text{Equivalent yield} = LTR + ((HTR - LTR) \times (CV@LTR - OCV/CV@LTR - CV@HTR))$$

The variable in the above formula are as follows:

LTR is the lower trial rate which is 7 per cent in the example.
HTR is the higher trial rate which in the example is 8 per cent.
CV@LTR is the capital value identified using the lower trail rate which in the
  example is £562,364.
OCV is the original capital value identified by the term and reversion valuation
  and which is £491,932.
CV@HTR is the capital value identified using the higher trail rate which in the
  example is £491,068.

When corresponding values from the example are inserted into the formula the following calculation emerges.

$$\text{Equivalent yield} = 7\% + (1\% \times (70,432/71,296)) = 7.99\%$$

The equivalent yield of 7.99 per cent could also be identified using an Excel spreadsheet in which the cells are linked to enable the 'goal–seek' function to carry out iterations on the cell containing the yield until a value of £491,932 (or very close) is reached in the cell containing the capital value. However derived, the figure of 7.99 per cent appears intuitively correct in this example where the bulk of the capital value is tied up in the reversionary period whose value was determined by an 8 per cent yield, i.e. the 8 per cent yield skews the equivalent yield towards it and away from the term yield which was 7 per cent.

Once identified, the equivalent yield can be inserted into either the term and reversion or the horizontal layer format, as either method will produce the same result as shown below. Because the equivalent yield in this case is very close to 8 per cent, that figure has been adopted below to demonstrate the principles. In that event there is no need to reproduce the term and reversion at 8 per cent as it was one of the trial rates conducted above and where the capital value identified was £491,068. As shown below there is an insignificant difference of £13 in the capital value produced when 8 per cent is used in the layer method because decimal rounding takes a slightly different effect at different points in each calculation.

Equivalent yield of 8% applied to the layer method

Hardcore annual rent passing	£35,000	
YP in perp. @ 8%	12.5	
Value of core		£437,500

Top slice rent anticipated in 2 years	£5,000	
YP in perp. @ 8%	12.5	
PV £1 in 2 years @ 8%	0.8573	
YP in perp. @ 8% deferred 2 years	10.7163	
Value of top slice		£53,581
Total capital value		£491,081

There are circumstances when it is not necessary to work through all of these stages to calculate the equivalent yield. Saunders (2010: 24–5) for example illustrates how the same yield can be selected without tortuous calculation and then applied in a multi-letting context such as when a large office block is gradually being let floor by floor over a relatively short timeframe.

The following example illustrated in Figure 8.6 is consistent with Saunders' work and reflects the gradual letting of three identical retail warehouses to reputable national retailers over a relatively short period. Assuming that the retailers will be paying an equivalent rent per square metre on long FRI leases, there is little justification for trying to distinguish the risk by adapting the yield

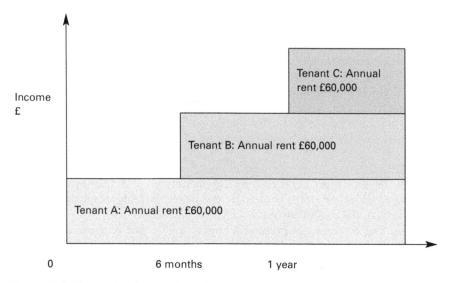

Figure 8.6 The gradual letting of retail warehouses

in each case. The only real differential is the staggered rate at which the tenants will occupy. The scenario envisages a rent already passing from retail tenant A, with rent from tenant B beginning in six months' time followed by tenant C six months after that.

The following calculation is the counterpart to the staggered letting pattern shown above.

Annual rent from tenant A		£60,000	
YP in perp. @ 7%		14.2857	
Capital value			£857,142
Annual rent from tenant B		£60,000	
YP in perp. @ 7%	14.2857		
PV £1 in 6 months @ 7%	0.9667		
YP in perp. @ 7% deferred 6 months		13.8100	
Capital value			£828,600
Annual rent from tenant C		£60,000	
YP in perp. @ 7%	14.2857		
PV £1 in 1 year @ 7%	0.9346		
YP in perp. @ 7% deferred 1 year		13.3514	
Capital value			£801,084
Total capital value			£2,486,826

Those readers coming to the subject of valuing reversionary properties using the traditional investment method for the first time might logically expect that one of the valuation formats (term and reversion, layer or equivalent yield) should be seen as the most correct approach. It might also be supposed that the professional body: the RICS or valuation tribunals would rule that one of the methods was preferred and that valuers should always use it rather than any other method. However this is intriguingly not the case, and there also appears to be disagreement between what practitioners do and what academics think they should do as Sayce *et al.* illustrates:

> In the investment marketplace the layer method using one equivalent yield tends to be the preferred method, the reason being that as only one valuation yield is used it makes the analysis of comparable evidence and other market transactions simpler. From an academic standpoint the term and reversion method treats the rentals according to their risk and growth characteristics and is thus a preferred method. (2006: 108)

The RICS (2010: 9) does go as far as commenting that neither the term and reversion or layer approach is entirely logical and that a '*simpler approach*' (the word 'superior' is not used) is to apply the same but higher capitalization rate in the form of the equivalent yield.

Depending on your viewpoint this might well be one of those areas where professional judgement should continue to be allowed to prevail in the absence of science. This viewpoint would champion the importance of continuity and 'how things are done' which has been a surprisingly durable quality in this area of practice. In this perspective valuers are therefore given leeway to form a judgement about which approach and which outcome is most credible in any given set of circumstances. A more hawkish viewpoint would suggest that there is room for improvement and evidence of inertia in practice and that a more consistent, transparent and logical way of conducting these valuations should be adopted.

The discussion on the different valuation methods in circulation and which should have primacy and the divergence between theory and practice raises all sorts of conjectures and research agendas. There may come a time when greater clarity and direction is given to valuers on these issues but that time has not so far been reached. In the interim period perhaps Scarrett (2008: 94) provides the most practical way to proceed, suggesting that to deviate from market derived yields by adjusting for the term and reversion (or core and top slice) introduces a degree of subjectivity for which there is no market evidence. Scarrett therefore suggests that it is safer and more defensible to adopt an equivalent yield to value both tranches of income.

8.8 Over-rented property

Property markets are affected by variations in supply and demand which are influenced by fluctuations in the wider national and global economies. Various terms are used to describe these fluctuations such as 'boom and bust', 'peak and trough' and 'market cycles' and which signify that markets can be volatile and risk cannot entirely be removed.

A number of research studies including RICS *et al.* (1994) have been undertaken to try to unravel the fluctuations in property markets and to try to suggest ways that they might be smoothed out or at least predicted so that preventative action could be taken. However because there are so many interacting variables, the best that these studies could do was to describe some of the relationships between the variables. It was confirmed that there are lengthy periods of market growth followed by shorter periods of 'market correction' when the market contracts only for it to begin to recover again several years later. However a hidden formula was not discovered which could predict the timing, depth or duration of these episodes.

Readers might at this point ponder upon the credit crunch induced recession which took hold in late 2007 and was thought to have been triggered by what at first appeared to be an obscure sub-prime mortgage lending problem in parts of the United States. Before the recession it was difficult to find an economist, academic, professional or politician who was predicting that there would be a serious and lasting recession which would have such far-reaching consequences.

Given that fluctuations are an inherent characteristic of all markets, including property markets, there will be occasions when investment properties have been let during buoyant market periods which several years later appear to be over-rented simply because the market has gone into a recessionary stage. Beginning first with the term and reversion format, the following examples will show how the traditional investment methods discussed earlier in the chapter can provide capital values for over-rented properties.

An over-rented property simply describes one which is let at a rental value higher than the current market would justify and thus there is an expectation that the rent will fall at the next review. The situation is common in recessionary

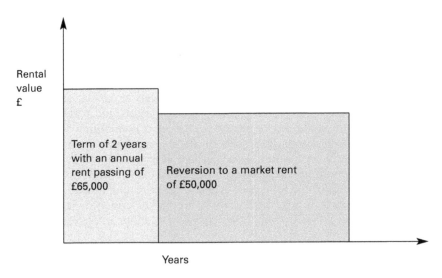

Figure 8.7 Term and reversion and an over-rented property

situations where there is considerable risk to investment properties because a recession inevitably adversely affects the business performance of tenants, some of who may fail. Alternatively companies may contract or consolidate by exercising break clauses when they occur, requiring properties to be re-let at the lower market rent.

Consider for example a shop which was leased to a retailer on a long lease at an annual net rent of £65,000 with five-year rent reviews, the next of which will occur in two years' time. Under the lease terms, the tenant has an option to exercise a break clause at that point. In the recessionary climate which is assumed to prevail, the likelihood is that the landlord will probably have to agree to the rent reverting to the current market rent of £50,000.

The alternative is that the tenant will exercise the break clause and in which case the best the property could achieve on re-letting is £50,000. Thus in order to avoid the potential of a void period and the cost of re-letting, the landlord would probably have to accept a reduction in the rent at the next review. The pattern is illustrated in Figure 8.7.

In the corresponding calculation below, the valuer has decided that the risk to the term income is quite high as other retailers have recently gone into receivership and so a relatively high yield of 10 per cent is used to capitalize the term income. If the retail tenant is able to maintain trading for the next two years to the reversion, the rent will fall and the situation is likely to be less risky from that point onwards as reflected in the lowering of the yield to 8 per cent.

Term of 2 years
Net annual rent	£65,000	
YP for 2 years @ 10%	1.7355	
Value of the term		£112,808

Reversion

Net rent anticipated		£50,000	
YP in perp. @ 8%	12.5		
x PV of £1 in 2 years @ 8%	0.8573		
YP in perp. @ 8% deferred 2 years		10.7163	
Value of the reversion			£535,815
Total capital value			£648,623

The layer method below can also be used to evaluate over-rented properties. The top slice in this scenario represents the over-rented layer which is sometimes referred to as the *overage* and which is treated differently to the core income. The arrangement is shown in Figure 8.8.

The counterpart calculation using the layer method is as follows and which uses the same variables from the business park example previously described.

Core rent

Estimated rental value (ERV)	£50,000	
YP in perp. @ 8%	12.5	
Value of the core		£625,000

Top slice

Rent passing	£65,000		
Less ERV	£50,000		
Overage		£15,000	
YP 2 years @ 10%		1.7355	
Value of the top slice			£26,033
Total capital value			£651,033

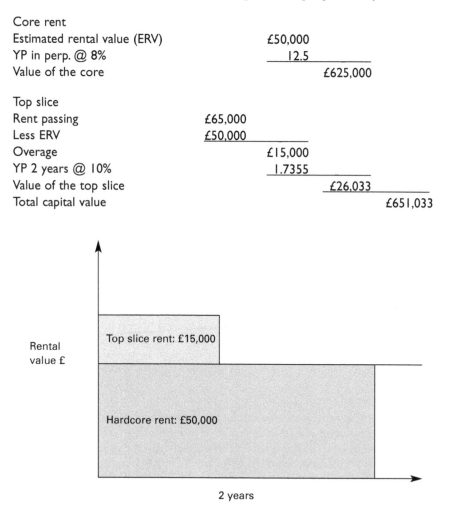

Figure 8.8 The layer method and an over-rented property

It is perhaps in the context of evaluating over-rented properties that it becomes clear why some valuers prefer to continue using this method in practice. The overage or top slice rent does look genuinely precarious in a recessionary context and there is every risk that it will evaporate at some point.

The fragility of the top slice rent during difficult economic conditions was illustrated in the UK in 2011 when some high profile business tenants sought reductions in the rents that they were paying in order to try to offset poor trading figures. Among these cases was a private health care company which sought a 30 per cent reduction in the rents being paid on numerous properties owned by a corporate landlord. In another example, an established national retailer claimed that the rents being paid on high street shops and retail warehouses were exorbitant and were forcing the company to downsize by exercising break clauses and not seeking to extend leases when they expired.

While the layer method may have some value in this type of situation, the weakness with the method is that it assumes that the full rental value of £50,000 in the example, will still be less than the passing rent of £65,000 at the rent review in two years' time. By that time markets could well have improved, so that the rent passing in the term was at least matched by the then reversionary rent. It is of course possible to impute a growth rate into the ERV so that a future point of convergence could be identified between it and the rent passing. However this type of explicit forecasting is not normally part of the traditional investment method which uses all risk yields to implicitly account for future growth.

8.9 Leaseholds and profit rents

The discussion so far has considered the straightforward relationship between a freehold owning landlord (a property investor) who has leased a building to a commercial tenant and there are no intermediaries. The discussion in this part of the chapter will now examine how traditional methods of valuation are brought to bear on leasehold interests when they are bought and sold.

Leasehold interests arise because, where the lease terms allow, they can be sold to intermediaries between the landlord and tenant. This can arise where a freehold has been let to a lessee who in turn has let the property to a sub-lessee. On a long commercial lease in a high value area, it is possible for a whole hierarchy of sub lessees to become established between the landlord and occupying tenant. There is no need to pursue that degree of complexity here, however it is important to emphasize the distinction between a lessee in occupation and where premises have been sublet by a lessee. Examples of the two situations are:

- A lessee occupies and pays an annual rent to the freeholder of £10,000. The market rent however is £15,000 so the valuation in this case would be based upon the profit rent, which is the difference between the market rent and the rent actually being paid, which in this case is £5,000 per annum.
- The property is sublet at an annual rent of £12,000 and the lessee does not occupy any of the premises. In this case the lease is valued on the net income received from the sub-lessee less the rent payable to the freeholder, which is £2,000 per annum.

Whichever permutation is followed, the income is said to be terminable for the simple reason that it will only exist for the duration of the lease or slightly shorter sub-lease. Despite their terminable nature, leases are traded as investment assets but they are not valued as highly as freeholds because of their wasting characteristic and the fact that the rights and responsibilities arising under a lease make them less versatile assets than freeholds.

The concept of a profit rent surfaced in the above discussion and it is simply the difference between the market rent and the rent actually paid by an occupying lessee or a sub-lessee. Where a profit rent exists, the tenant is making an annual saving because the rent paid is less that the full rental value. This situation often occurs when a tenant has been in occupation for a period of time and the rent has not been reviewed recently.

If an occupier wishes to sell a lease or sublease (the expression is to *assign* the lease), the valuation will capitalize the profit rent to arrive at a capital value for the unexpired term of the lease. This situation commonly arises in high streets or shopping malls, for example when a retailer, travel agency, bank or building society may have merged following which there is consolidation and branch closures. Where property is held on long leases the organization will typically wish to sell the leasehold interest in properties that are now surplus to the company's requirements. The situation can also occur for office space where floors in office towers or units on business parks may no longer be needed by a company and they may look to assign their lease.

The first priority for such a company in this situation is to cover the remaining rental obligations on the unexpired term of a lease. If that can be done with a rent achieved from a sub-lessee which is above the rent payable to the landlord then a profit rent has arisen. However during recessionary periods and for none prime property, it may be difficult to dispose of a leasehold interest and the best that may be achieved is a zero profit rent or even the mitigation of a loss on the rental obligations remaining.

The calculation below begins an exploration of the principles of valuing leaseholds. The scenario is based upon a shop which is let on a full repairing and insuring lease with 4 years remaining on the lease. The annual rent being paid by the tenant is £50,000 but the market rent is estimated to be £60,000. A valuer takes the view that the market would value this asset on a 9% yield and so the calculation would appear as follows.

Market rent	£60,000
Rent passing	£50,000
Profit rent	£10,000
YP 4 years @ 9%	3.2397
Capital value	£32,397

By selecting a yield of 9 per cent the valuer is implicitly absorbing a number of risks against a benchmark of a comparable freehold asset where the yield might be much lower at say 5 or 6 per cent. As Saunders (2010: 122–3) illustrates, if there were lease restrictions or planning restrictions on the use class, this would effectively screen out various categories of potential sub-lessee, reducing the marketability of the lease. In that scenario, there could be a dual effect on the valuation in that the margin of the profit rent could be reduced and the yield increased to reflect the added risk of finding a sub-lessee who met the criteria and was willing to take on a lease which had only four years to run. The valuation would then generate a significantly reduced capital value for the lease as shown below.

Market rent (unrestricted)	£60,000	
Rent subject to lease restrictions	£55,000	
Rent passing	£50,000	
Profit rent		£5,000
YP 4 years @ 10%	3.1699	
Capital value		£15,850

The valuation above adopts a YP single rate approach with an all risks yield of 10 per cent to reflect the combination of risks suggested by the short lease and characteristics of the particular property. Given that the lease is a wasting asset it is arguable that a prudent investor would not contemplate this purchase unless it were devalued further or that part of the profit rent could be invested and shown to compound over four years to replace the initial capital invested. For these reasons leaseholds are more properly valued using a dual-rate YP adjusted for tax, the constants for which can be sourced from valuation tables. The YP dual rate with tax is based upon two computations, the first of which is the YP capitalizer which is the same as the single rate YP which has been covered earlier. The second element is an annual sinking fund (ASF) adjusted for tax, hence the expression 'dual rate'.

The ASF in the dual-rate approach is a compounding sum which is assumed to be invested each year to ultimately replace the capital originally paid for the asset by the time the lease expires. This approach recognizes the fact that the value of leaseholds depreciate as the remaining term diminishes towards expiry when no value remains. The dual-rate concept therefore assumes that the purchaser of a lease is acting prudently by gradually putting aside some income to replace the original price paid for the asset.

Conventionally the ASF is assumed to be invested in a relatively risk free but low interest bearing account and that is why rates of anything between 2.5 per cent and 4 per cent tend to appear in this type of valuation. The sinking fund is assumed to attract tax to reflect some realism and so that the net of tax fund accumulates sufficiently to replace the value of the depreciating asset.

There has been debate about the relevance of the ASF with its tax adjustment and authors such as Scarrett (2008: 98) doubt that property investors actually go to the lengths of arranging such funds. However the theoretical approach is useful for investors who wish to ascertain the margin by which they might devalue a leasehold asset relative to freehold alternatives. Thus while attaching a sinking fund with allowance for tax adds complexity and it is practically tempting to abandon the approach, this text will persevere with the theory which does have some relevance for the prudent property investor.

The principle underpinning the dual-rate approach is that it is supposed to put leasehold investments on a par with freehold investments. To achieve this,

Table 8.2 Yield adjustments for leaseholds

Property characteristics	Additional risk premium for leasehold interests	Sinking fund
Prime commercial property	2%	3%
Older commercial property in secondary locations suffering from depreciation and obsolescence	3–4%	3%

the yield structure used in the valuation of freeholds must be adjusted when applied to leasehold interests. Thus in traditional leasehold valuations, the leasehold yield is marked up against the freehold yield to reflect the additional risks involved as shown in Table 8.2.

The additional risk premium for leasehold property arises because of a number of practical considerations regarding the characteristics of leaseholds. These include the additional management challenges posed by leaseholds one of which is that there could be liability for dilapidations claims from the landlord at the end of a lease. There could also be problems with liquidity, as leasehold interests will generally be more difficult to sell than freeholds because some investors will be deterred by the lease complexity and wasting nature of the asset. If the lease terms allow, a tenant could sublet the property and that might undermine the security of the investment. There can be difficulties in obtaining possession of leasehold property and the redevelopment and refurbishment options which may exist for freehold owners are reduced considerably for leaseholders.

Example 8.4 below is a dual-rate leasehold valuation in which a tax rate of 40 per cent is used for illustrative purposes, but which could of course be changed to suit the particular rate of tax prevailing. The example encompasses the 'grossing up' of the annual sinking fund so that it will be sufficient for reinvestment after tax has been deducted.

Example 8.4 Leasehold valuation

The capital value is sought for a leasehold interest in a shop which has five years' remaining and which is subject to an annual head rent of £50,000 net. The annual market rent is estimated to be £65,000 and the capitalization rate for a fully rented freehold interest in a similar shop is 5 per cent.

Dual rate, with sinking fund tax adjusted		
Annual market rent	£65,000	
Less head rent	£50,000	
Profit rent		£15,000
YP 5 years @ 7% + 3% (40% tax)		2.6047
Capital value		£39,071

The calculation can be deconstructed to show that part of the profit rent of £15,000 is notionally being invested at 3 per cent to ultimately replace the capital sum of £39,071 after five years. The first step is to identify the annual sinking fund (ASF) which would need to be invested over five years at 3 per cent to replace £1. This can be derived by formula (shown in Chapter 3) or sourced from valuation tables where the ASF is shown to be 0.1883546 rounded up to 0.1884 for this example. That figure is then multiplied by the capital which needs to be replaced as follows.

$$£39,071 \times 0.1884 = £7,361$$

The sum of £7,361 now has to be grossed up to allow for 40 per cent tax otherwise it would underperform and not replace the capital after five years. The formula to identify the gross adjustment factor in which t is the tax rate is:

$$1/(1 - t)$$

When applied to this example the gross adjustment factor will be:

$$1/(1 - 0.4) = 1.6667 \text{ (rounded up)}$$

£7,361 is then multiplying it by 1.6667 to produce a grossed-up annual sinking fund of £12,269 which will recover the capital sum at 3 per cent over five years allowing for 40 per cent tax. Assuming that figure is invested the amount remaining from the profit rent is £15,000 less £12,269 which is £2,731 and which represents a 7 per cent annual return on the initial capital outlay of £39,071.

The devaluing effect of making an allowance for a sinking fund with tax allowance is revealed by comparison with the capital value shown below which arises from the same circumstances but where the YP single rate is used. The capital value below however, might be an imprudent value to pay for this wasting asset.

Single rate			
Annual market rent	£65,000		
Less head rent	£50,000		
Profit rent		£15,000	
YP 5 years @ 7%		4.1002	
Capital value			£61,503

The discussion in this part of the chapter has now served its purpose by introducing the dual rate adjusted for tax approach to valuing leaseholds. This type of specialized valuation raises a number of further issues which extend beyond the scope of this book, such as judgements about the rate of interest to adopt for the sinking fund and the rate of tax applicable to that fund. Those readers who wish to pursue the topic in more depth than is possible here, could examine Enever *et al.* (2010: 113–19) or Baum *et al.* (2006: 126–42).

8.10 Premiums

Premiums can arise where negotiations between a landlord and tenant have culminated in the tenant paying a premium to a landlord so that a below market annual rent can be paid. The lessee, through the payment of a premium has technically purchased a profit rent and the landlord has received its capital equivalent in lieu of reduced future income. Another way to express this is that the landlord has agreed to take a capital sum in place of a portion of the future annual rents.

The principle of paying premiums can be extended to the point where a very considerable capital sum changes hands with the effect that the rent remaining to pass under the lease becomes a peppercorn rent. This is very nearly the case with most modern leasehold flats where the purchaser of what might be a 99- or 125-year lease might be paying £200,000 for a two bed flat (depending on the local residential property market) plus a ground rent under the lease of perhaps £200 per annum. Nearly all of the value of this type of long lease is therefore expressed in the initial premium paid by the buyer of the flat and once that commitment has been made there is a very low probability of the lessee defaulting on the annual ground rent of £200.

Saunders (2010: 112) suggests that the combination of this very low risk and the ability of the landlord to benefit from management charges and incentives for placing building insurance, results in low yields when ground rents on blocks of flats are valued for sale.

In commercial property situations the balance between the premium paid and the ongoing annual rent might not be quite as skewed as it is in the residential example above. However similar principles apply in the sense that the rent which will be paid by the tenant will be lower than the market rent and it is thus assumed to be more secure. The reduction of risk to the rental income would therefore be reflected a lower yield as illustrated in the following example.

Example 8.5 Calculation of a premium

A landlord is considering the grant of a 15-year lease on a shop whose market rent is £20,000 per annum. In negotiations the potential lessee has agreed to pay £15,000 per annum with the remainder paid in capitalized form up front in a premium. The landlord calculates the premium on the basis of a yield of 7 per cent with a sinking fund at 2.5 per cent and a tax liability of 40 per cent as follows.

Net annual market rent	£20,000	
Less rent to be paid	£15,000	
Profit rent		£5,000
YP 15 years @ 7% and 2.5% (tax 40%)		6.1371
Premium		£30,686

Working backwards in the calculation, the premium of £30,686 could be divided by the YP 15yrs @ 7 per cent and 2.5 per cent net of tax at 40 per cent to identify the profit rent confirming that the following relationship applies:

Reduction in annual rent = Premium/YP for the term of the lease

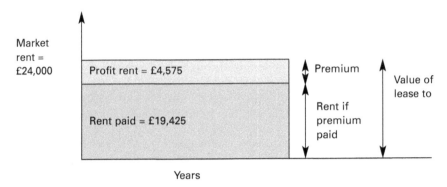

Figure 8.9 The relationship between premiums and profit rents

Example 8.6 Calculating the effects of a premium

A shop is to be let on a 10-year lease on FRI terms; the net annual market rent is £24,000 but the tenant has agreed to pay a premium of £20,000 at the commencement of the lease. Calculate the annual rent to be paid. Assume a yield of 8 per cent, a sinking fund of 2.5 per cent and a tax liability of 40 per cent.

Annual equivalent of premium = Premium/YP for 10 years @ 8% and 2.5% with 40% tax = £20,000/4.3713 = £ 4,575 (which is the annual reduction in the rent or profit rent)

Graphically the relationship is shown in Figure 8.9.

8.11 A critique of the traditional investment methods

At this point in the chapter it is possible to consider some of the strengths and weaknesses of the traditional methods of valuing investment property which have been explored. As will have become apparent, there are some grey areas in these techniques and this has led academics such as Crosby (1992) to question the validity of these methods because they do not explicitly forecast growth but imply it in a subjectively adjusted yield rate. More recently similar criticisms have arisen from Baum *et al.* (2006: 101–5) who note that this type of practice is historically derived from financial markets and is at odds with modern accounting principles for property where a more robust justification of yields is required. Baum *et al.* add that:

Some valuers still insist on using different rates to reflect some personal view on the security of income. This can be dangerous and can produce very peculiar results. (2006: 101)

The authors go on to illustrate how given the same set of circumstances the layer and term and reversion methods can produce quite different outcomes and it is not clear which outcome is more robust. This issue was identified in example 8.3 earlier in this chapter where more than a 10 per cent difference arose in the capital value of a retail warehouse when the two valuation methods were used. Questions have also been raised by authors such as Havard (2004: 24) about the logic of attaching a low yield and thus high capitalization rate to a lower than market term rent on the grounds of its alleged security. This may have the effect of overvaluing the term and undervaluing the reversionary income and overall this must distort the outcome of the valuation.

There has therefore been a debate involving academics and practitioners regarding the merits of continuing with this type of growth implied model, which relies heavily on the interpretation of comparable market transactions. The alternative is the so called growth explicit modern method which embeds explicit growth rates into discounted cash flows. In that approach a discount rate can be built up from an investor's cost of capital plus a risk premium. These alternative methods are discussed in Chapter 9 of this book and so readers will be able to make up their own minds on which they feel are the most defensible way to tackle the evaluation of property investments.

8.12 Summary

This chapter focused upon the traditional method of valuing investment properties which are those owned by a landlord and let to a rent paying business tenant. The discussion began by considering how the net rental income from recently let market rented properties could be capitalized into perpetuity using an all risks yield. The latter is derived from a valuer's analysis and interpretation of comparable transactions from the market set against the specific characteristics of the subject property. The situation becomes more complex for reversionary properties, where the rent passing under the lease is not the same as the market rent but could potentially revert to a market rent at the next rent review or when the lease expires (whichever is sooner).

For reversionary investments a valuer using traditional methods could use either the term and reversion approach or the layer method. Having made that choice a valuer must then exercise judgement by calibrating a yield to attach to the different tranches of income to reflect differential risk. Essentially where the income is thought to be at less risk the yield is reduced to approach the all risks yield used on market rented properties. Where the tranche of income is thought to be at more risk, a higher yield is attached to it, following the fundamental investment principle that as risk increases a higher rate of return is justified.

The yield adjustments made in these traditional valuation methods are a matter of judgement emphasizing art over science. Sceptics have suggested that the subtle adjustments to the yield to reflect differential risk are too subjective and lack transparency. This has led valuers and academics to explore ways of identifying an equivalent yield which is the same as an investment's internal rate of return and which can be used to capitalize the different income tranches arising from a reversionary property. There is agreement at least among academics that the use of an equivalent yield places both the term and reversion and layer methods on firmer ground because it enables a more direct comparison to be made between the more risky overall profile of a reversionary property with a less risky recently let market rented property.

Despite some of the misgivings attributed to the traditional methods discussed in the chapter they do have a degree of versatility and it is not surprising that some valuers have shown a continuing loyalty in their use. For example the layer and term and reversion approaches can be used to evaluate over-rented properties and the term and reversion approach can account for void periods when expenditure may be needed to refurbish a property. Hybrid versions of these methods can also be used to evaluate profit rents arising from leases as well as evaluating the effects that premiums can have on annual rents. Allowances for sinking funds and tax can also be built in to leasehold valuations if required.

Although there is some versatility and merit in these valuation techniques which explains why they continue to be options within the overall valuation toolkit, there remain reservations particularly around yield calibration. This has led to a search for more explicit methods of property investment appraisal which will be considered in Chapter 9 which follows.

References

Banfield, A. (2009) *Valuation on Quarterly in Advance Basis and True Equivalent Yield* (Reading: College of Estate Management).

Baum, A., Nunnington, N. and Mackmin, D. (2006) *The Income Approach to Property Valuation* (5th edn, London: EG Books).

Blackledge, M. (2009) *Introducing Property Valuation* (Abingdon: Routledge).

Crosby, N. (1992) *Reversionary Freeholds; UK Market Valuation Practice* (London: RICS).

Davidson, A. W. (2002) *Parry's Valuation and Investment Tables* (12th edn, London: EG Books).

Enever, N., Isaac, D. And Daley, M. (2010) *The Valuation of Property Investments* (7th edn, London: EG Books).

Havard, T. (2004) *Investment Property Valuation Today* (London: Estates Gazette).

Isaac, D. and O'Leary, J. (2011) *Property Investment* (2nd edn, Basingstoke: Palgrave).

RICS, Investment Property Databank and the University of Aberdeen (1994) *Understanding the Property Cycle: Economic Cycles and Property Cycles* (London: RICS).

RICS (2010) *Property Investment Valuation in the UK: A Brief Guide for Users of Valuations* (London: RICS).

RICS (2011) *RICS Valuation Standards – Global and UK* (7th edn, Coventry: RICS).

Saunders, O. (2010) *Valuation Calculations: 101 Worked Examples* (London: RICS).

Sayce, S., Smith, J., Cooper, R. and Venmore-Rowland, P. (2006) *Real Estate Appraisal from Value to Worth* (Oxford: Blackwell).

Scarrett, D. (2008) *Property Valuation: The Five Methods* (2nd edn, Abingdon: Routledge).

Shapiro, E., Davies, K. and Mackmin, D. (2009) *Modern Methods of Valuation* (10th edn, London: EG Books).

Self-assessment questions for Chapter 8

1 Explain what a YP is.

2 If a freehold property has an annual rental value of £30,000 and the yield for this investment is 8 per cent, what is:

(a) the Years' Purchase in perpetuity; and

(b) the capital value?

3 A shop is currently let to a retailer on a long lease under which the current net annual rent passing is £40,000. There is a rent review in three years' time when the rent is expected to increase to £50,000. Value the freehold interest in the shop using the term and reversion method assuming a term yield of 7.5 per cent and a reversionary yield of 8.5 per cent.

4 Using the same scenario for the shop above, produce a layer method evaluation using a 7.5 per cent yield to capitalize the core income of £40,000 and an 8.5 per cent yield for the top slice which is expected to add £10,000 to the annual rent in three years' time.

5 An office unit on a business park is fully let to a business tenant who is paying a net annual rent of £60,000. However since the lease was signed the property market has gone into decline and the current rental value for the property is £48,000 per annum. There is a rent review in three years' time which coincides with a break clause which the tenant could exercise. Value this over-rented property using the layer method. Adopt a yield of 7 per cent to capitalize the core income and a yield of 9 per cent to capitalize the overage.

Outline answers are included at the back of the book.

9

The investment method – discounted cash flow approaches

9.1 Introduction
9.2 Traditional and DCF approaches to property investment valuation
9.3 Basic investment appraisal techniques
9.4 Discounting and DCF
9.5 DCF to identify net present value (NPV)

9.6 DCF to identify the internal rate of return (IRR)
9.7 Summary
References
Self-assessment questions

Aims

This chapter discusses some of the shortcomings associated with the traditional investment method of valuation described in the previous chapter. This chapter then explores, with the aid of worked examples, some of the potential advantages of using a discounted cash flow approach. This type of appraisal can build in explicit assumptions about future costs, income and capital value, enabling property investors to decide whether, on the assumptions being made, a property investment will meet the required rate of return.

Key terms

>> **Discounted cash flow (DCF)** – the discounting of future cash flows to reflect their present value equivalent.
>> **Net present value (NPV)** – the total of the discounted future cash flows from an investment.
>> **Internal rate of return (IRR)** – the discount rate which generates an NPV of zero.

9.1 Introduction

This chapter discusses discounted cash flow (DCF) which is a technique used to assess the returns from a property investment or a property development project. The technique is now commonly used by property valuers and investment analysts either in the form of commercial software packages or in-house formats constructed using Excel spreadsheets.

The chapter will examine arguments for using DCF to appraise property investments in place of the more traditional methods discussed in the previous chapter. This is not to say that the latter methods are redundant, as valuers might still prefer to use the traditional methods either as a check upon the output from a DCF analysis or because the particular appraisal is relatively straightforward and the use of the more elaborate DCF might be deemed unnecessary.

As will be discussed in the early part of the chapter, when companies or individuals are faced with very straightforward business decisions they might prefer to use much simpler appraisal methods such as payback. However, the main theme of the chapter is to consider some of the shortcomings of adopting that type of assessment and, using worked examples, will illustrate the property contexts in which a valuer might choose to use DCF.

A DCF analysis can be used to identify the net present value (NPV) of the cash flow expected from a project or it can be used to identify the precise rate of return which a cash flow will produce and which is called the internal rate of

Figure 9.1 Cannon Place, a modern office development above Cannon Street Station in the City of London

return (IRR). Both types of DCF will be discussed in the chapter with examples to illustrate the principles at work.

Large commercial investment properties such as those shown in Figure 9.1 will generate substantial annual rental incomes over their lifetimes. It is this type of income stream which can be evaluated in a DCF format to identify the capital value of the property for property investors.

9.2 Traditional and DCF approaches to property investment valuation

The traditional investment method of valuation discussed in the previous chapter, forms part of the valuation toolkit from which a valuer will select the most appropriate method to suit the specific task. Traditional methods are sometimes referred to as 'implicit' because the valuer has selected the all risks yield, implying that all relevant factors have been embodied in this figure.

The valuer's professional body, the Royal Institution of Chartered Surveyors (RICS) (2010a: 4) confirms that the traditional method still has its merits and may be applicable where there is plenty of market comparable evidence and where the valuation is relatively straightforward. While it does have its merits, the traditional investment method lacks a degree of versatility and transparency especially when an investment is expected to generate varying costs and incomes over different time periods.

The traditional method is perhaps not the best method for making comparisons between alternative investment opportunities. In those circumstances a valuer might choose to use DCF which is a technique which has crossed over from the world of business into property appraisal. DCF brings all future revenues and expenditure to present day values using a given rate of interest known as the 'discount rate'.

One of the early drivers behind the adoption of DCF in property appraisal was an expectation on the part of large corporate clients, that a more explicit appraisal method be used to supplement the less explicit all risks yield approach which is a feature of the traditional method of valuation. Among the merits of DCF is that it sets out very clearly the predicted incomes and expenditures over the project time period. This has made the technique particularly applicable for appraising large commercial property investments which may be purchased and held for several years before disposal.

The DCF method explicitly takes account of the time value of money and it can also be used to compare capital projects and factor in assumptions about rental growth or how inflation might affect costs over time. DCF can be used to evaluate very complex properties such as shopping centres, where there are many variables to be taken into account. Blackledge (2009: 241) is one among a number of authors who are persuaded by the arguments for using DCF approaches in place of the traditional Years' Purchase investment method. However having carried out a DCF, the valuer should check if the resulting initial yield is acceptable and defensible in the light of market evidence.

Before going on to consider how DCFs are constructed and used in a property context, the following section summarizes some more basic methods of investment appraisal to provide a contrast with the DCF method.

9.3 Basic investment appraisal techniques

Investment appraisal techniques need a clear criterion to assess the expected returns from an investment opportunity such as the purchase of an income producing commercial property. Various types of appraisal have evolved which focus upon monetary performance rather than trying to become too involved in assessing the qualitative characteristics of the asset. Those using these techniques therefore have to add the wider perspective by forming judgements and making assumptions which stem from the context and type of investment. However, in the end, the outcome of the appraisal is still presented in monetary terms.

A number of investment appraisal techniques have emerged in the world of business to try to provide objective comparison between alternative investment projects. Some of these techniques are quite basic, but simplicity is sometimes a virtue particularly when an investment opportunity is being examined for the first time and when a broad brush indicator is required to see if further analysis is worthwhile. Two of these basic approaches are now discussed, the first of which is the payback period method and the second is the rate of return on investment method.

Payback method

This method involves the calculation of the number of years that it takes to pay back the original investment in a project. The criterion is simple in this type of analysis in that the shorter the payback period the better the project. Thus on this basis either project A or B in Table 9.1 could be chosen as they have both nominally paid back their initial investment of £100,000 by the end of year 2.

This type of analysis is crude in that it does not take into account the scale and timing of the cash flows, for instance the high cash flows in the early years or projects B and C compared to project A. The method does not consider strengthening cash flows after the payback point has been reached as is the case for project C below, and thus longer-term profitability is ignored. The advantage of the payback approach is its simplicity and its ability to recognise the time factor, although in a crude way.

Table 9.1 Comparing three investments on a payback basis

	A	Projects *B*	*C*
Investment required (£)	100,000	100,000	100,000
Cash flow (£)			
Year 1	10,000	70,000	70,000
Year 2	90,000	30,000	0
Year 3	20,000	20,000	30,000
Year 4	0	0	70,000
Total cash inflow	120,000	120,000	170,000
Payback period	2 years	2 years	3 years
Ranking	Equal 1st	Equal 1st	3rd

Rate of return method

This approach expresses a rate of profit as a percentage of the cost of an investment:

$$\frac{\text{Profit}}{\text{Cost}} \times 100\%$$

The cost figure is calculated by the capital employed in the project. A target return is set and if the profitability exceeds this figure, then the project is acceptable. This is a replica of the traditional all risks yield in perpetuity:

$$\frac{\text{Net income}}{\text{Capital value}} \times 100\%$$

The capital value in this context is the price paid for the investment and the yield is an initial yield and this type of appraisal could therefore also be thought of as a market valuation. In business finance the calculation can be done on various bases including profit before interest and tax (PBIT) have been deducted or net profit after tax has been deducted. In this type of analysis the profit is usually assessed as the average achieved over the project life. Interest is the interest outstanding on debt raised by the company. The capital employed may be shown gross or as an average figure over the life of the asset deducting each year for depreciation.

Investment	**£80,000**
Cash inflows (£)	
Year 1	£40,000
Year 2	£60,000
Year 3	£40,000
Year 4	£20,000
Total cash inflow	£160,000

Assuming there is no resale or scrap value for the investment then the original £80,000 is lost through depreciation. The average annual profit is:

$$\frac{£160,000 - £80,000}{4 \text{ years}} = £20,000$$

Annual return on the investment before tax and any interest payment is:

$$\frac{£20,000}{£80,000} \times 100\% = 25\%$$

In this model depreciation is on a straight-line basis and thus there is an equal amount of the total depreciation each year. The advantage of this method is that it uses the same criterion related to profitability both for projects and the overall business. The choice of target rate could be the same rate as the firm sets for overall profitability. The disadvantage of using this method is that it ignores the time value of money. The use of a straight-line approach to depreciation may not realistically reflect the actual rate of depreciation of the asset.

Both the payback and rate of return methods discussed above might be thought of as good, basic, broad-brush business appraisal techniques. However they do come with a number of simplifications and in particular they ignore the time value of money. Property appraisers will therefore try to go beyond these basic levels of appraisal when trying to assess development or property investment opportunities which will commit considerable sums of money for what might be lengthy periods of time. One of these arguably more sophisticated approaches is discounted cash flow and which is now discussed.

9.4 Discounting and DCF

DCF is an important aid in the evaluation of investment opportunities in that it explicitly takes account of the time value of money. The latter arises because £1 available today is worth more than £1 receivable in a year's time, even ignoring an inflation effect. Essentially if £1 is immediately consumed, the benefit will have been obtained a year earlier or alternatively the £1 could have been invested to earn interest over the year. In property valuation the traditional Years' Purchase approach takes into account the time value of money, whereas the basic business appraisal methods considered above do not.

DCF discounts to the present day, all sums of money, incoming and outgoing, which the investor incurs. For single sums, the Present Value of £1 formula is used and which is:

$$\frac{1}{(1 + i)^n}$$

This formula is the inverse of the Amount of £1, or compound interest formula discussed in earlier chapters. Where the same amount is being received or spent for a series of years, then the present value of £1 per annum can be used; this is more familiarly known as the Years' Purchase (YP). It can be seen from Table 9.2 that it is simply the sum of a series of individual Present Values. The example uses the rate of 8 per cent and assumes a regular annual income of £1 over 4 years so that the present value of this modest income stream is calculated to be £3.31 (rounded).

Table 9.2 Present value and Years' Purchase compared

PV of £1 in 1 year @ 8% =	0.9259
PV of £1 in 2 years @ 8% =	0.8573
PV of £1 in 3 years @ 8% =	0.7938
PV of £1 in 4 years @ 8% =	0.7350
YP 4 years @ 8% =	3.3120

The answer could also be found in *Parry's Tables* (Davidson, 2002) by consulting the Years' Purchase (single rate) tables or by using the YP formula which is:

$$\frac{1 - \dfrac{1}{(1 + i)^n}}{i}$$

The use of the YP is perfectly satisfactory where there is certainty that a future series of costs or incomes will remain constant. Thus in a term and reversion valuation where a rent is passing and can be expected to continue for a set number of years the YP approach is acceptable. It is true therefore that the traditional investment method estimates the present value of future periodic incomes and therefore DCF is just what valuers have been doing for years. However future costs and incomes arising from a project will not always be constant and this is where DCF can go beyond the traditional method by capturing and making explicit irregular patters of income and expenditure.

One of the key decisions to make when constructing a DCF is the discount rate to use. This aspect is seldom fully grasped by those coming into contact with DCF for the first time because the discount rate appears to be arbitrary or a slightly mysterious given value. To fully understand the significance of the discount rate, individuals would normally have to run through a series of DCFs at different discount rates to strengthen their understanding. Some find the expression 'target rate' helpful while others use the expression 'hurdle rate' as an analogy for the discount rate in that to be successful the hurdle has to jumped over.

In essence the investor chooses the discount rate to represent an acceptable rate of return relative to the risks involved, the cost of capital and likely returns on other ventures. For example if an investor could borrow money for 5 per cent and which could be reinvested in corporate bonds at 6 per cent the investor would be making the difference of 1 per cent from recycling the money in a relatively low-risk vehicle.

The notional 6 per cent in this example is sometimes referred to as the opportunity cost of capital. It is not the same as the 'risk-free rate' which is commonly benchmarked against the rate achievable on medium dated government gilt-edged stock. The risk-free rate is often below the cost of capital and to continue this example, it might be say 3 per cent. An investor would obviously be unwise to source capital at 5 per cent and then invest it in gilt-edged stock earning 3 per cent as there would be an obvious loss equating to 2 per cent.

An investor whose cost of capital was 5 per cent would probably want considerably more than a 6 per cent return if the money were to be invested in a speculative property development where the peer group of developers would not undertake such a project for less than a 15 per cent return. Thus in a DCF appraisal of a property development, an investor might well discount the expected costs and returns at 15 per cent to see if the project was able to achieve that rate of return.

If, for academic purposes, the discount rate of 15 per cent were to be disaggregated its components might look as follows:

The cost of capital @ 5%
The opportunity cost of investing is low-risk bonds @ 1% (6% minus 5%)
A risk premium @ 9% (the difference between low-risk bonds at 6% and
    high-risk development at 15%)

The 15 per cent discount rate represents quite a stringent test to evaluate the expected future costs and incomes, reflecting the considerable risks involved in developing a speculative project. If however the investment opportunity had been a completed development which was fully let to reliable business tenants and thus was already producing an income which was likely to continue, the risks would be significantly reduced. The risk premium might then be much lower at say 2 per cent producing an overall discount rate of 8 per cent. Armatys *et al.* (2009: 215) take the logic one step further by suggesting that if an anticipated cash flow is discounted at the cost of capital which is assumed to be 5 per cent in this example, the resulting NPV would represent the profit element. A fuller discussion on the significance of the NPV will follow later in this chapter.

It is the use of a discount rate in a DCF appraisal which is thought to make it a more robust and credible evaluative technique than the payback period and return on investment methods considered earlier in the chapter. However, because borrowing rates (the cost of capital) change over time, then so do discount rates. In practice valuers do not always have to concern themselves with the composition of a discount rate for each project, as large corporate clients regularly update their own discount rates to reflect their own combinations of costs of capital, opportunity cost and risk perception.

Before considering the different forms that DCF can take and examining examples, it should be remembered that like other forms of appraisal a DCF analysis is only as accurate as the data that are put into the calculation. The RICS (2010b: 4) sets out the headings which they expect a competent valuer to investigate when constructing a DCF to ensure that all of the necessary data is captured and calibrated properly. Among other things, the valuer is expected to investigate and confirm the physical attributes of the subject property, the tenure basis for the valuation, the rental value, management charges, finance, gearing, taxation and applicable inflation rates. These issues are properly concerned with maintaining high professional standards and thus they reach beyond the introductory nature of this chapter.

It is perhaps sufficient at this stage to state that even armed with the ability to construct a DCF there remain the challenges of credible data capture and calibration of variables combined with future uncertainty. Despite robust forecasting, there will inevitably be change in the values ascribed to variables at the outset when the capital investment project is being evaluated.

While DCF does not solve the problem of future uncertainty it can explicitly model different scenarios with regards to the quantum and timing of costs and revenues expected from a project. Thus like the sensitivity analysis considered in Chapter 7 for the residual valuation, DCF appraisals can also be subjected to 'what if' scenarios where key variables are altered to see what effect the changes will have on the outcome.

9.5 DCF to identify net present value (NPV)

As discussed above one of the key decisions when assembling a DCF is to adopt a discount rate which in one figure embodies the investor's cost of capital, opportunity costs and risk premium. Essentially the discount rate could be expected to increase when the cost of borrowing is high and when the risks associated with the project are significant. Alternatively the discount rate will be lower when the cost of capital has reduced and when the project or investment is not especially risky. When the discount rate has been decided upon, the future costs and incomes expected from the project can be interplayed over the project time horizon to produce a result in the form of the net present value (NPV).

For those coming new to DCF there is often a common misapprehension regarding the significance of the NPV and it is easy to see why many think that it is the profit or loss arising from the venture. For example, if a DCF appraisal had discounted a multimillion pound project at 10 per cent to produce an NPV of £500, some might incorrectly jump to the conclusion that the project was not worth undertaking because it had only made £500 profit.

Those who have studied or used DCF will know that the real significance of the £500 is that it is a positive sum, confirming that the project income had paid back all of the investor's expenditure as well as the equivalent of a 10 per cent annual return. The £500 represents a small bonus on top of that return, although it also signifies that the investment has only just achieved its target rate by a small margin and this would be true even if the NPV were only £1.

If the NPV had been £500,000 then the investment would have easily achieved its target rate with a considerable margin to spare. The £500,000 would by any measure, be a considerable bonus on top of the returns already achieved and subsumed in the 10 per cent discount rate.

Alternatively if the NPV was minus £500 it would signify that the investment had marginally failed to achieve a 10 per cent return but that it had come very close to achieving the target rate. If of course the NPV had been minus £500,000 then the investment had failed to achieve the target rate (the investor's expectations) by a considerable margin and should probably be abandoned.

To illustrate these principles Table 9.3 represents the investment of £100,000 in an 8 per cent interest bearing account with interest being paid to the investor each year. The investor is content to take the interest payments of £8,000 each year and has decided to leave the capital in the account for six years before withdrawing it.

The cash flow in Table 9.3 confirms that the investor earned 8 per cent per annum as depicted by the annual income of £8,000 and recovered the initial capital invested at the end of year 6. When the cash flow is discounted at 8 per cent the NPV is zero (the £2 shown is due to rounding in the calculation) signifying that the investor made an 8 per cent per annum return on the investment.

The same would be true if the investor chose not to take the annual interest payments but left them in the account to compound at 8 per cent per annum and then to withdraw the ensuing capital sum at the end of year 6. This approach is shown below in Table 9.4 and again it is clear that the investor earns 8 per cent per annum and recovers the initial capital invested. When this pattern of investment and withdrawal is discounted at 8 per cent it also results in a zero

Table 9.3 DCF appraisal of a £100,000 investment over six years at 8 per cent where annual income is taken

Year	Event	Expenditure £	Income £	Net cash flow £	PV £1 @ 8%	DCF £
0	Capital invested	100,000	0	−100,000	1	−100,000
1	Interest received	0	8,000	8,000	0.9259	7,407
2	Interest received	0	8,000	8,000	0.8573	6,858
3	Interest received	0	8,000	8,000	0.7938	6,350
4	Interest received	0	8,000	8,000	0.7350	5,880
5	Interest received	0	8,000	8,000	0.6806	5,445
6	Interest received	0	8,000	8,000	0.6302	5,042
	Capital withdrawn	0	100,000	100,000		63,020
					NPV =	2

Table 9.4 DCF of a £100,000 investment over six years at 8 per cent where no income is taken

Year	Event	Expenditure £	Income £	Net cash flow £	PV £1 @ 8%	DCF £
0	Capital invested	100,000	0	−100,000	1	−100,000
1	No interest taken	0	0	0	0.9259	0
2	No interest taken	0	0	0	0.8573	0
3	No interest taken	0	0	0	0.7938	0
4	No interest taken	0	0	0	0.7350	0
5	No interest taken	0	0	0	0.6806	0
6	No interest taken	0	0	0	0.6302	0
	Capital withdrawn	0	158,687	158,687		100,005
					NPV =	5

NPV (the £5 shown is due to rounding of the figures in the calculation) thus proving that the investment makes an 8 per cent per annum return.

Readers who want to review more examples of compounding and discounting in order to strengthen their understanding of the time value of money valuation mathematics generally could examine Fraser (2004: 9–23) or Baum *et al.* (2006: 3–24).

A property-related example is now considered in Table 9.5 to enable some reflection upon the conclusions which might be drawn from the NPV which that DCF has generated. The DCF calculation depicts a potential house purchase for £190,000 by a buy-to-let investor who requires a minimum of 10 per cent return on this type of investment. It is assumed that there will be £10,000 acquisition costs to add to the purchase price so that the overall expenditure will be £200,000.

The investor's research suggests that the house could be rented out for £900 per month, so that the gross income in the first year is expected to be £10,800. From this gross income the investor is budgeting for 35 per cent outgoings on

Table 9.5 DCF appraisal of a buy-to-let housing investment

Year	Expenditure £	Income £	Net cash flow £	PV of £1 @ 10%	DCF £
0	200,000	0	−200,000	1	−200,000
1	3,780	10,800	7,020	0.9091	6,382
2	3,893	11,124	7,231	0.8264	5,975
3	4,010	11,458	7,448	0.7513	5,595
4	4,131	11,802	7,671	0.6830	5,239
5	4,255	12,156	7,901	0.6209	4,906
6	4,382	12,521	8,139	0.5645	4,594
7	4,514	12,897	8,383	0.5132	4,302
8	9,649	364,961	355,312	0.4665	165,753
				NPV	2,746

items such as building insurance, repairs, allowances for depreciation and void periods between tenancies.

The investor plans to increase the rent annually by 3 per cent to keep pace with predicted inflation and then to dispose of the property at the end of year 8 when it is anticipated that the capital value will have appreciated by 8 per cent per annum. This is arguably an optimistic growth rate in housing values, but the investor has examined the long-term trend in house prices in the area and is satisfied that this is achievable. The investor expects some exit costs amounting to £5,000 to dispose of the house in year 8 and these have been added to the outgoings shown for that year.

The positive NPV arising from the DCF in Table 9.5 is the sum of the discounted cash flows and which signifies that the investor's target rate of return at 10 per cent would be met with a surplus of £2,746. The latter would be a small additional contribution to profit. Of course the outcome would rely on the assumptions underpinning the figures becoming reality over the eight-year holding period for the investment.

In contrast to the residential buy-to-let investment considered above, the following example in Table 9.6 illustrates how DCF can be used to assess the purchase price for a commercial property investment. The example is a large prime tenanted shop generating an annual rent of £150,000 per annum.

In the scenario, the property is considered to be under-rented as comparable market evidence suggests that its estimated rental value is £165,000. That figure is used to calculate the rent which is likely to be achieved when the rent is reviewed in two years' time by which time predicted inflation at 3.5 per cent per annum would produce an annual rental value of £176,752 as shown in the DCF below. The calculation underpinning that figure is: $1.035^2 \times £165,000 = £176,752$. If the average growth rate of 3.5 per cent persisted for the following five years to the next rent review in year 7 then the rent by that stage of £209,926 as shown below would be a function of: $1.035^5 \times £176,752$.

In Table 9.6 below the NPV of almost £2.5 million represents the maximum that a property investor could pay inclusive of purchaser's costs, to acquire the investment property while still achieving the target rate of return of 8 per cent.

Table 9.6 DCF appraisal of an under-rented shop

Rent passing in year 1	£150,000	Estimate rental value in year 1	£165,000
Annual rental growth	3.5%	Exit yield	7.5%
Discount rate	8%	YP in perpetuity therefore	13.3333

Year	Income £	PV of £1 @ 8%	DCF £
1	150,000	0.9259	138,885
2	150,000	0.8573	128,595
3	176,752	0.7938	140,306
4	176,752	0.7350	129,913
5	176,752	0.6806	120,297
6	176,752	0.6302	111,389
7	176,752	0.5835	103,135
8	209,926	0.5403	113,423
	2,799,006	0.5403	1,512,303
		NPV =	2,498,246

The following example in Table 9.7 assumes a similar shop but this time the property is considered to be over-rented relative to its estimated rental value. Over-rented properties became common in the wake of the credit crunch when commercial property rental values fell in many locations in the UK between 2008 and 2010. Saunders (2010: 100) is one of a number of authors who show how to take account in DCF appraisals of the strong possibility that commercial tenants will exercise break clauses to vacate over-rented properties or that they will choose not to renew leases when they expire. The strong likelihood of a void period when rates and re-letting fees fall on the freehold owner, can be explicitly modelled in DCFs as shown for year 3 in Table 9.7.

Table 9.7 DCF appraisal of an over-rented shop

Rent passing in year 1	£150,000	Estimate rental value in year 1	£135,000
Rental growth from year 4	3.5%	Exit yield	7.5%
Discount rate	8%	YP in perpetuity therefore	13.3333

Year	Expenditure £	Income £	Net cash flow £	PV of £1 @ 8%	DCF £
1	0	150,000	150,000	0.9259	138,885
2	0	150,000	150,000	0.8573	128,595
3	50,000	0	− 50,000	0.7938	− 39,690
4	0	135,000	135,000	0.7350	99,225
5	0	135,000	135,000	0.6806	91,881
6	0	135,000	135,000	0.6302	85,077
7	0	135,000	135,000	0.5835	78,773
8	0	135,000	135,000	0.5403	72,941
9	0	160,338	160,338	0.5002	80,201
	0	2,137,835	2,137,835	0.5002	1,069,345
				NPV =	1,805,232

In Table 9.7 the NPV of just over £1.8 million represents the maximum that a property investor might pay to acquire this over-rented property, inclusive of purchaser's costs. If the property could be acquired for less than this figure the difference between whatever was paid and £1.8 million would represent a bonus on top of meeting the target rate of return of 8 per cent. Of course if the investor paid over £1.8 million the target rate would not be met.

The NPVs arising from the examples above provide a clear indication of whether to accept or reject a project and this works well when there is only one project to appraise. In reality a project will face competition from other project opportunities, simply because investors are unlikely to have sufficient funds to take on all projects which their analyses indicate to be acceptable. This fact of life is referred to as 'capital rationing' and involves a restriction of choice when resources are limited.

To a large extent the use of DCF indicates which project is the strongest performer, as the size of the NPV will be an indication on how easily it has or has not met the investor's target rate. Consider for example two projects each of which has an asking price of £1 million and each of which will generate an income stream over the next 10 years and which when discounted at 10 per cent produces positive NPVs. The first project's NPV might be £100,000 while the second project's NPV might be £50,000. In a capital rationing scenario it is fairly obvious that the first project would be chosen.

The position is less clear cut when the asking prices for the two projects are different and when the timescales involved differ and when the NPVs are both positive and broadly similar. In that scenario it is advisable to supplement the NPV by identifying the Internal Rate of Return (IRR) for both projects to create some precision around what each project is actually achieving in percentage terms. The discussion now therefore turns to consider how DCFs can be used to identify project IRRs.

9.6 DCF to identify the Internal Rate of Return (IRR)

The NPV generated from a DCF gives a clear guide on whether the investor's target rate of return will be met. Investment analysts would probably investigate further by trying to identify the specific percentage rate produced from an investment. This is referred to as the Internal Rate of Return (IRR) and it is also the discount rate at which the NPV is zero. In the DCF example above at Table 9.5 the investor's proposed buy-to-let venture was discounted at 10 per cent and it produced a positive NPV of £2,746 signifying that the investment would generate returns above the target rate. A negative NPV would have indicated that the target rate would not have been achieved and that the investment was earning something less than 10 per cent.

The IRR is the precise rate of return and it may be obtained using Excel or a programmable calculator or *Parry's Tables*. Should a check be required to ensure that the figure identified is correct, the IRR can be calculated using a formula. The formula requires two discount rates to be selected by trial and error, one giving a positive NPV, the other a negative NPV as shown in Table 9.8. The formula then interpolates between the two NPV values to identify the IRR.

Table 9.8 Calculating the IRR using two trial discount rates

Year	Expenditure £	Income £	Cash flow £	PV of £1 @ 10%	DCF £	PV of £1 @ 12%	DCF £
0	200,000	0	-200,000	1	-200,000	1	-200,000
1	1,500	8,400	6,900	0.9091	6,273	0.8929	6,161
2	1,530	8,568	7,038	0.8264	5,816	0.7972	5,611
3	1,561	8,739	7,178	0.7513	5,393	0.7118	5,109
4	1,592	8,914	7,322	0.6830	5,001	0.6355	4,653
5	1,624	9,092	7,468	0.6209	4,637	0.5674	4,237
6	1,656	9,274	7,618	0.5645	4,300	0.5066	3,859
7	1,689	9,459	7,770	0.5132	3,988	0.4523	3,514
8	3,723	361,325	357,602	0.4665	166,821	0.4039	144,435
				NPV @ 10%	2,229	NPV @ 12%	-22,419

In the example above, the NPV at a trial rate of 10 per cent has generated a positive NPV while a trial rate of 12 per cent has generated a negative NPV. Given that the IRR is the rate at which the NPV is zero, it will be at a rate somewhere between 10 per cent and 12 per cent and it can be calculated by using the following formula:

$$R_1 + [\,(R_2 - R_1) \times \frac{NPV\ @\ R_1}{NPV\ @\ R_1 - NPV\ @\ R_2}\,]$$

Where R_1 = the lower discount rate, which in this case is 10 per cent.
R_2 = the higher discount rate, which in this case if 12 per cent.
NPV @ R_1 = NPV at the lower discount rate, which in this case is £2,229.
NPV @ R_2 = NPV at the higher discount rate, which in this case is – £22,419.

Inserting the actual values for the variables into the formula produces:

$$10\% + (2\% \times \frac{2,229}{24,648}) = 10.18\%\ (\text{rounded up})$$

A further example of using DCF to identify the IRR follows in Table 9.9 where there is an opportunity to invest in a property which will generate an annual income of £70,000 for 5 years before being disposed of. In this case the two trial rates are 8 per cent and 9 per cent indicating that the IRR lies somewhere between these two values.

Inserting the two trial rates and the resulting NPVs from Table 9.9 into the IRR formula produces the following.

$$8\% + (\,1\% \times \frac{17,613}{42,761}) = 8.41\%\ (\text{rounded up})$$

Table 9.9 Calculating the IRR arising from NPVs at two trial discount rates

Year	Particulars	Expenditure £	Income £	Net cash flow £	PV of £1 @ 8%	DCF £
0	Purchase price	1,000,000	0	−1,000,000	1	−1,000,000
	Purchase costs	50,000	0	−50,000	1	−50,000
1	Rent	0	70,000	70,000	0.9259	64,813
2	Rent	0	70,000	70,000	0.8573	60,011
3	Rent	0	70,000	70,000	0.7938	55,566
4	Rent	0	70,000	70,000	0.7350	51,450
	Rent	0	70,000	70,000	0.6806	47,642
5	Sale proceeds	0	1,187,686	1,187,686	0.6806	808,339
	Sale costs	29,692	0	−29,692	0.6806	−20,208
					NPV =	17,613

Year	Particulars	Expenditure £	Income £	Net cash flow £	PV of £1 @ 9%	DCF £
0	Purchase price	1,000,000	0	−1,000,000	1	−1,000,000
	Purchase costs	50,000	0	−50,000	1	−50,000
1	Rent	0	70,000	70,000	0.9174	64,218
2	Rent	0	70,000	70,000	0.8417	58,919
3	Rent	0	70,000	70,000	0.7722	54,054
4	Rent	0	70,000	70,000	0.7084	49,588
	Rent	0	70,000	70,000	0.6499	45,493
5	Sale proceeds	0	1,187,686	1,187,686	0.6499	771,877
	Sale costs	29,692	0	−29,692	0.6499	−19,297
					NPV =	−25,148

Table 9.10 sets out a further example of using DCF to identify the IRR arising from a commercial property investment which is generating a significant annual rent. The property could be a newly built and recently let large office development in a prime location, representing the type of purchase that a large financial institution might undertake. The purchaser plans to hold the property for five years before selling it for a capital value based upon predicted rental growth and an exit yield. The latter reflects the fact that after five years the building is no longer new and will be slightly less attractive relative to newer stock which will probably have been developed by that stage.

The discount rate of 8 per cent in Table 9.10 reflects a trade-off between the risk involved and investor expectations on the returns from this type of asset class relative to returns which could be achieved on other investment opportunities at the time. Because the building has already been developed and let to an assumed reliable business tenant, the project has already passed through the most risky stages and so a higher discount rate commensurate with carrying out development is not applicable in this example.

Using the IRR function in Excel, the NPV above equates to an IRR of 7.97 per cent rounded up. Thus this investment does not meet the investor's target rate and either there would need to be some negotiation around the purchase price (which would have to reduce by around £39,000) or the investor would

Table 9.10 A DCF appraisal of a major property investment

Purchase price	£25,806,452	Forecast annual rental growth	3.5%
Annual rent £	£2,000,000	Estimated rental value on sale	£2,375,373
Initial yield	7.75%	Anticipated exit yield	8.25%
Discount rate	8%	Sale price	£28,792,400
		Sales costs	2%

Year	Expenditure £	Income £	Cash flow £	PV of £1 @ 8%	DCF £
0	25,806,452	0	−25,806,452	1	−25,806,452
1	0	2,000,000	2,000,000	0.9259	1,851,800
2	0	2,000,000	2,000,000	0.8573	1,714,600
3	0	2,000,000	2,000,000	0.7938	1,587,600
4	0	2,000,000	2,000,000	0.7350	1,470,000
5	0	2,000,000	2,000,000	0.6806	1,361,200
6	575,848	28,792,400	28,216,552	0.6302	17,782,071
				NPV =	−39,181
				IRR =	7.97%

accept the investment as it is so close to the target rate of 8 per cent as to be within an acceptable tolerance. A strict interpretation would be that the investor should look at alternative investment opportunities which might meet the target rate.

By now it will probably have become apparent that with a little thought DCF can be used to tackle a wide variety of property appraisals, especially those where initial capital investment needs to be juxtaposed against a future revenue stream and often a capital disposal after a period of time. Scott (2008: 477) for example shows how DCF can be used to value hotels. The RICS (2010b) provides helpful guidance and examples for valuers on how to structure their DCFs in the context of commercial property valuation work. Because the RICS guidance is aimed at a professional practitioner audience it is neither possible nor necessary to delve into the depth and detail that it provides in this introductory book.

Continuing on the theme of versatility, the following example in Table 9.11 illustrates how DCF can be used to evaluate property development and a subsequent holding period when the property becomes an investment. The scenario envisages the acquisition of an undeveloped plot of land on a retail warehouse park followed by the construction and then letting of a small terrace of retail warehouses. The developer then becomes an investor by holding the properties up until the first rent review in year 6 when the properties will be sold at a capital value reflecting their reviewed rent at that stage.

Because this is a speculative development there is considerable risk and so the investor has discounted the cash flow at 20 per cent. In fact it is possible to disaggregate the development part of the cash flow and to discount that at a different discount rate to reflect the higher risk than for the subsequent holding period when a lower discount rate would be applicable to reflect the reduced risks by that stage of the project. However for simplicity in the example, the two stages in the life of the venture have been discounted at the higher

Table 9.11 DCF appraisal of the development and ultimate disposal of retail warehousing

Value		Costs	
Rental value per m²	£150	Asking price for land	£1,500,000
Gross floorspace m²	3,000	Land purchase costs @ 5% of land cost	£75,000
Net floorspace m²	2,850	Total for land therefore	£1,575,000
Annual rental income	£427,500		
Initial yield	7.50%	Building costs per m²	£490
YP in perpetuity	13.3333	Building costs applied to gross floorspace	£1,470,000
Capital value	£5,699,986	Ancillary costs @ 5% of building costs	£73,500
Developer's discount rate	20%	Professional fees @ 12% of building and ancillary costs	£185,220
		Contingencies @ 5% of building costs, ancillaries and professional fees	£86,436
Anticipated annual inflation rate	3.10%	Planning and building regs consent fees	£50,000
Inflated rent in 5 years time	£498,000	Letting fees @ 10% of annual rent	£42,750
Anticipated yield in 5 years	8%	Total costs excluding land therefore	£1,907,906
YP in perpetuity	12.5		
Capital value in 5 years	£6,225,000		
Disposal costs @ 5%	£311,250		

Year	Expenditure £	Income £	Net cash flow £	PV of £1 @ 20%	DCF £
0	1,575,000	0	−1,575,000	1	−1,575,000
1	1,907,906	0	−1,907,906	0.8333	−1,589,858
2	0	427,500	427,500	0.6944	296,856
3	0	427,500	427,500	0.5787	247,394
4	0	427,500	427,500	0.4823	206,183
5	0	427,500	427,500	0.4019	171,812
6	311,250	6,652,500	6,342,402	0.3349	2,123,685
				NPV =	−118,928

rate of 20 per cent. A summary of the scheme's characteristics are set out at the top of Table 9.11 following which there is a DCF of the project.

The negative NPV generated by the DCF in Table 9.11 indicates that the target rate of return of 20 per cent has not been met but this does not automatically mean that the scheme should be abandoned. There are a number of variables which could be revisited and prime among these is the £1.5 million asking price for the site. If that single item can be negotiated down by around £119,000 which would be an 8 per cent reduction on the asking price, the scheme would meet the investor's expectations. Even if a lesser reduction were possible, then a few other cost savings might enable the scheme to meet its target rate.

Because most DCFs will be constructed using Excel spreadsheets Shapiro *et al.* (2009: 181) suggest that the 'goal–seek' function in Excel can be used to identify the numerical value for a variable which would generate the desired outcome. Thus in the above example the spreadsheet cell containing the negative NPV value could be calibrated to zero in 'goal–seek' which can then iterate a selected variable to identify a value for it which will produce a zero NPV. In the simple example above a number of variables suggest themselves for this exercise such as the annual inflation rate which underpins rental growth and which in the exercise is assumed to be 3.1 per cent. 'Goal–seek' could investigate to see what that variable would need to be so that the investor's target rate was met in the form a zero NPV. DCF and its creative use within Excel spreadsheets thus becomes as much a diagnostic tool as a strict financial appraisal method.

9.7 Summary

The early part of this chapter contained a critique of traditional property investment valuation methods such as term and reversion and capitalisation using an all risks yield. It was acknowledged that while those methods still have considerable merit and remain a part of the valuer's toolkit, they are perhaps not the best methods for dealing with complicated cash flows over time. DCF is now a more widely used appraisal technique particularly for large value commercial properties. The widespread use of DCF in property appraisal has been fuelled by the availability of PCs and the collective consciousness of the property valuation community on how to build and interpret DCFs using Excel spreadsheets. There are also commercial software packages available which can run property investment analyses and which arguably save time constructing elaborate spreadsheets and increase consistency of approach.

DCF is as much about understanding the process of discounting and what the resulting NPV and IRR signify, as it is about research to identify the variables and then to calibrate them against the backdrop of an uncertain future. It is for this reason that despite its technical veneer, DCF like other methods of valuation is as much an art as a science. What could be said is that it aspires to transparency, as the users of a DCF valuation can clearly see the assumptions upon which it is based. Like other valuation techniques, DCFs can be subject to 'what if' scenario testing and variables such as inflation, which lie behind rental growth assumptions, would be prime candidates for exploring variations.

References

Armatys, J., Askham, P. and Green, M. (2009) *Principles of Valuation* (London: EG Books).

Baum, A., Nunnington, N. and Mackmin, D. (2006) *The Income Approach to Property Valuation* (5th edn, London: EG Books).

Blackledge, M. (2009) *Introducing Property Valuation* (Abingdon: Routledge).

Davidson, A. W. (2002) *Parry's Valuation and Investment Tables* (12th edn, London: EG Books).

Fraser, W. D. (2004) *Cash-Flow Appraisal for Property Investment* (Basingstoke: Palgrave Macmillan).

RICS (2010a) *Property Investment Valuation in the UK: A Brief Guide for Users of Valuations* (London: RICS).

RICS (2010b) *Discounted Cash Flow for Commercial Property Investments* (London: RICS).

Saunders, O. (2010) *Valuation Calculations: 101 Worked Examples* (London: RICS).

Scott, B. (2008) 'Hotels', in R. Hayward (ed.), *Valuation: Principles into Practice* (6th edn, London: EG Books).
Shapiro, E., Davies, K. and Mackmin, D. (2009) *Modern Methods of Valuation* (10th edn, London: EG Books).

Self-assessment questions for Chapter 9

1 A calculation is needed to show in today's terms the value of an annually receivable sum of £35,000 for the next 10 years, discounted at an annual interest rate of 7 per cent. Identify, name and use the relevant formula to calculate this sum.

2 Apart from using the formula above, there are two other ways that the answer to question 1 above can be found. Identify those two methods and use them to prove that your answer to question 1 is correct.

3 An investor who has £180,000 to invest is exploring whether to purchase a house for £170,000 plus fees and other purchase costs of £10,000. The investor plans to let the property for £1,000 per month, although recognises that there will be significant outgoings which will consume 40 per cent of that income each year. A local lettings agent has suggested that rents on these types of properties have risen at 3 per cent per annum and that it is reasonable to assume that this trend will continue. Forecasters are also suggesting that following a property recession the capital value of these types of properties looks set to increase by 5 per cent per annum. The investor plans to hold the property for six years and then to dispose of it on the assumption that disposal costs will be 5 per cent of the property's value at that stage. Produce a discounted cash flow to establish whether the proposal would achieve the investor's target rate of return of 10 per cent.

4 Using the same scenario as above produce a discounted cash flow to establish whether the investor's proposal would achieve a revised target rate of return of 6 per cent.

5 Using the IRR formula below and the discount rates and NPVs identified in your answers to questions 3 and 4 above try to identify the IRR for the investor's buy-to-let idea described above.

$$R_1 + [(R_2 - R_1) \times \frac{\text{NPV @ } R_1}{\text{NPV @ } R_1 - \text{NPV @ } R_2}]$$

Outline answers are included at the back of the book.

10

Yields, gearing and growth

10.1 Introduction
10.2 Inflation
10.3 Cost of capital
10.4 Risk premium
10.5 Gearing

10.6 The equated yield
10.7 The implied growth rate
10.8 Summary
    References
    Self-assessment questions

Aims

This chapter investigates the yield as an interest rate on property investment which theoretically compensates an investor for inflation, the cost of capital and the risk involved in investing in a particular asset. The concept of gearing which reflects the balance of debt and equity used to fund a venture is also tackled in the chapter. Finally the chapter considers the concept of the equated yield and the implied annual growth rate which would be needed to meet an investor's required rate of return.

Key terms

>> **Equated yield** – the internal rate of return (IRR) generated by an investment after an explicit growth rate has been applied to the anticipated income stream.

>> **Implied growth rate** – in a property investment context an investor's target rate of return implies that there will be some income growth in future so that the investor's expectations will be met. There are a number of formulas (which will be considered in this chapter) which can be used to calculate what that implied rate of growth would actually need to be to meet an investor's specific target rate.

>> **Weighted average cost of capital** – because property assets tend to be very expensive their development or acquisition will normally require a combination of debt (borrowing) and equity (the investor's or developer's own money). The interest charged on the debt will normally be higher than the opportunity cost of using equity which is a rate of interest that could be earned in a risk-free account. Because there is usually a higher reliance on debt relative to equity, the weighted average cost of capital will skew towards the borrowing rate and there are some examples of the calculation in this chapter.

>> **Gearing** – also referred to as leverage and which describes the balance of funding between debt and equity to support development or the acquisition of investment properties. Thus where 90 per cent of the money is borrowed and 10 per cent is equity, the developer/investor is said to be highly geared. There is a higher return to equity in this scenario if the development or investment asset performs as expected. However high gearing is risky and if the asset underperforms the high reliance on debt can quickly become burdensome for the borrower.

10.1 Introduction

A central theme in this chapter is the yield, which is an interest rate reflecting a rate of return for money invested in a property asset. However as was noted in Chapter 8 there are different types of yields in property and this can cause confusion especially when an individual is new to the subject. Inevitably there is a need for some specialized vocabulary building, which in this chapter includes the *equated yield* which is the internal rate of return from an investment after a growth rate has been factored into the future income stream.

Another way of thinking about yields is that they reflect what an investor expects as a rate of return for investing in a particular asset. The framing of expectations around a yield in any particular set of circumstances requires the synthesis of a number of factors. It will be explained in the chapter that some comparison needs to be made with the rate of return on other assets relative to their particular risk profiles. Inflation also has to be taken into account as well as the investor's cost of capital, as the acquisition or development of property will normally involve some borrowing and some equity each of which has a different interest rate.

The yield which reflects an investor's expectations is theoretically compensating simultaneously for all of these things. However, it will be seen that it is not possible to provide a 'one size fits all' solution to the calibration of the yield in every case, as different investors and developers have different risk tolerances, costs of capital and which are affected by the rise and fall of base rates.

The discussion begins by looking at inflation in a property context before moving on to consider the cost of capital and risk premiums all of which have a bearing on the returns expected from property. There follows a section on gearing which is the balance between debt and equity when funding property developments or investment acquisitions. The chapter rounds up on a mathematical theme where formulas are considered which structure a relationship between the investor's yield expectations and what level of growth is then required in an asset to achieve those expectations. There are five self-assessment questions at the end of the chapter, the solutions to which can be found towards the end of the book.

10.2 Inflation

Inflation can have a corrosive effect on the real value of assets and incomes, although if the value of those assets or incomes grows annually at the same rate as inflation, there is a neutral effect. Thus if the value of a house rises by 4 per cent in a year when the inflation rate also happened to be 4 per cent then the house owner is neither better nor worse off in real terms. Regarding incomes, if an employee's annual wage increased by 2 per cent in a year when the inflation rate was 4 per cent the employee would be 2 per cent worse off in real terms. Of course if the figures were reversed the employee would be 2 per cent better off in real terms.

A long standing and widely accepted measure of inflation is the Retail Price Index (RPI) which records price changes in a representative 'basket of goods' which an average person might purchase. In that manner the RPI is felt to be a reliable barometer of the cost of living. For this reason pensions and contracts involving financial transactions are often 'index linked', guaranteeing that the pensions or payments under a contract will increase at the same rate of inflation measured by RPI over time.

There is an alternative measure of inflation which is the Consumer Price Index (CPI) which excludes a number of items considered by RPI. For that reason the CPI tends to produce a lower numerical representation of inflation than RPI. CPI is not used so widely as a benchmark for inflation in contracts, perhaps because there is a latent suspicion that CPI is under-recording the real phenomenon of inflation. In most of the business and property world the key measure of inflation remains RPI and that will be the measure adopted in this text. Table 10.1 below is based upon data collated by the Office for National Statistics (2011) and it shows how inflation as measured by RPI has performed between 1980 and 2010 in the UK.

Recognizing that high inflation can have a damaging effect on the economy, successive governments have tried to keep inflation under control by setting

Table 10.1 Inflation as measured by the Retail Price Index 1980–2010

Year	Inflation rate (RPI)	Index	Year	Inflation rate (RPI)	Index
1980	18.0%	100	1996	2.4%	228.8
1981	11.9%	111.9	1997	3.1%	235.9
1982	8.6%	121.5	1998	3.4%	243.9
1983	4.6%	127.1	1999	1.5%	247.5
1984	5.0%	133.5	2000	3.0%	255.0
1985	6.1%	141.6	2001	1.8%	259.6
1986	3.4%	146.4	2002	1.7%	264.0
1987	4.2%	152.6	2003	2.9%	271.6
1988	4.9%	160.1	2004	3.0%	279.8
1989	7.8%	172.5	2005	2.8%	287.6
1990	9.5%	188.9	2006	3.2%	296.8
1991	5.9%	200.1	2007	4.3%	309.6
1992	3.7%	207.5	2008	4.0%	322.0
1993	1.6%	210.8	2009	−0.5%	320.3
1994	2.4%	215.9	2010	4.6%	335.1
1995	3.5%	223.4			

Average over all 31 years: 4.6%
Average over the final 10 years: 2.8%

what is seen as an acceptable threshold (such as 2 per cent) beyond which measures could be taken to try to curb inflation. However this is easier said than done and Table 10.1 illustrates that inflation has varied between 18.0 per cent in 1980 and –0.51 per cent in 2009.

If the time series were extended further back it would show that inflation reached 24.2 per cent in 1975 as the result of a number of factors including global economic phenomena. However the average figure of 4.6 per cent over 31 years and 2.8 per cent over the last 10 years at least provides some parameters on how inflation *might* behave going forward. However history is only a guide in this respect and it would only take a surge in food prices or oil prices on world markets to adversely affect domestic inflation rates.

The precise rate of annual inflation can therefore be unpredictable and susceptible to global price shocks and commodity shortages. However as Table 10.1 illustrates there was only one year when the cost of living actually fell back as reflected by –0.51 per cent rate in 2009. For this reason investors are constantly reassessing the performance of investment assets against inflation to see if those assets are performing better than or at least in line with the inflation rate. Investors will tend to dispose of assets which perform below the inflation rate as they are not achieving any real growth and to look for investments which exhibit real growth.

This raises the question of whether there is any truth in the cliché that property is 'a hedge against inflation'. The answer of course depends on the property type, the location and over what time frame the comparison is to be made. Table 10.2, for example, contains average terraced house prices recorded by the Department for Communities (2011) over 11 years for the four constituent countries of the UK. The average annual change in price over that period is in each case above the average annual inflation rate which as Table 10.1 above revealed was 2.8 per cent.

The data below could of course be converted into an index if that presentational format were preferred, but it would still confirm that the increase in average terraced house prices over this period has comfortably outstripped

Table 10.2 Average terraced house prices and annual percentage changes

Year	England Price £	Annual change	Wales Price £	Annual change	Scotland Price £	Annual change	Northern Ireland Price £	Annual change
2000	82,298		47,771		54,831		50,252	
2001	92,193	12.0%	53,079	11.1%	58,190	6.1%	57,302	14.0%
2002	105,739	14.7%	59,577	12.2%	55,118	–5.3%	56,379	–1.6%
2003	129,298	22.3%	75,629	26.9%	72,215	31.0%	65,320	15.9%
2004	151,410	17.1%	97,512	28.9%	90,824	25.8%	74,764	14.5%
2005	161,039	6.4%	108,451	11.2%	101,629	11.9%	89,551	19.8%
2006	170,607	5.9%	115,502	6.5%	105,354	3.7%	115,694	29.2%
2007	186,837	9.5%	124,824	8.1%	127,136	20.7%	159,946	38.2%
2008	188,139	0.7%	121,408	–2.7%	135,090	6.3%	142,874	–10.7%
2009	185,737	–1.3%	116,939	–3.7%	140,974	4.4%	118,885	–16.8%
2010	212,846	14.6%	124,940	6.8%	153,440	8.8%	113,367	–4.6%
	Average	10.2%	Average	10.5%	Average	11.3%	Average	9.8%

inflation. A similar exercise could of course be conducted for other house types such as detached or semi-detached houses or flats, with broadly similar results arising.

Of course averages across whole countries are indicative of general trends and there will inevitably be some localized housing markets in each country where local housing markets may have underperformed relative to the benchmark of inflation. Values also fell around the time of the credit crunch (2008–2009) and so if a comparison was made only across those two years, then in some of the housing markets house prices would not have performed better than the inflation rate.

The general picture however which emerges from the above is that if a sufficient time horizon such as 10 years is considered, then house prices do seem to have comfortably outperformed inflation.

Regarding commercial property, the IPD (Investment Property Databank) has been monitoring the long term financial performance of 11,276 commercial properties, which is widely agreed to be a representative sample of all commercial properties in the UK. The IPD index suggests that commercial property when measured over a reasonable time frame could also be said to be a hedge against inflation. However as for housing, it is inevitable that there will be some poor performing properties concealed within the averages which may not perform as well as inflation. There will also be inevitable differences in financial performance across different property sectors and if the sample were disaggregated it would be found that industrial property has performed marginally better than retail property, which in turn has performed better than offices. Geographical and qualitative differences between properties held in such a large sample are also facts of life which would not be readily apparent in the averaging process.

Notwithstanding the above comments on statistical averages, the IPD (2000) property index is accepted as being generally representative of the financial performance of commercial investment properties. Over the period 1980–2010 the IPD index rose from 100 to 1,403.4 reflecting an average annual rise of 9.2 per cent (rounded up). In simple terms this means that for every £1 invested in an average commercial investment property the investor notionally received a 9.2 per cent return based partly on annual income and partly on annual capital growth (so called annualized returns). Thus the IPD index has easily outstripped annual inflation, which over the same period (as Table 10.1 above revealed) rose by an annual average of 4.6 per cent taking the inflation index from 100 in 1980 to 335.1 in 2010.

In common with the housing market however, if the comparison had been made over a much shorter time frame such as the two years around the credit crunch, the losses made on commercial properties at that time would suggest that commercial property was not a hedge against inflation. Thus a longer term perspective needs to be taken with commercial and residential property before deciding whether 'bricks and mortar' are a good hedge against inflation.

As well as providing a comparison with inflation, the IPD index enables comparisons to be made between commercial property and alternative investments such as bonds (government gilt edged stock) and equities (FTSE company shares) as follows.

- The property index rose from 100 to 1,403.4 from 1980 and 2010 suggesting an average annual rise of 9.2 per cent (rounded up).
- The bonds index rose from 100 to 1,784 from 1980 and 2010 suggesting an average annual rise of 10.1 per cent (rounded up).
- The equities index rose from 100 to 3,350.5 from 1980 and 2010 suggesting an average annual rise of 12.4 per cent (rounded up).

The summary comparison above suggests that commercial property as an investment has performed less well than alternative investment opportunities, however this is a simple comparison which is silent about risk. Although equities have apparently performed more strongly there is more risk of a total loss with that type of intangible investment and thus given the increased risk there should be a commensurately higher reward. Bonds have less risk as they are government backed and thus far the government has never failed to redeem bonds, hence the expression 'gilt-edged stock'. The reduced risk therefore explains their lower reward relative to equities.

Freehold property is a tangible asset and so whatever the financial performance there still remains a site and usually a building which could be exploited in a number of different ways. Property returns are also loosely correlated with those of bonds and shares and thus investors who wish to diversify their portfolio would include some property investments to achieve this diversity which reduces risk. This issue is perhaps extending a little beyond the scope of this book but readers who might want to go further on this aspect could look at Isaac and O'Leary (2011) for example.

A time series compiled by the Office for National Statistics (2011) showing annual inflation from 1949 to 2010 reveals that there was only one year (2009) when there was negative inflation and even then it was only –0.5 per cent. There is therefore historical evidence that 'prices go up' and this reduces the spending power of money. A prudent property investor would therefore include an inflation allowance when deciding upon a target rate of return.

Different investors will anticipate inflation differently depending on whether they take a pessimistic or optimistic outlook on the economy while others will pragmatically adopt the Treasury forecast for the particular year. Table 10.1 above reveals a relatively low average inflation rate of 2.8 per cent in the 10 years leading up to 2010 whilst a longer-term perspective from 1980 revealed a higher average annual rate of 4.6 per cent. Given those parameters an investor might therefore form a judgment on what was a reasonable inflation expectation.

10.3 Cost of capital

There are two aspects to the cost of capital depending on whether an investor already has the money, in which case it is referred to as equity, or whether the investor is borrowing the money, in which case it is debt. If the investor already has the money the cost of capital is the opportunity cost of investing it in a safe interest-bearing account. This might be a bank or building society account or gilt-edged stock but the effect will be similar in that the money will earn the minimum rate of interest available in the market at the particular time. The rate of interest is therefore sometimes referred to as the risk-free rate. This element exists as compensation to an investor who has invested money and cannot therefore use it while it is on deposit.

The risk-free rate will move in harmony with any changes to the base rate made by the Bank of England Monetary Policy Committee. So for example when the Monetary Policy Committee decides that base rates should be 1 per cent to assist the management of the national economy, the best risk-free rate that could be earned in the market will be slightly above that. Depending on the size of the deposits which savers/investors could make, the best that they might therefore achieve in that scenario would probably be somewhere between 1.5 per cent and 2 per cent, which represents the opportunity cost of their equity.

However, most investments of any scale will necessitate some borrowing to supplement an investor's equity stake. The obvious example is a house purchase where the purchaser might be contributing a relatively small equity stake whilst borrowing might represent the larger part of the expenditure. Lenders will typically source capital from the money markets at LIBOR (London Interbank Offer Rate) which is a fractional margin above the base rate. However when recycling the money in the form of loans to borrowers the banks will normally add a risk premium depending on who the borrower is and what the money is being used for. Traditionally this risk premium might be between 3 and 5 per cent over LIBOR, although if the money were being borrowed for something particularly risky, such as developing speculative offices in an untried location, the margin above LIBOR might extend beyond 5 per cent.

Baum *et al.* (2006: 49) confirm that there is little point in borrowing money at say 8 per cent and then investing it in an asset which will provide an annual return of 8 per cent. An investor would simply be treading water in such a scenario and while the cost of capital is being met there is no incentive for the investor to borrow the money in the first instance. There would therefore have to be a mark up above the investor's cost of capital or if not then, the capital value of the asset would need to be maturing to be redeemed as a capital gain at a later date.

As mentioned above most property investors and developers will combine some equity with borrowed funds to carry out a development or to purchase completed and tenanted schemes. The discussion later in this chapter on gearing (see section 10.5) suggests that it makes sense for developers or investors to keep the equity stake to modest proportions, thereby using it as leverage for a larger borrowed element. So for example an investor who is to purchase a commercial investment property for £10 million (inclusive of all purchase costs) might contribute £1.5 million of equity to supplement a loan of £8.5 million. The opportunity cost on the equity might be 1.5 per cent while the borrowing rate on the loan might be 8 per cent. As Fraser (2004: 110) confirms the investor's weighted average cost of capital for this purchase would be:

$$((1.5/10) \times 1.5\%) + ((8.5/10) \times 8\%) = 7.025\%$$

If the annualized return on the property represented by its rental income plus capital growth equated to 7 per cent, there would have to be some other reason why an investor would take on such a venture. The latter might be the promise of realizing some latent development value in the site at a future date or perhaps that the property had some potential for future rental growth.

The average weighted cost of capital will be specific to particular investors and developers who will have varying amounts of equity at their disposal and differential access to the most preferential borrowing rates in the market. There is also a temporal dimension in that as base rates move, so will the risk-free rate and the borrowing rate.

10.4 Risk premium

As noted above there is little incentive for an organization or individual to invest in or to develop a scheme which produces a return that is exactly the same or lower than the cost of capital. There has to be some incentive and an allowance for inflation otherwise the venture is pointless in the absence of some other special reason. This is where the concept of risk premium comes in.

There is thought to be a trade-off between risk and reward and for additional risk a greater reward is expected by an investor or developer. Even then different organizations and individuals have different tolerances to risk. Risk-averse individuals and organizations will require higher rates of return to tempt them away from risk-free investments than will risk seeking individuals or organizations.

Different types of ventures present different types of risk and there is even a distinction drawn between *systematic risk* (which are those that all similar assets face such as market turbulence) and *unsystematic risk* (which are specific risks raised by the peculiarities of the property or venture).

Consider for example the risks posed to a property investor who is purchasing the freehold of a recently let commercial property to a blue-chip company on a long FRI lease. Although the investor is probably looking at a reasonably secure income stream with potential capital growth, there remain some risks. The latter includes liquidity risk, which is the difficulty of reconverting this high value, specialized, non-divisible asset into cash at short notice. There are a limited number of potential purchasers for this type of asset so the market is not competition rich and sales can take a considerable length of time to broker. However the risks involved in purchasing this already income-bearing asset are significantly less than those faced by a developer who is embarking on a speculative development in an untried location. The risk premium in the first example would therefore be quite modest whereas in the second example the risk premium would need to be significant to reflect the number and extent of the risks involved.

In a property context Baum *et al.* (2006: 70) have identified different types of risks which include:

- Tenant risk: the risks of voids or default on the rent perhaps due to company failure.
- Sector risks: some sectors of the economy may be more prone to financial turmoil and therefore tenant default during periods of economic contraction or cuts in public spending.
- Legislation and tax risk where changes in these regimes may adversely affect property.
- Planning risk which might create external change in the environment or which might affect the type and scale of development envisaged by a developer on a site.

- Legal risk: perhaps undiscovered legal constraints on the legal title of land or legal challenge from a third party for an unanticipated reason.

Baum (2009: 142–3) has extended this concept by apportioning a percentage rate or slice of the risk attributable to each factor which when added to the risk-free rate obtainable on gilts, produces an overall discount rate. However in the end, the calibration of the elements of the risk premium will involve a degree of subjectivity and comparison with other more or less risky ventures which the organization or individual has experience with. While this type of exercise is useful in helping an investor identify and think about the types of risk involved in a venture, it is not possible to be overly prescriptive on what risk premiums should be in each case.

Perhaps a more pragmatic approach is to consider what property investors have historically tolerated as an overall rate or return and which subsumes within it an allowance for risk. The IPD index above revealed that over a lengthy period it seems that property investors were earning an average annual rate of return of around 9 per cent on a wide category of commercial property. If the cost of capital to those investors had been say 5 per cent and that they had built in some allowance for inflation at say 2 per cent it could be deduced that the risk premium was 2 per cent.

Of course the relationship is not that mechanical, and indeed there are other factors which could be factored into the equation such as an allowance for depreciation. What might be said is that the presence of this background data does provide a relative benchmark for other types of venture. Thus if tenanted commercial properties are returning an average of 9 per cent then an investor could consider other investment media which promises this rate of return and whether the risks are commensurate. Similarly a developer who creates the property assets in the first instance should expect a higher rate of return than the investor, given the wider range of risk exposure which development entails. It is not surprising therefore that development appraisals will factor in a developer's return in the order of 15 to 20 per cent depending on the particular project.

10.5 Gearing

Gearing, which is called leveraging in the United States, describes the ratio between borrowing (debt) and a developer's or investor's own money (equity) which in combination enable the funding of development or the acquisition of property investments. Getting the balance right between debt and equity to fund a particular venture is crucial in determining the returns (or losses) to an investor.

During periods of financial uncertainty, the banks, building societies and financial institutions who lend against property make the decision easier on what the debt to equity ratio should be in any particular case by lowering the ceiling on loan to cost ratios. Thus if the cost to acquire a major investment property is £10 million then during difficult market conditions a lender might go as far as lending 65 per cent of the purchase price of the asset, i.e. a 65 per cent loan to value ratio or LTV. The purchaser will have to contribute the remaining 35 per cent from equity or alternatively source those funds from expensive 'borrowing of the last resort' in the form of mezzanine finance.

To illustrate the gearing effect, an investor is exploring the opportunity of purchasing a large country house for £1,000,000 as the market for this type of asset in the particular location is strengthening and an annual growth rate of 10 per cent in value is forecast. The investor plans to keep the house for two years before selling it on. The property will be let out for most of that time and the rental income will pay for building maintenance, insurance, stamp duty, fees associated with purchase and disposal and to cover interest forgone on the investor's equity stake in the house. This is something of a simplification to enable a focus on the gearing effect.

The investor is assumed to have a good track record in this type of venture and therefore a bank is willing to provide a considerable fixed rate interest only loan at 7 per cent to fund this type of acquisition. The investor, who could contribute up to £400,000 towards the purchase if required, decides to model a couple of gearing options to see which one makes the most financial sense.

Option 1 Purchase the £1 million house with equity of £400,000 and a £600,000 loan

House sale price achieved after 2 years reflecting 10% annual growth	£1,210,000
Repay loan which was 60% of the original house price	£600,000
Account for 2 years' interest-only loan payments at 7%	£84,000
Balance	£526,000
Profit after deducting original equity stake of £400,000	£126,000

Return on capital invested over 2 years = $\dfrac{£126,000}{£400,000}$ = 31.5%

Equivalent to an annual rate of return of: 14.67%

Option 2 Purchase the £1 million house with equity of £100,000 and a £900,000 loan

House sale price achieved after 2 years reflecting 10% annual growth	£1,210,000
Repay loan which was 90% of the original house price	£900,000
Account for 2 years' interest-only loan payments at 7%	£126,000
Balance	£184,000
Profit after deducting original equity stake of £100,000	£84,000

Return on capital invested over 2 years = $\dfrac{£84,000}{£100,000}$ = 84.0%

Equivalent to an annual rate of return of: 35.6%

The comparison above reveals that the higher gearing in Option 2, where a higher proportion of debt to equity was used, enabled a higher rate of return on equity where the investment had performed positively. Thus in Option 2 an initial equity investment of £100,000 saw the return of the equity stake plus £84,000 on top, i.e. £184,000. The annual interest rate which has been earned by investing £100,000 over two years in this investment could be identified by the following calculation.

$$(1 + i)^n \times £100,000 = £184,000$$

$$(1 + i)^2 = £184,000/£100,000$$

$$1 + i = 1.84^{1/2}$$

$$i = 0.356 = 35.6\%$$

In this example, the investor who had £400,000 of equity to invest, would achieve superior returns on that money if it were used to fund four house acquisitions of £1 million using the £100,000 stake as leverage in each case rather than investing the whole £400,000 in one venture as in Option 1 above. This is essentially the principle underpinning buy-to-let investment, where it often makes more financial sense for small investors to use their limited equity to lever in larger loans. The ambition (which is not always realized) is therefore to use a bank's or the building society's money to make more money.

However, high gearing, such as the 90/10 relationship shown in Option 2 above, is very risky, as the borrower is carrying a large debt on which the interest has to be serviced and the capital eventually repaid. The higher the gearing the more dependent the investor becomes on the financial performance of the asset. High gearing also exposes the smaller equity element to more risk because it is the first element of funding to evaporate when things go wrong. It is not surprising therefore that during periods when the property values fall that highly geared developers and investors are at considerable risk from financial collapse. This is especially true where loans are on a floating rate basis and interest rate changes also conspire against overstretched borrowers.

To illustrate the risks involved, the calculations below reflect the same scenario and gearing ratios as above but where the value of the £1 million house did not perform as expected. In this scenario, the house had lost 5 per cent of its original value when sold after two years. It does not require a major recession for this type of event to occur, and this would be a modest fall in value perhaps reflecting a dormant or slow market. Note the considerable losses in the highly geared scenario where all of the equity is lost and in addition a further £76,000 of debt is accumulated.

If the developer had used the 400,000 as leverage for four such schemes, the relatively mild down turn in the market would have seen the loss of £400,000 of equity invested plus £304,000 of debt (4 × £76,000), i.e. an overall loss of £704,000. In the less highly geared Option 1 scenario, the original £400,000 invested would have reduced to £266,000 so by comparison a smaller loss of £134,000 would have been made.

Option 1 but where the value of the property falls over two years by 5%

Purchase the £1 million house with equity of £400,000 and a £600,000 loan

House sale price achieved after 2 years reflecting a 5% fall in value	£950,000
Repay loan which was 60% of the original house price	£600,000
Account for 2 years' interest-only loan payments at 7%	£84,000
Balance	£266,000
Loss after deducting original equity stake of £400,000	£134,000

Loss on capital invested over 2 years = $\dfrac{£134,000}{£400,000}$ −33.5%

Option 2 but where the value of the property falls over 2 years by 5%

Purchase the £1 million house with equity of £100,000 and a £900,000 loan

House sale price achieved after 2 years reflecting a 5% fall in value	£950,000
Repay interest loan which was 90% of the original house price	£900,000
Account for 2 years' interest-only loan payments at 7%	£126,000
Balance	−£76,000
Loss including the loss of the equity stake of £100,000	−£176,000

Loss on capital invested over 2 years = $\dfrac{-176,000}{£100,000}$ −176.0%

10.6 The equated yield

Forecasted growth can be built into DCF cash flows so that the internal rate of return (IRR) which arises is referred to as the *equated yield*. The latter is the yield resulting from explicit growth in income. Because this type of exercise is forward looking it is a form of financial modelling which is exploring the overall return to an investor if a particular growth of rental income is realized. The expression 'what if' is sometimes used in this context, as the analysis is trying to find out what the IRR/equated yield would be if the growth in rental income were X per cent.

Equated yield analysis requires the adoption of a realistic judgement of what the annual growth rate might be and which might be derived from assessing historic growth trends for the particular asset class. Once the expected annual growth rate has been identified it can then be applied to the original income using the compound interest formula which is the Amount of £1. The tranches of rental income reflecting growth can then be inserted into a DCF to identify the IRR which would then result. Property investors who have specific minimum rates of return in mind could therefore model at different rental growth rates to see whether an investment was likely to deliver their required rate of return.

To illustrate the process a vendor is offering the freehold of a recently completed office building for sale with offers invited in excess of £2,500,000. This investment opportunity has recently been let at a market rent of £187,500 on a 20-year lease with five-year rent reviews. A property investor who is interested in the property has undertaken some preliminary research and feels that this type of asset could realistically achieve annual rental growth in the region of 4 per cent. On the basis that the property would be sold at the end of the lease, the investor has applied the 4 per cent growth rate to see if the investment property would meet the investor's minimum IRR/equated yield of 10 per cent for investments like this as follows:

Purchase price: £2,500,000   Initial annual rent: £187,500
Trial equated yields: 9% and 11%   Rent review frequency: 5 years
Expected rental growth rate per annum: 4%   Disposal of the asset in year 21
Investor's minimum rate of return: 10%
Initial yield: 7.50% and so the YP in perpetuity is: 13.3333
Exit yield: 9.00% and so the YP in perpetuity is: 11.1111

DCF with a trail rate of 9%

Years	Amount of £1 @ 4%	Cash flow £	PV £1 @ 9%	Deferred YP	PV of slice £
0	n/a	−2,500,000	1		−2,500,000
1–5	n/a	187,500	1	3.8897	729,319
6–10	1.2167	228,131	0.6499	2.5279	576,692
11–15	1.4802	277,538	0.4224	1.6430	455,995
16–20	1.8009	337,669	0.2745	1.0677	360,529
21	2.1911	410,831	0.1637	1.8189	747,261
				NPV =	369,796

DCF with a trail rate of 11%

Years	Amount of £1 @ 4%	Cash flow £	PV £1 @ 11%	Deferred YP	PV of slice £
0	n/a	−2,500,000	1		−2,500,000
1 – 5	n/a	187,500	1	3.6959	692,981
6 – 10	1.2167	228,131	0.5935	2.1935	500,405
11 – 15	1.4802	277,538	0.3522	1.3017	361,271
16 – 20	1.8009	37,669	0.2090	0.7724	260,816
21	2.1911	410,831	0.1117	1.2411	509,882
				NPV =	− 174,645

Having identified a positive and negative NPV using the two trial rates in the DCFs above, the investor can use the interpolation formula to identify the IRR as follows:

$$\text{IRR} = 9\% + (2\% \times (369{,}796/544{,}441)) = 10.36\%$$

In this case the investor's minimum target rate of return of 10 per cent is just met with a very small margin to spare. This might cause the investor to do a number of things including seeking to negotiate on the asking price for the property to improve the margin. The investor might also model at progressively lower rental growth rates such as 3.5 or 3 per cent to see whether even in those slightly more pessimistic scenarios the overall rate of return would still be 10 per cent or above.

The two DCFs above reflect five-year rent review periods during which the income cannot change. The cash flows for each five-year period have been inflated by the amount of £1 at the investor's envisaged growth rate of 4 per cent to the beginning of each period. The period cash flows are valued by capitalizing them at the trial rates for the respective five-year periods (YP 5 years at 9 per cent and 11 per cent). These are multiplied by the respective PV of £1 value to give the deferred YP which is multiplied by the inflated cash flow to give the value of the deferred slice. The values of the deferred slices are added together to give the overall net present value in each of the DCFs.

In the scenario the disposal of the asset is assumed to take place in year 21 and so the proceeds from that disposal are discounted at both trial rates for that length of time. Thus the present value arising from of the sale of the asset in 21 years' time in the 9 per cent trial-rate version above is shown to be £747,261. The latter is based upon the capitalized rental value which is assumed to have grown by 4 per cent per annum over 20 years to have reached £410,831. An exit yield of 9 per cent is used for that process and which reflects a slackening from the initial yield of 7.5 per cent to reflect the fact that the building will have aged 20 years and would then be far less competitive in market terms than it once was due to obsolescence. The figures used to generate the deferred YP in year 21 are therefore:

PV of £1 in 21 years at 9% = $1/((1 + 0.09)^{21})$ = 0.1637 (rounded to four decimal places)

Capitalization at 9% = 1/0.09 = 11.1111 YP in perp. (rounded to four decimal places)

The deferred YP in perpetuity is therefore: $0.1637 \times 11.1111 = 1.8189$ (rounded to four decimal places)

The present value of the sale is therefore: $1.8189 \times £410,831 = £747,261$ (rounded up to the nearest pound).

For presentational purposes the figures in this example have been rounded up to 4 decimal places and so a recalculation with a calculator or in Excel without rounding will give a slightly different (but essentially the same) answer.

The calculation to identify the equated yield required a positive and negative NPV to enable interpolation between the two figures. Two trail rates of 9 per cent and 11 per cent were employed for this purpose and interpolation then identified the yield which is the IRR and which is 10.36 per cent. If a DCF were run using the IRR as the discount rate, the NPV arising would be zero confirming that the investment made no more nor less that that rate of return. Of course Excel can identify the IRR on the basis of one trial run and in that context the interpolation formula becomes a secondary checking option.

10.7 The implied growth rate

In section 10.6 above the scenario was exploring whether on the basis of an assumed and explicit annual rate of rental growth, the purchase of an investment property would meet an investor's minimum rate of return, which in that example was 10 per cent. The challenge can be approached differently, so that given the asking price for an investment, it is possible to identify the annual rate of rental growth which would be needed in order to deliver the investor's target rate of return.

There is something to be said for this approach because the future is uncertain and even on the basis of the best research and forecasting, there will remain some uncertainty around rental growth rates in the future. Thus this approach inputs the known variables which are the asking price for the investment, the passing rent and the rent review periods to see what rate of rental growth would be needed to meet the investor's minimum target rate of return.

When that rate of growth is identified the investor could stand back and consider whether such a rate of growth was a reasonable or unreasonable expectation. If historically the rate of growth on a particular type of property has been say 3 per cent but that to meet investor expectations the growth rate on the asset would need to be say 6 per cent, i.e. twice the historic rate, the investor should see that this was stretching credibility. In that scenario either the asset's asking price would have to be reduced to balance the equation or the investor could move on to consider other, perhaps more credible, investment opportunities.

To illustrate the concept of the implied growth rate, a corporate property investor is considering the purchase of the freehold of a shop which was recently let on a 15-year lease with five-year rent reviews. The retail tenant is paying a market rent of £40,800 and agents acting for the vendor have received lots of expressions of interest and are confident that the asking price of £680,000 will be met. Before making a commitment, the investor decides to use the formula below which will reveal the annual growth rate required to enable the asset to achieve the investor's minimum rate of return of 10 per cent for this type of asset.

$$(1 + g)^t = \frac{\text{YP perp. @ } k - \text{YP } t \text{ years @ } e}{\text{YP perp. @ } k \times \text{PV } t \text{ years @ } e}$$

Variables which will need to be transposed into the equation to identify the growth rate: g are k, t and e and these are as follows:

k is the capitalization rate which in this example is: $\dfrac{£40,800}{£680,000} = 0.06 = 6\%$

e is the investor's minimum target rate of return and which is 10% in this example.

t is the frequency of rent reviews under the lease and which is 5 years in the example.

When inserted into the formula the following calculation emerges in which for presentational purposes there has been rounding up to 4 decimal places. At this point some readers may wish to refamiliarize themselves with the formulas for YP in perp. and YP for n years covered in Chapter 3 of this book.

$$(1 + g)^t = \frac{16.6667 - 3.7908}{16.6667 \times 0.6209} = \frac{12.8759}{10.3484}$$

$$(1 + g)^5 = 1.2442$$
$$1 + g = 1.2442^{1/5}$$
$$g = 0.0447 = 4.47\%$$

The annual rental growth rate required in order that the investor's overall rate of return of 10 per cent is met is therefore 4.47 per cent, which at first sight appears to be a fairly modest expectation. However during periods of recession there can be zero or negative growth and (as discussed in Chapter 8) properties can be deemed to be over-rented, so that on rent review the rental value does not increase. Where a high value transaction is envisaged organizations such as IPD can be commissioned to undertake bespoke analysis and forecasting for an investor to try to identify what realistic growth assumptions could be made in any particular case.

If the investor were in any doubt about the rate of growth identified from using the formula above, it is possible to induce the 4.47 per cent growth rate into a DCF as follows to prove the relationships at work. In the DCF the 10 per cent discount rate is the investor's minimum rate of return. Because of the rounding of decimal places at various points the NPV identified by the DCF below and which represents the capital value or asking price in the scenario, differs by £198. However the test does confirm that 4.47 per cent is the rate of growth which this asset would need to achieve in order to meet the investor's minimum rate of return of 10 per cent.

Years	Amount of £1 @ 4.47%	Cash flow £	PV £1 @ 10%	Deferred YP	PV of slice £
0–5	1	40,800	1	3.7908	154,665
6–10	1.2444	50,772	0.6209	2.3537	119,501
1–15	1.5485	63,179	0.3855	1.4614	92,330
16–perp.	1.9270	78,622	0.2394	3.9900	313,702
				NPV =	680,198

There is an alternative formula which some might prefer and which gives the same result as follows:

$$k = e - \frac{e[(1 + g)^{t} - 1]}{(1 + e)^{t} - 1}$$

$$0.06 = 0.1 - \frac{0.1 \times [(1 + g)^{5} - 1]}{(1 + 0.1)^{5} - 1}$$

Which when transposed gives:

$$\frac{0.1 \times [(1 + g)^{5} - 1]}{0.6105} = 0.1 - 0.06$$

$$\frac{(1 + g)^{5} - 1}{6.105} = 0.04$$

$$(1 + g)^{5} - 1 = 0.2442$$

$$1 + g = 1.2442^{1/5}$$

$$g = 4.47\%$$

10.8 Summary

This chapter examined the yield as an interest rate used to reflect the returns from investing in property assets. It was found that theoretically at least the yield should compensate for a number of things including an investor's cost of capital, an allowance for inflation and a reward to taking on the specific bundle of risks posed by an asset. In theory therefore it should be possible to structure an overall yield by adding together the constituent parts.

Whilst it might be possible to pin down an investor's or developer's cost of capital and to make a reasonable allowance for inflation, it is not easy to identify and then be definitive about an allowance for different aspects of risk. For that reason it is probably as instructive to compare what other investors or developers have sought as an 'in the round' return from similar assets in similar circumstances. It is also helpful to look at whether the same return could not be made on other perhaps less risky investment opportunities.

There is a complex interplay of factors and a dynamic quality regarding yields so that it would be too prescriptive to state that an investor must always expect an X per cent return for investing in property type Y in location Z. After all, different investors and developers have different attitudes to risk and interest rate change will inevitably affect each investor's cost of capital. Thus each investment opportunity has to be looked at in the light of its specific time frame and the risk and reward trade off suggested by the asset. Historic investment patterns provide a guide in this respect but they do not neatly solve the challenge of what rate of interest to expect in any particular case.

The chapter ended on a mathematical theme where assuming that an investor was able to commit to a specific target rate of return, it was shown that it is then possible to calculate the annual growth in the asset which would be needed to satisfy the investor's expectations. There are formulas which come into play and the outturn figures can then be run through a discounted cash flow as a way of cross checking the result. The purpose of this type of analysis is perhaps to support better decision-making so that by trying to weigh up whether on historical performance the growth expectations in newly acquired assets were more or less likely to be met.

References

Baum, A., Nunnington, N. and Mackmin, D. (2006) *The Income Approach to Property Valuation* (5th edn, London: EG Books).

Baum, A. (2009) *Commercial Real Estate Investment: A Strategic Approach* (2nd edn, London: EG Books).

Department for Communities (2011) *Table 511 Housing Market: Simple Average House Prices, by Dwelling Type and Region, United Kingdom, from 1986* (London: Department for Communities). Available in e-format at: www.communities.gov.uk

Fraser, W. D. (2004) *Cash-Flow Appraisal for Property Investment* (Basingstoke: Palgrave Macmillan).

IPD (2011) *IPD UK Annual Property Index: Results for the Year to 31 December 2010* (London: Investment Property Databank Ltd). Available in e-format at: www.ipd.com

Isaac, D. and O'Leary, J. (2011) *Property Investment* (2nd edn, Basingstoke: Palgrave Macmillan).

Office for National Statistics (2011) *Retail Price Index (RPI) All Items Percentage Change over 12 Months: Table RP04* (Cardiff: Office for National Statistics). Available in e-format at: www.statisitcs.gov.uk

Self-assessment questions for Chapter 10

1 A property investor is in negotiations to purchase the freehold of a tenanted retail warehouse for £800,000 inclusive of all purchase costs and stamp duty. A bank is willing to lend 80 per cent of the money at an annual interest rate of 9 per cent and the investor will contribute the remaining 20 per cent which could have been invested in gilt edged stock to earn 1.5 per cent. What is the investor's average weighted cost of capital for his venture?

2 Three years after the purchase described above, the investor sells the retail warehouse for £1 million. What has been the return on the investor's equity overall and as an annual rate of return? It can be assumed that during the intervening years the rental income from the retail warehouse paid for the annual interest on the interest only loan.

3 A property investor is to purchase for £910,000 the freehold of an investment property which has been let to a business tenant for 10 years at a market rent of £65,000. There is a rent review after 5 years and it is assumed the rent will then be increased to reflect an annual growth rate of 3 per cent. It is assumed that the property will be sold in year 11 to reflect an exit yield of 9 per cent which will capitalize the rental value at that time which will have grown over the preceding 10 years by 3 per cent per annum. The investor is trying to determine the equated yield and has begun the process below by running two trail rates at 8 and 11 per cent. Complete the cash flow for the second trail rate at 11 per cent to identify the net present value (NPV) there.

Trial rate @ 8%

Years	Amount of £1 @ 3%	Cash flow £	PV £1 @ 8%	Deferred YP	PV of slice £
0	n/a	−910,000	1		−910,000
1–5	n/a	65,000	1	3.9927	259,526
6–10	1.1593	75,355	0.6806	2.7174	204,770
11	1.3439	87,354	0.4632	5.1467	449,585
				NPV =	3,881

Trial rate @ 11%

Years	Amount of £1 @ 3%	Cash flow £	PV £1 @ 11%	Deferred YP	PV of slice £
0	n/a	−910,000			
1–5	n/a	65,000			
6–10	1.1593				
11	1.3439				
				NPV =	

4 Having obtained the NPV for the 11 per cent trial rate above use it along with the NPV for the 8 per cent trail rate in the IRR formula below to identify the project's equated yield.

$$R_1 + [\ (R_2 - R_1) \times \frac{NPV\ @\ R_1}{NPV\ @\ R_1 - NPV\ @\ R_2}\ ]$$

5 Assuming that in the above scenario the investor's target rate of return was 11 per cent use the formula below to identify what the implied rental growth rate would need to be. Earlier in the chapter where this topic was explored k was shown to be the capitalization rate which is the initial rent divided by the capital value, e is the investor's target rate of return and t is the rent review period. The growth rate g is therefore the variable to be identified.

$$(1 + g)^t = \frac{YP\ perp.\ @\ k - YP\ t\ years\ @\ e}{YP\ perp.\ @\ k \times PV\ t\ years\ @\ e}$$

Outline answers are included at the back of the book.

11

Conclusions

11.1 Introduction
11.2 Consolidation on some key themes
11.3 Issues and opportunities for valuers

11.4 Summary
References

Aims
This chapter aims to consolidate understanding around some of the key themes which have been discussed in the book. The chapter also identifies some issues where it could be expected that there will be further development in thinking and practice. It is likely that these issues will resurface for those readers who will go on to study the subject of property valuation at a higher level.

Key terms

>> **Facilities management** – from a property perspective, facilities management seeks to ensure that premises are procured and managed in an optimal way to support the core activities and objectives of an organization.

>> **Densification** – the process by which not particularly well-planned council housing estates can be redeveloped at higher density, providing more but better dwellings on a site. Creative agreements can be engineered between the local authority land owner and private housebuilders in which the land owned becomes leverage for involving a private developer. A local authority is sometimes able to achieve regeneration objectives through densification.

11.1 Introduction

This brief concluding chapter has selected a number of themes which have arisen in the book and upon which some consolidating comments can be made. The chapter also identifies some issues which are likely to develop further in future and which are likely to surface as topics for those who go on to study property valuation and closely related subjects in more depth.

11.2 Consolidation on some key themes

One of the core themes in the book was the exploration of the valuer's toolkit, which could be thought of as the five methods of valuation combined with the valuation tables and their formulas. The valuation tables have evolved to support valuation calculations and given the widespread availability of PCs it is the formula equivalent of the tables which are now more likely to be used within Excel spreadsheets.

In essence a valuer exercises judgement when deciding which method of valuation is applicable to the circumstance encountered and then conducts the calculation with the aid of the valuation tables. There is therefore a judgement stage followed by a calculation stage. While some properties will have similarities and the context might suggest an obvious approach, a valuer will still need to exercise choice each time on how best to use the valuation toolkit. In the background is the RICS Valuation Standards (2011) which is more familiarly known as the Red Book and which sets out minimum standards and core principles which valuers have to remain cognizant with. The Red Book however is not overly prescriptive as it still leaves a lot of discretion in the hands of the valuer.

The five methods of valuation have developed in response to the different types of property and circumstance found in the market. The first of the five methods considered in the book was the comparison method, which most would be familiar with in a housing context, where values are often derived from the analysis of recent sales of similar properties. Comparison has wider applicability than the residential market and for example, it can be applied to development land or commercial property where data on rental values and yields can be derived from market comparison. Where markets are active there will probably be sufficient data for valuers to analyse and apply to the property being valued. The courts and tribunals have signalled through their judgements that they prefer a straightforward valuation approach wherever possible and this is one of the reasons why comparison will always be a consideration for the valuer.

Even when a valuer decides that the comparison method is not applicable to the particular circumstances, it will still play a role in framing the variables in a valuation conducted using an alternative valuation method. Thus in a residual valuation for development purposes, variables such as the building costs per square metre will be benchmarked against the construction costs incurred on similar projects. Similarly, the gross development value of an envisaged development must in the end bear some comparison with contemporary market values for similar developments.

Although comparison is a legitimate approach to valuation it is not just a matter of reducing previous transactions to a unit of comparison and mechanically applying the variable to the subject property. Valuers have to remain alert to rising or falling trends in the particular market. For example a house may have been sold for £200,000 one year ago but this does not necessarily mean that it or houses very similar to it will realize the same figure now. Markets move and circumstances change and this is where judgement is needed by the valuer to adjust the variables arising from comparison.

Despite its merits, comparison cannot be used as the principal method in all circumstances and four further methods of valuation then become choices for the valuer. Chapter 5 looked at the profits method which is often used to value leisure properties where the value of the premises is directly connected to the financial performance of the business. Chapter 6 examined the contractor's method where there is no market for the particular property type and there are no accounts which could be used to support a profits method evaluation. The contractor's method is more formally known as the depreciated replacement cost method and it works from the basis of the cost to provide a modern replacement building which is then depreciated to reflect the actual subject building.

Chapter 7 considered the residual valuation method which is used in development situations to assess the value of development sites given their development potential. The latter is often confirmed by a planning consent which establishes the quantum and type of development and which enables a valuer to identify the gross development value of a scheme. The residual valuation was found to be particularly sensitive to relatively minor changes to its large value variables, and for that reason the concept of sensitivity testing is a valid addition to this type of appraisal.

Chapter 8 discussed the traditional investment method which capitalizes rental income using the Years' Purchase (YP) multiplier. It was found that the YP is the reciprocal of an interest rate which is calibrated by a valuer based upon knowledge of yields on similar property investments in the market. The valuer might adjust the yield (and therefore the YP multiplier) to reflect the perception of risk to the income stream and thus the yield calibration implies the risks involved. This approach has been criticized as a 'dark art' because the margin of adjustment made to the yield by the valuer can seem arbitrary and lacking in explicit justification. However the method is still widely used especially for straightforward investment valuations.

Chapter 9 considered a more explicit approach to investment valuations which sets out future income from an investment property in a discounted cash flow format. The calibration of the discount rate absorbs the investor's cost of capital and in addition it reflects the trade-off between risk and reward suggested by the asset. This type of valuation is felt to be applicable to high value property investments around which financial modelling of different rental and capital growth rates can be explored.

Some readers who may be new to the subject of property valuation may have imaged that they were coming to a body of knowledge which was fixed, largely governed by mathematical formulas and which gave rise to absolutely certain valuation figures. However those readers may have experienced something of a culture shock because while there is some truth in the above preconceptions, valuations are in fact only best estimates which come with an implied tolerance. The process is not as scientific as might be imagined and as was discussed in the book, valuers are constantly required to use their creative powers of interpretation to get the best out of the valuation toolkit.

At various points in the discussion it was stressed that valuation is an art rather than a science and that part of the practice of that art requires skilled and experienced practitioners to form judgements around which method of valuation to use in the circumstances encountered. Sometimes valuers have to make assumptions or create delicate fictions to overcome imperfections found in the market, such as a lack of market transactions for the particular property type. Valuers therefore have to be creative individuals as well as being competent with formulas and figures.

It was also explained that as valuers develop their careers they will tend to specialize and to become knowledgeable about particular sectors of the market and particular geographical contexts. Indeed it was found that there is no such thing as one cohesive property market but a number of sub market divided by tenure and building type and it would not be reasonable for valuers to move across all of these boundaries in a seamless manner. The valuer's professional body, the RICS, reminds valuers in the Red Book that they should think very carefully before undertaking a commission which takes them outside of their usual sphere of activity.

> The valuer must have sufficient local, national and international (as appropriate) knowledge of the particular market, and the skills and understanding necessary, to undertake the valuation competently. (2011: 14)

The RICS's Valuer Registration Scheme has been put in place to ensure that this type of advice is adhered to by valuers in their day to day activities both in the UK and overseas where RICS is rapidly becoming a global brand.

11.3 Issues and opportunities for valuers

Sustainability is an agenda which will continue to evolve and which valuers will have to continuously monitor as knowledge develops on how to translate sustainability accreditations attached to properties into tangible value added. These challenges could also be seen as opportunities which will widen the employability of valuers beyond providing traditional services such as valuing property investment portfolios for corporate clients.

There are a number of areas where valuers will increasingly be called upon to give advice and which include valuing and advising on funding for different affordable housing formats which the UK government have been promoting for a number of years. As the government's Community Infrastructure Levy is taken up by more local authorities there will be a need for robust valuation advice on development viability and site values.

Some local authorities are also beginning to explore how to use their land assets creatively in the context of densification projects where private development partners are brought in to assist with housing estate renewal. One such example is within the London Borough of Greenwich where the authority has been tackling regeneration at the Kidbrooke Estate which it owns. The cost to bring the existing council housing stock shown in Figure 11.1 up to decent homes standards would have been prohibitive and so an ambitious renewal programme was embarked upon based upon the principle of densification. In simple terms densification means that land is redeveloped so that it can be used more efficiently for new housing but that this does not necessarily mean that the resulting development is overly dense. In fact a more attractive environment can usually be created with careful design.

To tackle this type of financially demanding regeneration project, local authorities need the support of central government via the Homes and

Figure 11.1 Council housing requiring renewal at the Kidbrooke Estate in the London Borough of Greenwich

Communities Agency and private sector partners. At Kidbrooke the council were able to establish such a partnership using their status as freehold owner as leverage. Berkeley Homes was chosen from among a number of private sector bidders to become the council's partner to implement a renewal master plan for what is to become Kidbrooke Village. New housing in phase 1 of the project is shown in Figure 11.2 and it suggests that the partnership is achieving success in tackling the significant regeneration challenges posed by the old estate.

The partnership deals such as those struck at Kidbrooke require careful structuring between the principle partners, which will normally include a local authority, central government agencies, a major housing association and crucially a private developer with a good track record. Brokering these creative deals requires business skills and credible financial evaluation which will include scenario testing. There is therefore a significant role for valuers to play in supporting negotiations and demonstrating that the partners can achieve their financial as well as policy objectives in the light of the risks involved.

There will also be financial modelling opportunities for valuers who will be able to advise clients on the cost benefit relationships between the costs of retro-fitting buildings to attract a sustainability accreditation against a value uplift. Discounted cash flows provide a convenient way to model this type of scenario, enabling comparisons to be made with the do-nothing, redevelop or retro-fit options.

Figure 11.2 New housing emerges from partnership working at Kidbrooke Village

Commercial and residential property has always been interlinked with the banking system which remains the principal source of loans for development and acquisition. Using debt to support the purchase or development of property enables leveraging which can maximize the returns on the developer's or investor's equity contribution. The credit crunch from early 2008 however reminded the financial services and property sectors that risks are an inherent characteristic of markets.

Valuers have an ongoing role in looking at the risks involved in projects and property lending and in trying to advise clients on how best to mitigate against identified risks. Sometimes the best objective advice a valuer can give to a client is not to undertake a project or to borrow heavily, because the circumstances are sometimes too risky. Professional and impartial advice can sometimes appear to be negative, but if it protects clients from complacency and financial difficulty then it is in the end good advice.

Valuer advice on risk and borrowing is as applicable to the large investor as the small investor who might be interested in buy-to-let property investment. The weight of valuation advice, research and publication is weighted towards large lot commercial property investment but there remain opportunities for valuers to expand their activities in the sizeable private rented residential sector. Good professional advice backed by financial modelling will help small investors to make better borrowing and acquisition decisions with what is probably limited equity in most cases.

Facilities management was not a topic discussed in this book because it is a specialism which becomes relevant and to which connections can be made once general valuation principles have been understood. It is flagged up here as a topic which likely to surface for those who will go on to study property valuations at a higher level and where the financial principles being explored in this book can be extended and applied. For example large companies will increasingly need to know whether it is more financially viable to rent premises rather than to try to purchase them or whether they would be better advised to sell their premises and to lease them back under satisfactory terms. These are among the challenges that lie ahead.

11.4 Summary

This chapter provided some consolidating comments on selected themes which arose in the book and which included the scope and application of the valuation toolkit. The chapter also identified some topics which are likely to develop further and which are likely to surface again for those who will go on to pursue the subject of property valuations at a more advanced level in an academic or practical setting.

References

RICS (2011) *RICS Valuation Standards – Global and UK* (7th edn, Coventry: RICS).

Solutions to self-assessment questions

Solutions to self-assessment questions for Chapter 2

Question 1 Key factors which in combination affect property values

Some of the key factors which affect property values and which a property valuer will normally be aware of include:

General or systematic factors

- The national and international economic situation.
- Existing supply of the particular type of property.
- Government policy, tax regimes and interest rates.
- The condition of the local economy.
- The geographical strengths and weaknesses of the location.
- Fashion and trends in demand for the particular type of property.

Specific characteristics of the property:

- State of repair/conditions and decor internally and externally.
- Size, floorspace, number of bedrooms.
- Costs-in-use, sustainability rating (if any).
- Condition and capacity of building services and facilities.
- Building age and design, presence or absence of alterations and/or extensions.
- Fixtures and fittings.
- Development potential.
- Quality and attractiveness of the immediate local environment.
- Proximity to local services.

Question 2 Explaining the term 'invested stock' and who the investors are

Invested stock is properties which are purchased by investors for the promise of rental income from leasing and potentially capital gains when the property is sold on. In the commercial property sector invested stock could be shops, offices, industrial or warehouse units and which will normally be owned by a corporate landlord such as a pension fund or an insurance company or a Real Estate Investment Trust. It is estimated that 43 per cent of all commercial properties are owned on this basis.

In the residential sector invested stock are those dwellings which are rented privately and are sometimes referred to as buy-to-let properties. These dwellings account for 15.5 per cent of all homes in the UK. Investors in this sector tend to be smaller landlords as the large corporates who dominate the commercial property sector have not shown much enthusiasm for investing in residential property.

Question 3 Common circumstances in which a bank might become the client of a valuer

When a developer wishes to carry out a development there will normally be a heavy reliance on borrowed money which will usually come from a bank. To reduce risks, a bank will seldom provide a developer with all of the money required and will expect the developer to contribute some equity. However, the banks needs to know what proportion could reasonably be offered to the developer as a loan and this will in some way be related to the value of the scheme. This is one of the circumstances where the services of a valuer will be called upon by a bank, who will tend to take a cautious view by working to the lower of two independent valuations when lending the money.

Question 4 Explaining the significance of the four Cs in a property lending context

The four 'Cs' essentially summarize a lender's assessment of a borrower's loan application. Thus a lender such as a bank will be interested in whether:

- The borrower has sufficient *character* to be trusted with large sums of money as revealed in the presence or absence of a track record for successfully completing profitable developments on time and within budget.
- Whether there is a sufficient *cashstake* or equity being contributed by the borrower towards the particular scheme.
- Whether the borrower has the *capability* of servicing the loan, which stems from the borrower's business plan which should show the cash flow from the development.
- The borrower can put up sufficient *collateral* to support the scale of loan being sought and which may include the site or other uncharged properties or other assets which the borrower may own.

Question 5 The connections between a valuer's work and CSR and BREEAM

Most organizations now have corporate social responsibility (CSR) policies which extend to procuring buildings which are sustainable and which contribute gains across the triple bottom line of social, environmental and economic. One way to demonstrate in a practical way that organizations are developing, purchasing or using sustainable buildings is for those companies to seek sustainability accreditations for their buildings and which might be a 'good' or 'very good' or 'excellent' rating under BREEAM (Building Research Establishment Environmental Assessment Method). A BREEAM rating can now be found on any new quality commercial building. In the residential sector the equivalent accreditation is the Code for Sustainable Homes which awards a star rating up to six stars which is a zero-carbon home.

At present valuers are expected to show awareness of these accreditations in valuation work, but the precise conversion of these accreditations into the uplift in the value of a property has yet to be developed.

Solutions to self-assessment questions for Chapter 3

Question 1 Whether the valuer should be concerned about the client's claim

The question raises a whole a number of legal issues and more would need to be known about the specific circumstances to be definitive. However, there are some general considerations which would arise in this type of argument and which would have a bearing upon whether the valuer was deemed to have acted in a negligent manner. A key principle is that the valuer was not commissioned to undertake a forecast of how the market would perform over two years and cannot therefore be held accountable for market movements. The valuation was valid at the valuation date and not two years hence. If the valuation was carried out in a competent manner and no obvious factors were overlooked and that the guidelines in the RICS Red Book were followed, the valuer will have a good defence. The valuer's defence will be even stronger if it can be shown that the valuation fell within a bracket of reasonableness which can be assumed in this case to be +/− 10 per cent of what a reasonably competent valuer would have arrived at.

Question 2 Explaining what a statutory valuation is

Statutory valuations need to be carried out because either an Act or statutory instrument requires a valuation to be undertaken for a specific purpose or that the implementation of an Act or statutory instrument has a financial consequence which triggers the need for a valuation. Examples include valuations to determine the rateable value of non-domestic property, valuations to assess the compensation payable for land taken in compulsory purchase or where commercial or residential leases are being extended under relevant legislation.

Question 3 Filling in the gaps in the statement.

The missing parts of the statements are shown underlined as follows.

The _RICS Valuation Standards_ _which is more familiarly known_ as the Red Book recognizes four bases of valuation which are:

1 A valuation to determine market value.
2 A valuation to determine market rent.
3 A valuation to determine worth or investment value.
4 A valuation to determine fair value.

Question 4 The VRS and who it applies to

The RICS's *Valuer Registration Scheme* (VRS) was introduced from 2010 to strengthen the reputation of valuers and to enable the RICS to monitor the standards being achieved by its registered valuers. RICS members who carry out Red Book valuations must be registered under the VRS.

Question 5 Identifying the correct formula to calculate the answer

This is the calculation of what £5,000 will compound into over 12 years in an account earning annual interest at 9 per cent (where tax is not considered). The relevant formula is the *Amount of £1* which is $(1 + i)^n$ where $i = 0.09$ and $n = 12$. When these variables are transposed into the formula the answer is as follows:

$$£5,000 \times (1 + 0.09)^{12} = £14,064$$

(b) The present value of £17,000 receivable in 6 years' time at 8 per cent requires the use of the *Present Value of £1* formula which is $1/(1 + i)^n$ and where $i = 0.08$ and $n = 6$. When these variables are transposed into the formula the answer is as follows:

$$£17,000 \times \frac{1}{(1 + 0.08)^6} = £10,713$$

(c) The sum which will have compounded on the basis of £10,000 being invested each year for 12 years at 7 per cent can be calculated using the *Amount of £1 per annum* formula which is $(1 + i)^n - 1/i$ where $i = 0.07$ and $n = 12$. When these variables are transposed into the formula the answer is as follows:

$$£10,000 \times \frac{(1 + 0.07)^{12} - 1}{0.07} = £178,885$$

Solutions to self-assessment questions for Chapter 4

Question 1 The capital value of the investment property

Given the market yield of 7 per cent the capital value can be found by producing the YP in perpetuity from $1/0.07 = 14.2857$ and then to use it to multiply the net rent of £125,000 to give a capital value of: £1,785,713.

Question 2 The rental valuation for the high street shop

The rental value of £550 per m² in terms of zone A (ITZA) in this high street can be represented by X in the calculation below. The shop, whose dimensions are 6 metres frontage by 16 metres depth, could be zoned using 6 metre depths to identify its value by halving back as follows:

Zone A: 6m × 6m = 36m^2 @ Xm^2 = 36X
Zone B: 6m × 6m = 36m^2 @ 0.5X/m^2 = 18X
Zone C: 6m × 4m = 24m^2 @ 0.25X/m^2 = 6X
Total depth = 16m   60X

The annual rental value of the shop is therefore 60 × £550 per m^2 ITZA from comparables = £33,000.

Question 3 The usual outgoings and who is reliable for them given an FRI lease

The principal outgoings when a full repairing and insuring (FRI) lease is discussed are the internal and external repairs and building insurance premiums. The FRI lease commits the tenant to paying for these outgoings so the rent received by the landlord is said to be the net rent and it may be used for capitalization purposes.

Question 4 The circumstances in which the comparison method is used

The comparison method is essentially a like-for-like comparison. In property it is appropriate to use the comparison method where properties share similar characteristics and where there have been recent market transactions to provide comparable data. This could apply where there is an active market in development land for housing and where a value per hectare or per habitable room can be identified and legitimately used as the unit of comparison. Comparison falls back to fulfil a secondary checking role particularly for development appraisals where unique development proposals do not really have any direct comparisons. Comparison can still play a role in calibrating the variables in a development valuation and for example may help a valuer frame the gross development value of a scheme by looking at recent sales or lettings of similar properties.

Question 5 The other factors valuers need to consider when using the comparison method

Valuation is often described as an art requiring the judgement of the valuer and so while there might be comparable data from similar properties in terms of a value per square metre or value per hectare, the valuer has to remain aware that all properties will in the end be unique and quite subtle differences can affect value. Thus in a residential context although flats in a block may have the same internal space, number of bedrooms and lease terms, there will still be differences between them. These differences will affect value and include the floor the flats are on and thus the types of views obtainable, whether there are balconies, aspect and internal decorative order. Valuers therefore must make reasonable adjustments to comparable market data to suit the specifics of the subject property.

Solutions to self-assessment questions for Chapter 5

Question 1 The circumstances in which a valuer might choose to use the profits method

The profits method of valuation is used where the value of a property is based upon the profit earning potential of a business operating from the premises. The profits method is used where the uniqueness of the property makes it difficult to identity direct comparisons from market transactions. The uniqueness may come about because a business has a localized monopoly perhaps due to a licence or a restricted location or because the design of the building is only applicable to a specific use.

Examples of properties which are evaluated using the profits method are sometimes categorized as leisure properties and which include hotels, casinos, marinas, golf courses, pubs, bowling alleys and night clubs. However, the method can extend beyond the leisure sector to perhaps more mundane properties such as petrol filling stations and car parks whose value relies upon the income that they are able to generate.

Question 2 Identifying the total room revenue and room yield for an 80 bed hotel

No. of rooms available per year	Average overall occupancy rate	Single occupancy rate	Average single room rate per night	Double occupancy rate	Average double room rate per night	Total room revenue	Room yield
80 × 365 = 29,200	67% × 29,200 = 19,564	70% × 19,564 = 13,695	£50 × 13,695 = £684,750	30% × 19,564 = 5,869	£70 × 5,869 = £410,830	£684,750 + £410,830 = £1,095,580	£37.52

Question 3 Identifying the capital value for the 80 bed hotel

Total hotel income = Total room revenue/0.7 =	£1,565,114
Deduct expenses and operating costs of 80%	£1,252,091
Net profit/Divisible balance =	£313,023
Landlord's share of the divisible balance @ 50%	£156,512
Capitalize @ 8.5% YP = 11.7647	£1,841,311

Question 4 The special qualities required of a valuer when using the profits method

The valuer would need to be a specialist conversant in and experienced with the types of properties being valued. The valuer would need to maintain a degree of market awareness as incomes on some of these property types can be quite volatile from year to year, especially for properties in the leisure-related industry.

The valuer must have gained experience and have the ability to read and interpret business accounts. The valuer has to think about what could sustainably be achieved by the business entity occupying the subject property given its management by a hypothetical reasonably efficient operator and that the premises are assumed to be properly equipped. The valuer must maintain an overview by showing awareness of alternative uses and potential values for the site.

Question 5 The advantages of using discounted cash flows for profits method appraisals

Discounted cash flow (DCF) enables explicit modelling of the anticipated growth of a business's turnover and hence expected growth in net profits going into the future. A DCF appraisal can be tailored to the specific time-frame required, discounting income and capital sums over that time-frame to present value, which reflects the current value of the enterprise. The discount rate used in a DCF subsumes an investor's rate of return and so once that is known, there is no need for a separate calculation to establish the return to the investor. A DCF could factor in abnormal costs which might arise at some point in the future such as the need for expenditure to refurbish a property. The attributes of DCF are discussed in more depth in Chapter 9 in the book.

Solutions to self-assessment questions for Chapter 6

Question 1 The alternative name for the DRC method of valuation

The alternative and perhaps more popular name for the DRC method is the *contractor's method* to signify the cost basis of this type of valuation. The contractor is therefore assumed to be a building contractor who provides an all-in price to construct the particular building against which a valuer produces a valuation.

Question 2 Appropriate properties and circumstances when the DRC method is used

The DRC method becomes applicable as a valuation method by default when other more straightforward methods cannot be relied upon. Thus the DRC method is sometimes referred to as a method of last resort. The method therefore tends to be used to value public and quasi public buildings including schools, hospitals, libraries, police stations and other specialized buildings which are not normally traded or leased in the open market. Thus for these properties there is no comparable data available as the basis for a more conventional valuation approach to be taken.

Question 3 The element in the DRC valuation which is not depreciated

The land value in a DRC valuation is not usually depreciated because the valuation assumes that a site has to be sourced at today's values to accommodate the replacement building. The replacement hypothetical building which would fulfil the same function as the current building could however be accommodated on a smaller site in a more cost effective location. That decision is based on the premise that the owner would act in a rational manner in the light of today's circumstances and given the opportunity to a use a site more efficiently.

Question 4 The other costs which may be factored in to a DRC valuation

This type of valuation works on the fiction of the hypothetical replacement building and so it is admissible to include those incidental costs which would arise if the modern equivalent building really were to be designed and built. Thus there needs to be an allowance for the fees to be paid to the fictitious professional team, an allowance for ancillary costs such as landscaping or laying out external parking areas, a contingency allowance which is normally made in development appraisals and the cost of finance which would arise to support the overall costs.

Question 5 Decapitalizing and the purpose that it serves

A DRC valuation identifies the capital value of a property, i.e. the combined value of the building and the land upon which it sits. However for purposes such as determining the rateable value of a property an annual rental value is required, as rates are levied on a rate in the pound multiplied by the annual rental value of a property. Given that the DRC method is used precisely because there is no market for the particular property and therefore no rental value comparisons, the capital value has to be decapitalized to identity what a notional tenant might pay to rent the building. Because there have been numerous court cases contesting this matter, the government decided to set statutory decapitalization rates for particular categories of buildings so that some consistency could be brought to bear on the process. So assuming a building had a statutory decapitalization rate of 3.33 per cent and that its capital value was £800,000 its notional annual rental value for rating purposes would be £800,000 × 0.0333 = £26,640.

Solutions to self-assessment questions for Chapter 7

Question 1 The purpose and context in which the residual valuation might be used

The residual valuation method can be used to identify the site value for a development by deducting the costs of development (including profit but excluding land costs) from the Gross Development Value (GDV). If the site value is already known because it has already been purchased or will only be sold for a fixed price, then the residual method can be adjusted to identify the development profit by residualizing that element. The residual method will tend to be used by valuers when the direct comparison method could not reasonably be used because the development under consideration does not have any direct comparisons.

Question 2 The limitations associated with the residual method

Although the residual method is a recognized part of the valuer's toolkit which can legitimately be used for development appraisals, it does have some limitations which should be borne in mind when it is used. There are so many variables in the calculation that errors easily occur and thus robust quality control procedures would need to be in place when this method is used. As with all valuation methods, judgements have to be made by the valuer and quite small variances in these judgments when calibrating the key or so-called sensitive variables in the calculation can generate significant changes in the residual outcome.

The output from a residual calculation is a single spot figure suggesting a degree of accuracy that is unrealistic when in fact what might be more credible is a range of figures with probabilities. The residual calculation does not cope well with changes over time, in terms of rent levels, interest rates or the inflation of building costs. For this reason on major projects, a residual might be the first line of appraisal to establish whether there were any project viability and if so, a more detailed period by period cash flow could then be undertaken to add refinement to the appraisal. Cash flows can reflect a stream of income and costs through a project timeline and this will tend to give a more accurate reflection of interest charges on costs for a project.

Question 3 Does the scheme achieve a developer's profit equivalent to 15 per cent of the GDV?

Because the cost of the site is given at £2.2 million a simple residual approach could be constructed to identify the unknown variable which in this case is the developer's profit. The developer's aspiration is that the profit should be at least 15 per cent of the scheme's GDV but as the figures below show this aspiration is not met.

House type	No.	Unit sales value £	Totals £
Two bedroom houses	15	180,000	2,700,000
Three bedroom houses	20	250,000	5,000,000
Four bedroom houses	10	320,000	3,200,000
	45	GDV =	10,900,000

Land price £	2,200,000
Total scheme costs excluding land £	7,500,000
Scheme costs including land therefore	9,700,000
Profit residualized £	1,200,000
Profit as a proportion of GDV =	11%

Question 4 Identifying the site value given the developer's profit expectations and the imposition of a 25 per cent affordable housing policy

The changed circumstances would give rise to a calculation which made the site value the residual element as follows.

House type	Tenure	No.	Unit sales value £	Totals £
Two bedroom	*Market*	11	180,000	1,980,000
houses	*Affordable*	4	117,000	468,000
Three bedroom	*Market*	15	250,000	3,750,000
houses	*Affordable*	5	162,500	812,500
Four bedroom	*Market*	7	320,000	2,240,000
houses	*Affordable*	3	208,000	624,000
		45	GDV =	9,874,500

Developer's profit at 15% of GDV £	1,481,175
Scheme costs excluding land £	7,500,000
Total scheme costs excluding land £	8,981,175
Land value £ = GDV – total scheme costs =	893,325

Question 5 Identifying the net site value

Part (a) of this question required the present value of the site value of £893,325 in two years at 8 per cent. The present value of £1 formula would be used as follows:

$$\frac{1}{(1 + i)^n} = \frac{1}{(1 + 0.08)^2} = 0.8573 \times £893,325 = £765,848$$

Part (b) of this question required the calculation of the net site value after deductions have been made for solicitors and agents fees and stamp duty land tax. Given that the fees are benchmarked at 1 per cent and stamp duty at 4 per cent of the gross site value, the deductions are 5 per cent in total and calculation is as follows.

Net site value + 5% of net site value = gross site value
Net site value = £765,848/1.05 = £729,379
Deductions are therefore £36,469.

Note that this is not simply a matter of multiplying 5 per cent by the gross site value which would produce deductions of £38,292 and which would be incorrect.

Solutions to self-assessment questions for Chapter 8

Question 1 Explaining what a YP is

A YP is a capitalizing factor which converts a future stream of income to a present capital sum. It is the present value of an income of £1 per annum discounted on a year-to-year basis at the yield rate. Strictly it is the income per period discounted on a period-to-period basis so the same approach can be used so long as the income per period ties in with the number of periods involved.

Question 2 The YP and capital value for a freehold property

(a) The Years' Purchase in perpetuity for freeholds is $1/i = 1/0.08 = 12.5$
(b) The capital value = net rental income × YP in perpetuity = £30,000 × 12.5
= £375,000.

Question 3 The use of the term and reversion method to value a shop

The answer to the question requires a term and reversion calculation as follows:

Term of 3 years			
Net annual rent		£40,000	
YP for 3 years @ 7.5%		2.6005	
Value of the term			£104,020
Reversion			
Net rent anticipated		£50,000	
YP in perp. @ 8.5%	11.7647		
x PV of £1 in 3 years @ 8.5%	0.7829		
YP in perp. @ 8.5% deferred 3 years		9.2106	
Value of the reversion			£460,530
Total capital value			£564,550

Question 4 The use of the layer method to value the same shop

Hardcore annual rent passing		£40,000	
YP in perp. @ 7.5%		13.3333	
Value of the core			£533,332
Top slice rent anticipated in 3 years		£10,000	
YP in perp. @ 8.5%	11.7647		
PV £1 in 3 years @ 8.5%	0.7829		
YP in perp. @ 8.5% deferred 3 years		9.2106	
Value of the top slice			£92,106
Total capital value			£625,438

Question 5 Using the layer method to value an over-rented property

The business tenant has the leverage at the rent review in three years' time to exercise the break clause if the rent is not adjusted to the market rent of £48,000 per annum. The overage of £12,000 does not look as if it could realistically extend beyond that point. The layer method calculation would look as follows:

Core rent			
Estimated rental value (ERV)		£48,000	
YP in perp. @ 7%		14.2857	
Value of the core			£685,714
Top slice			
Rent passing	£60,000		
Less ERV	£48,000		
Overage		£12,000	
YP 3 years @ 9%		2.5313	
Value of the top slice			£30,376
Total capital value			£716,090

Solutions to self-assessment questions for Chapter 9

Question 1 Identifying and using the right formula

The formula which could be used to identify the present value of an annually receivable sum of £35,000 for 10 years at 7 per cent is called the *Present Value of £1 per annum* which is also referred to by its shorter title as *Years' Purchase* or *YP*. The formula, which appears in Chapter 9 and also in Chapter 3, is as follows:

$$\frac{1 - \dfrac{1}{(1 + i)^n}}{i}$$

The formula could be used to calculate the answer to the question by incorporating the interest rate i which is 7 per cent (0.07 as a decimal) and the time period n which in this case is 10 years as follows:

$$\frac{1 - \dfrac{1}{(1 + 0.07)^{10}}}{0.07}$$

The value which emerges from the above should be: 7.0236 (rounded up) and this is used to multiply the actual capital sum involved which is £35,000 to produce the answer: 7.0236 × £35,000 = £245,826.

Question 2 Two alternatives to the formula to identify (and check) the correct answer

The same answer as shown above in question 1 can be found by constructing a discounted cash flow (DCF) in Excel using the discount rate of 7 per cent over 10 years and the annually receivable sum of £35,000. Note that in these types of calculation the income is assumed to be receivable in arrears, so the first year's income is one year away and thus is discounted at 7 per cent on that basis. There is a difference of £4 in the answer which is due to the rounding which takes place within the DCF table below for formatting purposes.

Year	Cash flow £	PV £1 @ 7%	Discounted cash flow £
1	35,000	0.9346	32,711
2	35,000	0.8734	30,569
3	35,000	0.8163	28,571
4	35,000	0.7629	26,702
5	35,000	0.7130	24,955
6	35,000	0.6663	23,321
7	35,000	0.6227	21,795
8	35,000	0.5820	20,370
9	35,000	0.5439	19,037
10	35,000	0.5083	17,791
		NPV =	245,822

There is yet a further way to calculate the answer and that is to look up the constant in Parry's Tables (or similar valuation tables) where the Years' Purchase (single rate) tables reveal that the present value of £1 for 10 years at 7 per cent is: 7.0236 which when multiplied by £35,000 (as already demonstrated above) produces £245,826.

Question 3 Assessing whether the house purchase would meet a 10 per cent target rate

The expenditure of £180,000 shown in year 1 in the DCF below comprises the house purchase price of £170,000 plus £10,000 of purchase costs and fees. The property has a gross annual income of £12,000 but 40 per cent of this is spent on outgoings plus an allowance for void periods leaving a net income of £7,200. The gross rent increases each year by 3 per cent so that for example, the gross rent in year 2 is £12,360 but again the investor only retains 60 per cent of that income. In the final year after receiving the annual income the investor sells the property on the assumption that its value has increased by 5 per cent per annum, i.e. $(1.05)^6 \times £170,000 = £227,817$ (rounded up). The negative NPV of −£24,295 suggests that the investment does not satisfy the investor's target rate of return of 10 per cent.

Year	Expenditure £	Income £	Net cash flow £	PV of £1 @ 10%	DCF £
0	180,000	0	−180,000	1	−180,000
1	4,800	12,000	7,200	0.9091	6,546
2	4,944	12,360	7,416	0.8264	6,129
3	5,092	12,731	7,639	0.7513	5,739
4	5,245	13,113	7,868	0.6830	5,374
5	5,402	13,506	8,104	0.6209	5,032
6	5,564	13,911	8,347	0.5645	4,712
	11,391	227,817	216,426	0.5645	122,173
			NPV		−24,295

Question 4 Assessing whether the house purchase would meet a target rate of 6 per cent

The same data as in question 3 above applies but the discount rate of 6 per cent represents a lower investment threshold which the positive NPV of £10,557 suggests has easily been achieved. The question is of course what specific rate of return has been achieved and this is revealed in the answer to question 5 below where the IRR is identified.

Year	Expenditure £	Income £	Net cash flow £	PV of £1 @ 6%	DCF £
0	180,000	0	−180,000	1	−180,000
1	4,800	12,000	7,200	0.9434	6,792
2	4,944	12,360	7,416	0.8900	6,600
3	5,092	12,731	7,639	0.8396	6,413
4	5,245	13,113	7,868	0.7921	6,232
5	5,402	13,506	8,104	0.7473	6,056
6	5,564	13,911	8,347	0.7050	5,884
	11,391	227,817	216,426	0.7050	152,580
			NPV		10,557

Question 5 Identifying the IRR for the investor's buy-to-let idea

$$R_1 + [(R_2 - R_1) \times \frac{NPV @ R_1}{NPV @ R_1 - NPV @ R_2}]$$

$$6\% + [(10\% - 6\%) \times \frac{10,557}{34,852}] = 7.21\%$$

Solutions to self-assessment questions for Chapter 10

Question 1 Identifying the average weighted cost of capital

Retail warehouse purchase on the basis of:

80% debt @ 9%	7.2%
20% equity @ 1.5% opportunity cost	0.3%
Average weighted cost of capital therefore	7.5%

Question 2 Gearing

The retail warehouse is purchased for £800,000 using and equity stake of £160,000 plus a loan of £640,000. The retail warehouse is then sold three years later to generate the following calculation.

Retail warehouse sold after 3 years for	£1,000,000
Repay interest only loan which was 80% of the original price	£640,000
Balance	£360,000
Profit after deducting original equity stake of £160,000	£200,000

Return on capital invested over 3 years = $\dfrac{200,000}{160,000}$ = 125.0%

Equivalent to an annual rate of return of   31.04%

Question 3 Completing the discounted cash flow for the second trail rate of 11 per cent

Trial rate @ 8%

Years	Amount of £1 @ 3%	Cash flow £	PV £1 @ 8%	Deferred YP	PV of slice £
0	n/a	−910,000	1		−910,000
1–5	n/a	65,000	1	3.9927	259,526
6–10	1.1593	75,355	0.6806	2.7174	204,770
11	1.3439	87,354	0.4632	5.1467	449,585
				NPV =	3,881

Trial rate @ 11%

Years	Amount of £1 @ 3%	Cash flow £	PV £1 @ 11%	Deferred YP	PV of slice £
0	n/a	−910,000	1		−910,000
1–5	n/a	65,000	1	3.6959	240,234
6–10	1.1593	75,355	0.5935	2.1935	165,291
11	1.3439	87,354	0.3522	3.9133	341,842
				NPV =	−162,633

Question 4 Identifying the IRR/equated yield using the formula:

$$R_1 + [\ (R_2 - R_1) \times \frac{\text{NPV @ } R_1}{\text{NPV @ } R_1 - \text{NPV @ } R_2}\ ]$$

$$8\% + [\ (11\% - 8\%) \times \frac{3{,}881}{166{,}514}\ ]$$

$$8\% + [\ 3\% \times 0.0233\ ] = 8.07\%$$

Question 5 Identifying the implied growth rate given a target rate of return of 11%

$$(1 + g)^t = \frac{\text{YP perp. @ } k - \text{YP } t \text{ years @ } e}{\text{YP perp. @ } k \times \text{PV } t \text{ years @ } e}$$

In the question scenario the following applied:
The rent review period is 5 years, so $t = 5$
The investor's target rate of return is 11%, so $e = 11\%$
The capitalization rate k is: £65,000/£910,000 = 7.14%

$$(1 + g)^5 = \frac{14 - 3.6959}{14 \times 0.5935}$$

$$(1 + g)^5 = \frac{10.3041}{8.309}$$

$$(1 + g)^5 = 1.2401$$

$$1 + g = 1.2401^{1/5}$$

$$1 + g = 1.0440$$

$$g = 4.4\%$$

Bibliography

Armatys, J., Askham, P. and Green, M. (2009) *Principles of Valuation* (London: EG Books).

Askham, P. (2003) *Valuation: Special Properties and Purposes* (London: Estates Gazette).

Balchin, P., Isaac, D. and Chen, J. (2000) *Urban Economics: A Global Perspective* (Basingstoke: Palgrave).

Baldwin, C., Davies, F. and Petty, R. (2003) *A Valuation for All Seasons: A Practical Guide to Valuation for Housing Associations* (London: National Housing Federation).

Banfield, A. (2009) *Valuation on Quarterly in Advance Basis and True Equivalent Yield* (Reading: College of Estate Management).

Baum, A., Nunnington, N. and Mackmin, D. (2006) *The Income Approach to Property Valuation* (5th edn, London: EG Books).

Baum, A., Sams, G., Ellis, J., Hampson, C. and Stevens, D. (2007) *Statutory Valuations* (4th edn, London: EG Books).

Baum, A. (2009) *Commercial Real Estate Investment: A Strategic Approach* (2nd edn, London: EG Books).

Blackledge, M. (2009) *Introducing Property Valuation* (Abingdon: Routledge).

Bond, P. and Brown, P. (2006) *Rating Valuation: Principles and Practice* (2nd edn, London: EG Books).

Building Cost Information Service. Available at: www.bcis.co.uk.

Crocker, S. (2008) 'Public Houses', in R. Hayward (ed.), *Valuation: Principles into Practice*, (6th edn, London: EG Books).

Crosby, N. (1992) *Reversionary Freeholds; UK Market Valuation Practice* (London: RICS).

Davidson, A. W. (2002) *Parry's Valuation and Investment Tables* (12th edn, London: EG Books).

De Montford University (2008) *Review of Practice in the Use of Section 106 Agreements to Facilitate the Delivery of Affordable Housing in the East Midlands* (Leicester: De Montford University, Centre for Comparative Housing Research).

Department for Communities (2005) *Circular 05/2005: Planning Obligations* (London: Department for Communities and Local Government). Originally published by the Office of the Deputy Prime Minister. Available in e-format at: www.communities.gov.uk

Department for Communities (2010) *The Community Infrastructure Levy: An Overview* (London: Department for Communities and Local Government). Available in e-format at: www.communities.gov.uk

Department for Communities (2011) *Table 101 Dwelling Stock: By Tenure, United Kingdom* (historical series) (London: Department for Communities and Local Government). Available in e-format at: www.communities.gov.uk

Department for Communities (2011) *Table 511 Housing Market: Simple Average House Prices, by Dwelling Type and Region, United Kingdom, from 1986* (London: Department for Communities). Available in e-format at: www.communities.gov.uk

Derwent London plc (2010) *Report and Accounts 2010* (London: Derwent London plc).

Enever, N., Isaac, D. and Daley, M. (2010) *The Valuation of Property Investments* (7th edn, London: EG Books).

Estates Gazette (2011) 'Growth Slows as Yields Plateau', 14 May, 1119, p. 49.

Fraser, W. D. (2004) *Cash-Flow Appraisal for Property Investment* (Basingstoke: Palgrave Macmillan).

Havard, T. (2008) *Contemporary Property Development* (2nd edn, London: RIBA Publishing).

Hayward, R. (ed.) (2008) *Valuation: Principles into Practice* (6th edn, London: EG Books).

Healey, J. Rt. Hon. (2009) *Rates: Non-Domestic Valuations, House of Lords Written Ministerial Statement on 19.1.09* (London: Hansard).

Investment Property Forum (2005) *The Size and Structure of the UK Property Market* (London: Investment Property Forum).

IPD (2011) *IPD UK Annual Property Index: Results for the Year to 31 December 2010* (London: Investment Property Databank Ltd). Available in e-format at: www.ipd.com

Isaac, D. and Steley, T. (2000) *Property Valuation Techniques* (London: Macmillan).

Isaac, D. and O'Leary, J. (2011) *Property Investment* (2nd edn, Basingstoke: Palgrave).

Isaac, D., O'Leary, J. and Daley, M. (2010) *Property Development, Appraisal and Finance,* (2nd edn, Basingstoke: Palgrave).

Jones Lang LaSalle (2010) *The Central London Office market Q4 2010.* Available in e-format at: www.joneslanglasalle.co.uk.

Law, D. and Gershinson, J. (1995) 'Whatever Happened to ERP?' *Estates Gazette,* 16 September, pp. 164–5.

Lorenz, D. (2009) *The Application of Sustainable Development Principles to the Theory and Practice of Property Valuation* (Karlsruhe: University of Karlsruhe).

Mackmin, D. (2008) *Valuation and Sale of Residential Property* (3rd edn, London: EG Books).

Murdoch, J. (2008) 'Negligence and Valuations', in R. Hayward (ed.), *Valuation: Principles into Practice* (6th edn, London: EG Books).

Office for National Statistics (2011) *Retail Price Index (RPI) all Items Percentage Change over 12 Months: Table RP04* (Cardiff: Office for National Statistics). Available in e-format at: www.statisitcs.gov.uk

RICS (1994) *President's Working Party on Commercial Property Valuations: the Mallinson Report* (London: RICS).

RICS, Investment Property Databank and the University of Aberdeen (1994) *Understanding the Property Cycle: Economic Cycles and Property Cycles* (London: RICS).

RICS (2006) *The Analysis of Commercial Lease Transactions: Valuation Information Paper No. 8* (London: RICS).

RICS (2007) *Code of Measuring Practice* (6th edn, London: RICS).

RICS (2007) *The Depreciated Replacement Cost Method of Valuation for Financial Reporting: Valuation Information Paper 10* (London: RICS).

RICS (2008) *Valuation of development land: Valuation Information Paper 12* (London: RICS).

RICS (2009) *Sustainability and the RICS Property Lifecycle* (London: RICS).

RICS (2010) *Discounted Cash Flow for Commercial Property Investments* (London: RICS).

RICS (2010) *Property Investment Valuation in the UK: A Brief Guide for Users of Valuations* (London: RICS).

RICS (2010) *Rules for the Regulation of Schemes, 01 September 2010, Version 2* (London: RICS).

RICS (2010) *Valuation of Land for Affordable Housing* (London: RICS).

RICS (2011) *RICS Valuation Standards – Global and UK* (7th edn, London: RICS).

RICS (2011) 'The Valuation of Individual Trade Related Properties: Guidance Note 2', in *RICS Valuation Standards – Global and UK* (7th edn, London: RICS).

RICS (2011) *Why use a registered valuer?* (London: RICS). Available in e-format at: www.rics.org/vrs

Saunders, O. (2010) *Valuation Calculations: 101 Worked Examples* (London: RICS Books).

Sayce, S., Smith, J., Cooper, R. and Venmore-Rowland, P. (2006) *Real Estate Appraisal from Value to Worth* (Oxford: Blackwell).

Scarrett, D. (2008) *Property Valuation: The Five Methods* (2nd edn, Abingdon: Routledge).

Scott, B. (2008) 'Hotels', in R. Hayward (ed.), *Valuation: Principles into Practice* (6th edn, London: EG Books).

Shapiro, E., Davies, K. and Mackmin, D. (2009) *Modern Methods of Valuation* (10th edn, London: EG Books).

Thorne, C. (2008) 'Valuations for Financial Statements', in R. Hayward (ed.), *Valuation: Principles into Practice* (6th edn, London: EG Books).

University of Sheffield (2010) *The Incidence, Value and Delivery of Planning Obligations in England in 2007–08* (London: Department for Communities and Local Government). Available in e-format at: www.communities.gov.uk

Valuation Office Agency (2011) *Property Market Report 2011*. Available in e-format at: www.voa.gov.uk.

Wilkinson, S. and Reed, R. (2008) *Property Development* (5th edn, Abingdon: Routledge).

Index

affordable housing 26
  in residual valuations 109–12
all risks yield 50, 131, 132, 159, 164, 166
amortization 48
amount of £1 per annum 47, 51
  see also compounding
amount of £1 44–6, 51
ancillary costs 99–100
annual sinking fund 48
  in dual-rate valuations 154, 155–6
annuity £1 will purchase 48–9, 51

Bank of England Monetary Policy Committee 103, 187
bank lending 22
  and risk premium 187
  based on valuations 4
  capability 24
  cashstake 24
  character 24
  charge on housing association properties 26
  collateral 9
  gearing 189
bracket (of valuation accuracy) 3, 29, 41–3
building costs 98
Building Cost Information Service 98
building insurance 35, 60, 133–6
Building Research Establishment Environmental Assessment Method (BREEAM) 2, 18–19
building societies 26, 30, 189
business rates 32, 34, 74, 141
buy-to-let 14–15, 27, 127, 171–2, 174

capability *see* bank lending
capital gains tax 32
capitalizing 64, 69, 114, 126, 128, 194
cashstake *see* bank lending
character *see* bank lending

Code for Sustainable Homes 18, 208
collateral *see* bank lending
Community Infrastructure Levy (CIL) 100
comparables 3, 43, 54, 55–6, 63, 132
comparison method 6, 54–67, 94, 201
compounding 44, 46–7, 51, 154, 171
compulsory purchase 32
construction costs 1, 121, 201
Consumer Price Index (CPI) 183
  see also inflation
contingencies 100–1
contractor's method *see* depreciated replacement cost method
core rent *see* hardcore rent
corporate social responsibility (CSR) 2, 9, 18
correlation between investments 12, 16
cost of capital 36, 168–70
  see also weighted average cost of capital
council tax 32
credit crunch 23, 40, 119, 149, 185, 205

debt finance 22
decapitalization 87, 214
  rate 81
densification 200, 203
depreciated replacement cost (DRC) method 81–91
development appraisal 33, 94–6
  see also residual valuation
developer's profit 95, 104
discounted cash flow (DCF) 50, 77–8, 121–2, 162–4, 192–7, 204
discounting 44, 46, 51, 167–8
diversification of investments 8, 16–17
divisibility 10, 15
divisible balance 71, 74–7, 78–9
dual rate 154–6

earnings before interest, tax,
    depreciation and amortization
    (EBITDA)   69, 74
easements   19
equated yield   181–2, 192–4
equitable interests   19
equity   24, 26, 102, 119, 181–2,
    186–92
equivalent yield   145–9, 159
estimated rental value (ERV)   126,
    133
ex ante   4
ex post   4–5
existing use value (EUV)   94,
    117–18
    for social housing   26

facilities management   200, 205
fair maintainable turnover   68–9, 72,
    77
fair value   30, 37, 52
finance charges   102
financial institutions   22, 189
fire insurance   49, 60, 90–1
forecasting   5, 41
freeholds   18–19

gearing   182, 189–92
gilt-edged stock   15, 168, 186
globalization   33
goodwill   71–2
ground lease   19
ground rent   157
gross development value (GDV)
    94–8

hardcore rent   126, 143–4
housing association   26, 98, 204

illiquidity   10
implied growth rate   181, 195
inflation   14, 119, 131, 182–6
initial yield   37, 1312, 145
insurance companies   16
interest rates   46, 119
    quarterly equivalent to annual rate
    46
internal rate of return (IRR)   145,
    162, 174–7, 182, 192
International Valuation Standards
    Council (IVSC)   33

invested stock   12
investment market   12, 55, 130
investment method of valuation
    traditional   125–59
    discounted cash flow approach
    162–79
Investment Property Databank (IPD)
    132, 185
Investment Property Forum (IPF)
    12
investors   13–14, 16, 19, 50, 63–4,
    127

Landlord and Tenant Acts   19
Law of Property Act   19
layer method   126, 143–5, 148,
    151–2
lease
    internal repairing   135–6
    full repairing and insuring   133–5
leasehold property   17, 155–6
lending criteria   *see* bank lending
letting fees   109
letting terms   133
liquidity   155
loan to value ratio (LTV)   189
London Interbank Offer Rate
    (LIBOR)   187

Mallinson Report   40–1
market comparables   *see* comparables
market rent   30, 32, 35, 133
market value   34–7, 41, 43
marketing   34, 109
marriage value   37
mortgages   19, 26, 33, 39, 48–9,
    106

negative equity   39
net development value   108
net income   60, 93–4, 126, 128,
    133–4
net present value (NPV)   162, 170–9
non-statutory valuations   31, 32–33

opportunity cost   72, 119, 168, 181,
    186–7
outgoings   60, 126, 133–4, 136
overage   151–2
over-rented property   125, 149–52
owner-occupiers   10–13

payback method   165
pension funds   12, 16, 22
planning agreements   94, 99–100
portfolios   16–17
premiums 1 57–8
present value   46, 49, 106, 162,
    167–8, 170, 194
present value of £1   46–7, 51
present value of £1 per annum
    49–50, 51, 129, 167–8
prices   38–9
professional fees   101–2
profit margin   106
    see also developer's profit
profit rent   152–4
profitability   70–71, 73, 166–7
profits method   68–79
property
    characteristics   17–18, 155
    companies   12–13, 16, 19, 39
    cycles   11, 38
    market   8–17
    valuation   3, 30, 33–4, 40
purchaser's costs   106–7, 108,
    130–1

rate of return method   166–7
rates of return   129, 192
rating   *see* business rates
ratios
    gearing   73
    see also loan to value ratios
    profitability   189
Real Estate Investment Trusts (REITs)
    12, 16, 19
reasonably efficient operator   68, 72
Red Book   2, 29, 30, 33–7, 40, 41,
    42, 44, 52, 201
refurbishment   116–7
rent review   20, 25, 35, 58, 126,
    136–7, 143, 195–6
rental values   55, 58–9, 96, 114, 116,
    138, 201
repairs   60
residual valuation method   93–122
Retail Price Index (RPI)   183
    see also inflation
return on capital   36, 73
reversionary property   126, 140, 143,
    159

risk   112–15
    free rate   13, 154, 168, 186–7
    premium   188
Royal Institution of Chartered
    Surveyors (RICS)   2, 4, 18, 26,
    30, 33, 34, 35, 37, 38, 41, 42–3,
    52, 65, 70, 71, 94, 113, 164,
    203

sale and leaseback   13
security
    capital   14–15
    income   14–15
sensitivity analysis   94, 113, 115–6,
    169
shared ownership   26, 31, 110–1
single rate   49, 51, 154, 168
sinking fund   48, 154–6
spreadsheets   30, 44, 163, 178–9
statutory valuations   31–2
sustainability   2, 18–19, 102, 203
    see also Building Research
        Establishment Environmental
        Assessment Method
        (BREEAM); Code for
        Sustainable Homes; corporate
        social responsibility (CSR);
        triple bottom line
systematic risk   188

target rate   167–8, 170, 174, 186,
    195
tax liability   157–8
tenure   5, 17–18, 26
    see also property characteristics
term and reversion   126, 136–43,
    145–6, 148, 149–51, 168
top slice   126, 143–4, 145, 147,
    151–2
Town and Country Planning Acts
    20
    see also planning agreements; use
        classes
triple bottom line   2
    see also sustainability; corporate social
        responsibility (CSR)

uncertainty   122, 141, 144, 169
units of comparison   54, 55
unsystematic risk   188
use classes   21

use value   11
  see also existing use value
utility   4

valuation
  formulae   44–51
  negligence   3–4, 30, 40, 41–44
  non-statutory   *see* non-statutory
    valuations
  standards   *see Red Book*
  statutory   *see* statutory valuations
  tables   44–51
  toolkit   30, 31, 201
Valuation Office Agency (VOA)   32,
  65, 82
Valuer Registration Scheme   30,
  37–8, 203

weighted average cost of capital   181,
  187
worth   1, 5, 35–7, 41, 52

Years' Purchase (YP)   *see* present value
  of £1 per annum
Years' Purchase (YP) in perpetuity
  50–1, 63, 129–30
yield
  all risks   *see* all risks yield
  equated   *see* equated yield
  equivalent   *see* equivalent yield
  initial   *see* initial yield

zoning   54, 61–3